OUTRAGE
AND
HOPE

Also by Frederick Houk Borsch

The Son of Man in Myth and History
The Christian and Gnostic Son of Man
God's Parable
Introducing the Lessons of the Church Year
Coming Together in the Spirit
Proclamation 2 • Advent Christmas A (with Davie Napier)
Proclamation 3 • Pentecost C1
Proclamation 4 • Epiphany A
Power in Weakness
Anglicanism and the Bible (ed.)
Jesus: The Human Life of God
Many Things in Parables
The Bible's Authority in Today's Church (ed.)
Christian Discipleship and Sexuality

OUTRAGE

AND

HOPE

A Bishop's Reflections in
Times of Change and Challenge

Frederick Houk Borsch

Trinity Press International
Valley Forge, Pennsylvania

Trinity Press International, P.O. Box 851, Valley Forge, PA 19482-0851

Grateful acknowledgment is made to the following for permission to reprint previously published material by the author:

Los Angeles Times:
      "Reason to Use Our Franchise" (January 1, 1990); "We Do Have Power to End the Madness" (April 26, 1993); "The Cost of Guns" (May 16, 1994); "Who Are We?" (August 31, 1994).

Anglican Theological Review:
      "Jesus and Women Exemplars" (Supplementary Series 11: March, 1990); "The Ministry and Authority of Bishops in a Changing World and Church" (Vol. 77, No. 1: Winter 1995).

The Christian Century:
      "Where Was God When the Plane Crashed?" (Vol. 102, No. 9: March 13, 1985).

The Living Church:
      "Love Bade Me Welcome" (October 9, 1983)

Unless the author has made his own translation, scripture quotations are from the New Revised Standard Version Bible, copyright 1989, Division of Christian Education of the National Council of the Churches of Christ in the United States of America, U.S.A. and are used by permission.

Library of Congress Cataloging-in-Publication Data
Borsch, Frederick Houk.
      Outrage and hope / Frederick Houk Borsch
            p.   cm.
      ISBN 1-56338-170-2 (pbk. : alk, paper)
      1. Episcopal Church. Diocese of Los Angeles—
      History—20th century.   2. Church and social problems—
      California—Los Angeles Region.   3. Los Angeles Region
      (Calif.)—Church history—20th century.
      4. Borsch, Frederick Houk.   I. Title.
BX5918.L7B67 1996   96-10961
283' .7949—dc20   CIP

Printed in the United States of America

96 97 98 99 00 01 02 03 10 9 8 7 6 5 4 3 2 1

To the people of hope in Los Angeles

"…knowing that suffering produces endurance
and endurance produces character
and character produces hope
and hope does not disappoint us"

CONTENTS

3. Adelante! Ministries Today

Foreword

From lightning and tempest; from earthquake, fire and flood; from plague, pestilence and famine, GOOD LORD, DELIVER US. From all oppression, conspiracy and rebellion; from violence, battle and murder; and from dying suddenly and unprepared, GOOD LORD, DELIVER US."

So do members of my Church pray in what is known as *The Great Litany*. Yet no more than for Jesus, who prayed that "this cup might pass me by," are we always spared from calamities and tribulation. In the years since mid-1988, when I became Bishop in the Episcopal Diocese of Los Angeles, this region has experienced several major earthquakes, including the most severe earthquake in terms of damage costs in modern history. It has known the terrible social upheaval after the original acquittal of the officers involved in the Rodney King beating. There have been devastating fires, drought and then floods. With the rest of the country we have been part of a war in the Middle East, and, more than most parts, have felt the downsizing of the military after the collapse of communism in the Soviet Union. So there has been severe recession and powerful changes in the makeup of our economy.

Meanwhile, waves of newcomers have continued to come to Southern California, both legally and outside the law. Here and worldwide the plague of AIDS goes on. Caused in part by the increasing availability of guns, violence has grown—both everyday homicides and the bizarre and notorious murders of the parents of the Menendez brothers and of Nicole Simpson and Ronald Goldman. All this has taken place in a region of enormous diversity of race, ethnicity, language, sexual orientation and religion; where people are brought together by freeways, and are separated by freeways, geography and class into many enclaves—some of them extraordinarily privileged, others desperately poor.

When I was asked several years ago why I was going to El Salvador while there were so many problems in our own region, I could remind my challengers that Los Angeles was now home to more than four hundred thousand people from El Salvador. For economic and other reasons hundreds of thousands of persons from the Philippines and Mexico, and many others from every part of the world now live in Los Angeles.

Severely tested by environmental degradation, by poverty, by youth with too little hope in their future, and by a swiftly changing society and economy, Los Angeles is still a dynamic light industrial, entertainment and trading center with a relatively young workforce and more than seventy institutions of higher education. With its great diversity and business and personal links to the whole world, it has been called by some the Twenty-first Century world capital.

More than one out of every fifteen people in the United States now live in the five and one-half county region that is the Diocese of Los Angeles. The Episcopal Church here is not a large denomination, but in 150 congregations, and in our schools and service agencies and institutions, we have members who are of Asian background, Hispanics, Pacific Islanders, Native Americans, people from the Middle East, African-Americans, Africans, and many other "minority" persons who now are sometimes called Euro-Americans. People who call themselves conservatives, or liberals, or progressives, or who just want to be known as Christians live by the ocean, in the desert, in mountain regions, in crowded ghettos and barrios, on estates, in suburbs—in Beverly Hills, Pasadena, Santa Barbara, Santa Ana, Santa Monica, San Bernardino, the San Gabriel and San Fernando valleys, Orange County, South Central Los Angeles, Simi Valley, and what is known as the Inland Empire.

What is one to think? How is one to respond? What values and virtues should be held to? Where is God's presence in all this? Where are we to look for community, for justice, mercy, compassion and hope? While the Los Angeles area may experience some of these concerns and questions writ large, they are, of course, known in many other cities and towns, as well.

What is the role of communities of faith in these circumstances? What are some of the special challenges to clergy and to the Church, which is itself experiencing so many changes and challenges to belief? And how do we just get along from day to day? What makes us cry and sometimes laugh and go on caring and hoping?

The pages which follow are reflections about these times, about reasons for outrage, for fear and for hope, and for continuing to worship God and to pray and to serve together. Many of the commentaries, and those in the subsequent sections, first appeared in *The Episcopal News* of the Diocese of Los Angeles, or the op-ed pages of the *Los Angeles Times*, in *The Anglican Theological Review, The Christian Century, The Living Church, The Tidings, The Angelus,* a clergy newsletter, or were statements made at various news conferences. A number of them were written in immediate response to events or questions posed to me. They are in this sense a record of the times, but also an ongoing invitation to reflect together about who we are and who we are called to be. The book is dedicated to the many friends and colleagues of hope and faith who helped me to reflect and shape these pieces together, with particular thanks to Patti Benner, Bob Williams, Dan Crossland and Ruth Nicastro.

Because it presses home several of these concerns in a personal way, and was, indeed, a deliverance from sudden death, I begin with a reflection on a rather harrowing experience that happened a few years ago.

PART 1

Earthquake,
Fire & Flood;
War and More

Where Was God When the Plane Crashed?

W orld 30 going over the end." Those were the pilot's last words to the tower before the DC-10 went shooting off the end of the runway, up and over the breakwater and into Boston Harbor. Scheduled to preach in the Harvard University Chapel the next morning, I had flown out of Newark Airport on a sleeting, dark, late Saturday afternoon in January. I had wondered whether my flight would try to take off in such weather, but had reassured myself by remembering the airlines' overall safety record and by telling myself that "they know what they're doing. If it's really dangerous, they won't fly." We left Newark late, but uneventfully.

As we landed in Boston, I felt that the plane came in a little fast—hot, as they say—and farther down the runway than usual. But, surely, there could be no problem. Then, in the snowscape alongside the runway I saw one, two, then three of the turnoffs hurtle by and I knew we were in trouble.

There wasn't a sound on the plane. Either the other passengers did not realize what was happening or they had begun to freeze as I had. I saw the last of the runway go, and we began a series of sharp bumps. My prayer was short and primitive—that well-known one-word petition, "Help!" Then I felt the plane swerving to the left and ducked my head. There was a much heavier bump, after which we seemed to go up into the air and then slam down. My head banged into the seatback in front of me.

After the crash, my first emotion was relief. I didn't seem to be injured and the plane hadn't exploded. I looked around. One or more of the engines were roaring, and I could hear yelling from the back of the plane. Right around me, however, no one appeared to be injured and people were remarkably quiet. Remembering that there was a woman with a baby a row or two behind me, I got out of my seat and saw that they were all right. Other people were beginning to move about in the dim light. When someone said we were in the water, I looked out and saw it lapping several feet below the window.

There was no word from the captain or crew. It was another minute before I found out that the force of the crash had sheared off the cockpit and

3

thrown its crew into the harbor. It was the engine high and mounted on the tail which was still roaring, making it difficult to be heard. Probably it was helping to keep the few lights on, but I worried that it might explode and began shouting back and forth with several other passengers about how we might get a door open.

I happened to look down and saw my travel bag. Incongruously I thought of Sunday's sermon, which I was likely to live to preach. I unzipped the bag and took out my notes, while realizing it would need to be a very different sermon.

When someone told us we should try to get out the back, we got up and began to move in that direction. I saw I had a life vest on, but did not remember putting it on or having been told to. Several others, however, had theirs on as well. An older woman could not find one, and we found one for her.

Suddenly people began to surge toward the front again, saying we couldn't get out the back. I sensed a general feeling of panic beginning to mount, along with a determination to get out somehow. One of the flight attendants squeezed by, and several of us began to half shout at and half argue with her. Apparently she now realized that the engine blast made the back exit useless and that we would have to escape through the water.

The side door came open easily, and the escape chute inflated into a great yellow slide. I thought about trying to be a hero and helped a few people onto the chute. Then someone from behind pushed and said, "Get going." I did and sort of waddled down the wobbling chute. It was only a gradual incline because the water was nearly up to the door. I remember thinking rather crazily that this might be fun on another kind of occasion. We swung the chute toward the wing and were able to crawl over the side onto the slippery wing.

From the wing tip I had to wade only a few yards in thigh-deep water to reach the shore. I looked back at the huge broken machine, once so powerful, now helpless in the mud and water. The rear engine continued its wailing, sounding like a scene from the *Inferno*. It had sucked up the rear escape chute and then spewed little bits of hot rubber over the plane. The split-off front section looked as if it had been severed from the rest by a giant cleaver.

I clambered over the rocks and up onto the runway, nearly falling down several times on the icy tarmac. It seemed crazy that a plane would have tried to land on anything so slick. In the distance I could see a long line of emergency vehicles coming from the direction of the terminal.

By now there was a feeling of comradeship and pride among the passengers. We were alive, and there seemed to be but a few injuries. Only later was that good feeling fractured by the news that two people had been thrown from the plane and drowned. Only slowly, too, did we begin to realize how lucky we all were. If the pilot had not swerved, we would have crashed into the landing bridge covered with lights and high-tension wires. As it was, the right wing tip had come to rest only two feet away from it. We were lucky that the landing gear had sheared off and that we had not gone further out into the water.

But was it only luck, or was there more to our survival? I heard many complimentary references to God as we made our way safely to the terminal. Several people told me that they had joined me in one version or another of that fox-hole prayer. And friends later assured me that God had rescued me and did not want me to die. God had been my copilot.

It is a nice image: God as the stage manager of all of life's events, hearing our prayers and rescuing those especially favored or who still have work to do on earth. Isabel Peron had recently expressed that form of piety after, seemingly by chance, a bomb was found in the plane she was scheduled to fly. "God won't let you die five minutes before you're sup- posed to," she said.

Such a theology works best when things turn out well. I have found myself reflecting on it as I have heard prayers for safe travel, "O God, watch over Bill and Mary who are driving to Washington today." And later, "Thank you, Lord, for bringing Bill and Mary safely home." It certainly can be comforting to picture the Spirit of God hovering over all the traffic intersections that those we love must cross during a trip.

But there clearly is a theological problem here, for if God has kept Bill and Mary safe, has God then not also directed or allowed others to crash— hundreds every day? What of the two passengers who died when the jet went into the harbor? How are we to understand the fate of the many who have died, and will die, in other plane crashes? It is, of course, possible to maintain that those deaths are also part of God's plan, a design too intricate for us to comprehend. But such a view certainly is not easy to maintain in the face of the prolonged agony of some deaths, or of the suffering of children mangled in accidents.

For many in our time this view of God as the director of life's events has, of course, gone by the boards; even among those who have retained a religious vocabulary, the very idea of a God present in this way to our world often seems foreign. In biblical times mysterious divine powers were thought directly to control many events, from the daily rising of the sun, to earthquakes and plagues. Today most of us understand natural events quite differently. However difficult it may be to give a precise explanation for everything, we are trained to look for a closely knit relationship of causes and effects. We may think of God as the remote original, ultimate, or final cause of all that takes place. But God, for many people, seems further and further removed from the world of their experience.

Although there is much that we do not understand—of which we have not yet even dreamed—we must ask what kind of thinking and reflection we need to do in order to have a faith that is more than just a kind of fantasy about God, a faith in a real God in a real world.

Someone once sketched out for me the difference between what he called "Theology A and Theology B." Theology A goes like this: "If the children survive, if my doctor gives me a good report, if my business thrives, then I will give thanks and trust in God." Theology B says, "Even though I walk through the valley of the shadow of death...you are with me."

Although I am far from having all the answers, my faith tries to follow in the way of Theology B. When my plane rolled into Boston Harbor, God was not present to intervene and save me and others from the crash, but God nonetheless was not absent. Rather, God was and is mysteriously and powerfully with us, deep in the heart of life; participating in what happens with us and through us; offering faith and courage, even in the midst of tragedies; assuring us that the risk and pain of trying to care and to be creative are worthwhile. The God who cannot be seen is yet present as the Spirit of all that is, willing to share in all the consequences of creation—including evil and suffering—and seeking to transform them through love.

For some people such a God may seem rather weak, hardly better than no God at all. But for others this is the God who is always present to the world and to whom we are always present. Whether the plane lands or goes over the end, whether we live or die, this God—even in the valley of the shadow of death—is always with us. "In God we live and move and have our being" (Acts 17:28).

One of a Christian teacher's most painful and prophetic responsibilities is to point out that God and God's purposes often are not to be heard or seen on the surfaces of reality. Attempts to locate God there and to represent the Divine as one whose ways can be readily known and who can be directed by human prayers and actions border, as the Bible continually points out, on superstition rather than true faith. The thrust of a number of Jesus' parables seems to point faith away from surfaces to deeper mysteries about the manner in which God's ruling love and justice are breaking into the world. The God who is visibly absent to many human ways of trying to comprehend and control life is yet mysteriously present to the eyes and ears of faith.

This presence can be realized both amid the joy of life and in its agony. Central to the gospel's chief parable is the cross, God's signature in the world, expressing the divine willingness to share in the pain and tragedy of life—accepting them as part of God's own creative existence, while seeking to bring them new meaning. It is this presence which inspires trust and compassion, for we know that God is always working to redeem. This Spirit is present with the power to heal us spiritually and emotionally, and so sometimes physically as well. From God comes the power for life's greatest miracle; not some contravention of the natural order, but the possibility that men and women can find the trust, in the midst of mortal frailties and tragedies, to care for one another, to struggle for fairness, and to tell of the God who shares with them. This is the God who will never leave them alone.

Outrage and Hope in Los Angeles

Outrage. Feelings of sharp anger and profound sadness. These were the feelings of so many of us when we first watched the video of the beating of Rodney King. Rodney King did not live an exemplary life, but, whatever wrongs he had done, he was and is a fellow citizen and a human being. We know him as a child of God. As I watched the video there kept running through my head a phrase from the baptismal vows: "...and respect the dignity of every human being."

Outrage. Feelings of sharp anger and profound sadness were ours when we heard that the police officers, who had clearly gone well beyond the guidelines of their police rules by using excessive, unreasonable and, indeed, cruel force to subdue Rodney King, were acquitted of all charges, except for one that may or may not be retried. While we must give our support to the jury system of law, the message for so many persons of color and for persons of lower economic status in our city and country seems to be that it is permissible for police to use such force if they want to.

Outrageous have also been the immediate results of this jury decision, and one can only respond with great sorrow as our city burns. However much we share in the sense of outrage and the painful frustrations and disillusionments these acquittals have caused, it is tragic to watch as people burn and pillage. Many people in these local communities have now lost their jobs. Several have lost their lives. Many others are terrified, and they weep as they see what has happened to their neighborhoods. They worry as they think of the shortage of shops and stores and facilities which they will experience for years to come.

They and we all weep for the heightened racial tensions that have particularly targeted Korean shop and store owners and workers. The poor and the poor working people again suffer the most. Martin Luther King, Jr. was right to remind us again and again that violence, however understandable the anger that drives it, will always breed more violence.

These circumstances did not come about overnight or only because of Rodney King's beating and the acquittals. The hopelessness of many youth with poor educational and employment prospects, and the growing gap in this region between those who have and the have–nots have been developing for years. Many of us have helped to give the police the message that their primary job was and is to protect people of means, the wealthy and the propertied middle class, from those who have less or little—often identified as poorer people of color.

In a genuine democracy police would see themselves as protectors of all the people—particularly the weaker and disadvantaged. But those who are poor in Los Angeles and many people of color believe that the police view them as those who are to be "policed" and against whom excessive force can at times be used, evidently without restrictive punishment.

There are so many fine, courageous and dedicated police men and women, and one weeps also for them on these nights and days of anger, terror and criminal behavior. We all are dependent on the police—especially those who are, sadly, protected least. Many of us must recognize that it is we who have helped put the police into the position of defending some in society from others.

Now, however, the problems are so overwhelming that we are clearly all in this together. All of us are frightened, all outraged and deeply saddened and concerned for ourselves, our children, the future of Los Angeles and of our society. Some of us can continue to live in enclaves, build gated communities and private schools, and hire more protection, but none of us can escape the fear and the worry for the children and the future.

Maybe there is some hope in this. Maybe there is hope in the realization that, if we condone or don't care about what happens to one black man in a hard place in his life, sooner or later this will profoundly affect the lives of all of us. It is not always easy to discern a corporate moral order, but it does exist. In biblical terms, if the society fails to care for the poor, for the widows, the orphans and the strangers in their midst, that society will come to tragedy.

Now we are faced with the immediate task of restoring order and trying to pick up shattered and burnt out neighborhoods. The far larger task is to learn that we must live together. In countries poorer than ours no children go without care. There is a sense that they are everyone's responsibility. People there would be disgraced to see homeless and hungry people in their midst.

That is not just a dream for what could happen in our society— not a utopia. It is a vision of a preferable future in which we would care that all of us have a decent education and medical attention, and hope for some kind of work, and food and housing—a future in which everyone is equally protected by the police.

But now we are also afraid, and anxiety creates greed that even the very rich apparently cannot satisfy. Only a few moments of such reflection cause us to realize that our deepest problems are spiritual and that only a sense of being loved and of learning to care for others can heal us and our society.

There are things we can do now. Those of us resident in the city of Los Angeles can vote for Charter Amendment F in June and thus strengthen opportunities for change for which many of the police also hope. We can welcome our new Chief of Police and make it clear that we want protection and police support for everyone, not just some. We can ask for many more women police and more police representing our several racial and ethnic groups.

All of us in Los Angeles may participate in the Hope in Youth Campaign which can change the lives of many of our youth and their families.

We can listen to one another. This Church of ours is able to bring together many people from different ethnic groups and classes as we did on May 3. We can tell others that we care—that we understand their outrage and their hurt.

Those who have in this world can give of what they have for others. We can vote in such a way as to make it clear that we are prepared to make sacrifices for the sake of all of us together. There is no point in our just complaining about political leadership. Most people elected to public office are followers, not leaders. They follow the electorate much more than many people seem to realize. What could be more grassroots than many of our congregations telling them what they care about?

But congregations need to be much better educated about the issues that cause so much gross economic division, poverty and desperation in our society. Our Peace and Justice Commission can send educational materials to those who ask. If you do not have people in your congregation who know first–hand the reasons for anger and hopelessness in parts of our society, churches in our poorer areas can send representatives to speak with you.

Several months ago I sent materials to each of our congregations from Bread for the World. These materials described letter writing campaigns in which we all can be involved to help support changes in our laws and national budget. These changes would make enormous strides in overcoming the cycles of poverty, hunger and joblessness in our country.

We continue to look for more congregations who will join with us in support of Nehemiah West. Nehemiah West will build housing for low income families. This housing will be owned by the people living in it. This is probably the most important single thing we can do to help stabilize otherwise troubled neighborhoods.

Our splendid Neighborhood Youth Association, which works with youth in difficulty and their families, needs financial support and volunteers. Hillsides Homes is looking for people who want to participate in Advocates for Children.

Some of our congregations might wish to become a companion church with one of our churches in the impacted areas. Or you may wish to contact them directly about sending food or clothing to St. Martin's or St. Timothy's in Compton, St. John's, Advent, Christ the Good Shepherd, Trinity, St. Mary's, St. Philip's, or St. Nicholas (all in Los Angeles), St. Francis of Norwalk or Holy Faith in Inglewood.

With assistance from the Presiding Bishop's Fund, I am using my Discretionary Fund as a channel to send money to the clergy at a number of these churches so that they can directly help those in need in their areas. Those who wish to help in this way may contribute to my Bishop's Discretionary Fund.

We are also seeing how some of our business leaders and lawyers can be of help to those who need such assistance in obtaining loans and rebuilding.

We will do other things. But these are all important things that you and we can do now. We can channel our feelings of anger or sadness or guilt in constructive ways.

In the last few days Bishop Talton and I have been present with many of our people in the areas that suffered the most. We have heard their anger, frustration, fear and pain. We have also already heard of and seen many examples of courage and generosity—of individuals and congregations reaching out in care. This brings us hope. What we must do now is to join together with others in ways which will sustain this hope for our future together. Let us pray.

> God of mercy, who calls us to live lives of justice and compassion, we pray for all who suffer from the disorder and injustice of our society. We pray for those beaten and oppressed. We pray for those who have died. We pray for those who have lost their livelihoods and homes. We pray for those who are afraid. We pray for all our children. We pray for parents. We pray for the elderly. We pray for those who struggle to bring order and stability to our neighborhoods. We give thanks for people of courage and love. We pray against hopelessness. We pray that

11

we may learn better to live together as people caring for each other's needs and problems. We pray for the forgiveness of our sins. We pray for a peace of righteousness and fairness for us all. We pray in Jesus' name. Amen.

Rodney King and Dignity
Testimony to the Christopher Commission

We have a long distance to go to reach any ideal state of community in Southern California, but in our churches and in many other places there are daily examples of people of different cultures and groups sharing with and supporting one another.

In a number of ways the policemen and policewomen of Los Angeles are supportive and protective of this diversity and interaction. We can take pride in these numerous examples of support and cooperation among peoples in this diverse and complex region. The Christopher Commission has been created to help us find ways to restore that pride that has been harmed, for the pride itself can be both a resource and a guide to us in strengthening harmony, democracy and community in our city.

We all need to recognize, however, that the harm that has been done is severe, and that the source of that harm is a sickness that runs deep in our police department, in our society, and in the human heart. That sickness has a number of symptoms—among them insecurity and anger. At a deeper level, fear is both a symptom and a cause—making people afraid of what is different, afraid of each other. Out of the wisdom of our tradition we would understand the root cause to be sin—the desire to put self or one's family or group so at the center of concern that there is no real love and therefore no real understanding of others and no strong care for the larger community.

There is a question in our Christian baptismal covenant which calls upon us to respect the dignity of every human being. I do not believe the police officers involved in the now notorious action would have done what they did to Mr. King if they had had some similar thought in their heads and hearts that fateful night.

After the beating of Mr. King, I heard a number of stories from members of our churches. One that has particularly stuck in my mind was told by a distinguished lay official in our diocese—a black man who has lived in Los Angeles for a number of years. He told me of the times that he had been stopped for no apparent reason, ordered out of his car, spread-eagled and insulted. He told me it was hard to relate such stories because he found such instances so humiliating.

This is a well-dressed, well-educated man driving a nice automobile. One shudders when one thinks of the times and ways similar things have happened to other people because of their skin color or ethnic group.

Not only in Los Angeles but in many parts of our country, the major task of the police is too often seen as protecting the well-to-do and those who are relatively well off from those who have less or little. I think this attitude is pervasive and affects every aspect of police work from recruitment and training to organization and strategy. In subtle if not open ways it is an assumption encouraged by elected and non-elected officials. Because people of color are a disproportionate number of the less well-off in our society, the assumption fosters and reinforces prejudicial racial attitudes and actions.

I would argue that we must work hard to alter that assumption or all else we accomplish will end up only treating symptoms. In a true democracy all people should be entitled to equal police support and protection no matter what their economic circumstances. Indeed, there are obvious good reasons for holding that most police work should be dedicated to the support and protection of those in society who are more victimized and less able to protect themselves.

To be truly effective, the change in this ordering of priorities must come from courageous elected officials and from the people themselves. To begin with, however, it must be written into the training and policy of all police and receive especially effective expression from those who lead the department.

The power of police to protect the community is more effective the less violence is used. Every time violence is used, the effectiveness of the badge and the uniform is lessened because a stable and just order cannot, in the long run, be enforced by violence. This understanding does not mean that force can never be used, but it runs directly counter to the belief that the use of violence strengthens the authority and power of police by creating fear of them.

I believe the City of Los Angeles needs to have a genuinely independent Police Commission, chosen by elected officials, but then protected from any interference. This commission, using investigators other than the police themselves, needs to have the means to investigate all serious allegations against police behavior.

The alternative to this fully independent commission is that the elected officials themselves would become directly responsible for the conduct of the police. This solution has some merit, but elected officials should not attempt to have it both ways, holding a body other than themselves responsible while claiming authority over that body.

I also hope for three other changes in the local police department:

• More women police—I would say *many* more women police. I believe women police are and can be trained to be more likely to look for ways other than force and violence to resolve difficult situations.

• More police representing different racial and ethnic groups.

• More police out of cars, visible and known in the daily life of our communities.

What I am sure many of us look and hope for is a police department that can become more fully supportive of a multi-ethnic society and take pride in the strengths this brings to our region.

Our Racism

In 1939 the Daughters of the American Revolution refused Marian Anderson permission to sing in Constitution Hall. Hearing of this, Eleanor Roosevelt promptly resigned from the D.A.R. and helped arrange for Marian Anderson to sing at the Lincoln Memorial. There, in her pure and haunting contralto voice, she sang "My country 'tis of thee, sweet land of liberty, of thee I sing."

That moment in American history has been etched in my memory from the first time I saw the filmclip as a young teenager: The vision and longing for a land of liberty inclusive of all people—set poignantly against the reality.

There are many splendid American stories of sacrifices made, barriers overcome and solidarity achieved. But there are also so many bitter tales of displacement, broken treaties, dehumanization, slavery, lynchings, bigotry, discrimination, oppressive poverty and prejudice. Beginning in the sixties and through the seventies and part of the eighties some progress was made, particularly for African-American people who were able to gain a decent education, find reasonable job opportunities and become professionals or otherwise join the middle or upper-middle economic classes. Many others, however, found themselves still caught in cycles of poverty, now even further constrained by the loss of many of the jobs traditionally held by black males. And racism continued at every level in subtle but also overt and often destructive ways.

An all too real sign of this racism has been the manner in which police have been encouraged to see a central part of their work as the protection of the propertied classes and the "policing" of those with less in our society, often people of color. The beating of Rodney King, and what appeared to be the jury vindication of his police "handlers," seemed to many to be almost a caricature of this repeated history.

Few people want to believe that they have racist attitudes and engage in racist actions, but few are the people who escape them. Indeed the most dangerous racists in our society may be those who think they are not.

Some racist words and acts are, of course, overt and deliberate. When, in his Gettysburg address, Abraham Lincoln set forth the conviction that our nation was dedicated to the equality of all its people, the Chicago *Times* was among those who attacked the President for suggesting that this had been or should have been the cause of those who had died: "They were men possessing too much self-respect to declare the Negroes were their equals, or were entitled to equal privileges." Although such words and attitudes may be muted in public today, they are (directed against African-American people and other races and ethnic groups) still a very real part of our society.

Other racist acts and attitudes can be more covert. People are often uncomfortable with those different from themselves, so they do not live near them, or go to school with them, or promote or even hire them except perhaps for certain kinds of jobs. Such racism has become systemically institutionalized in our society. So much is this the case that it often goes unquestioned. A classic example of such racism in the life of our church is the manner in which we regularly deploy our clergy. Black clergy are for black congregations. An Asian-American clergyman or woman? Well, why would a predominantly white congregation consider having him or her? Providentially there are a few exceptions, but one needs less than one hand to count them.

Sometimes we may discern forms of racism which are more unintentional. Under the illusion that we are colorblind, we may overlook some of the assumptions we hold about others and our failures to perceive different cultural contexts. It is often just expected that minorities must try to fit into the ways and mores of the predominant group, regardless of the stress and loss of valuable insights and practices this expectation may cause. Many upper and middle-class white Americans, for example, have developed highly individualistic and often competitive attitudes toward life and work. Other groups may stress more communal and cooperative ways of living. One might argue over which approach is preferable, but the answer is far from self-evident, even though this is often assumed in the workplace and other environments.

The very standards according to which forms of inclusivity might take place are regularly set by the predominant group. Because these standards are usually unarticulated and often assumed, they are still more difficult to deal with. Such racism becomes fully institutionalized as it combines power with prejudice. In our church gatherings it is often just assumed that the procedures, theological imagery and understandings, and the liturgical language and music which derive from a European heritage should be accepted by Christians from all backgrounds.

Such racism can be and often is characterized as part of human nature and accepted as "the way things are." It is clear, however, that from the beginning the disciples of Jesus were meant to live differently. His own radically inclusive invitation to participate in the reign of God's justice and mercy, followed by St. Paul's vision of a oneness in Christ Jesus that subsumed the differences of ethnicity, gender and class, set forth a new hope for his followers and for humanity. But, despite a number of splendid instances of striving for such community, church history has regularly mirrored the racism and bigotry of its societies and often tragically reinforced them. The observation that eleven o'clock on Sunday morning is the most segregated hour in America is a painful truth for us to confess and confront.

There are so many challenges and opportunities before us. We know that we cannot speak to our society until we can witness to it. Alongside God's calling and grace and courage for us, we have enormous people resources in our church—the wisdom and leadership of different races, ethnicities, backgrounds and experience. This is among the reasons we must learn better to share and witness at diocesan and other levels beyond our vital ministries as congregations.

Our Diocesan Task Force on Inclusivity is at work examining our attitudes and structures at every level. We know that we have an enormous and primary task of just listening—really hearing one another. There is lack of understanding, and there are fears that can be overcome only by careful listening and prayer and looking to God together in order to know God's love in our lives. We want to shape better ways to do multicultural and crosscultural ministry. New programs are being established so that we can educate ourselves about these opportunities and about the problems of racism in our church and society.

There are ways that congregations and other groups can get on with this vital ministry using resources immediately at hand. Groups could take this commentary of mine and discuss it and build upon it with their own insights and calls to action.

Congregations are setting up companion relationships with other of our churches, or they are becoming involved in specific projects like the Hope in Youth Campaign or the work of our Economic Development Task Force. They are looking more carefully at themselves, their structures and attitudes, and their communities and neighborhoods for overlooked opportunities for service, outreach and invitation.

With our education department the Task Force will be providing additional ideas and challenges, along with written and people resources, to encourage new learning and cross-cultural sharing. The rewards and benefits of such sharing can bring splendid new friendships and opportunities to our lives.

All this could, of course, be one of those issues we take up for a while, and then let slip back as we return to older patterns and consciousness. But we had better not.

Though the Earth Be Moved

What next?" I asked a friend. "Killer bees," was the response. After drought, flood, fire, severe recession, civil upheaval, and devastating earthquakes, killer bees I think I can take. One can at least try to out-run the bees.

Among the extraordinary things about the earthquake was how intensely personal and communal it was at the same time.

It broke into each of our homes—for most of us into our bedrooms. Each of us remembers exactly where we were—who we held onto or how alone we were. We remember who we worried about first.

In my home—only a few miles from the epicenter—the noise and the shaking were violent and fierce. Stunned in the immediate aftermath, Barbara and I tried to remember the basics. Don't walk around without shoes. Watch out for broken windows or things that could still fall. Open cabinets with caution. Smell for gas. Fortunately I had purchased one of those lights which comes on automatically when the electricity goes off. The batteries in our radios were still working.

But I also remembered the extra water I had said I was going to purchase. And, as the immediate terror and euphoria at still being alive began to pass, I started to think of the possibility of yet another, perhaps larger quake. I thought of people dying, the injured, the elderly, the very poor, and those suddenly without homes or food, of damaged churches.

Our young dog had disappeared. I found him a few minutes later hiding in the furnace closet, the door of which had been thrown open. Perhaps not a bad place to seek safety.

As daylight came there were other almost comic scenes—a library alcove three feet deep in books on the floor. Amid all the shards of glass in the kitchen, cans and packages of food were strewn about with a broken jar of olives and another of pizza sauce spread decoratively upon them.

Person after person had similar stories of terror, fear and worry to tell. There was relief to be alive and even attempts at humor—trying to get back to some sense of normalcy amid the aftershocks. It was something that had happened to all of us at once. For days there was little else we talked about.

We were reminded of how closely we are bound together, and, however resourceful we were and are, we learned again how much we need one another and depend on the common fabric of society and services we have established. Forced back onto surface streets again, and watching through the eyes of television, we could see who needed help the most, and were asked again how it is we want to try to live together and be part of one society.

Some of us, whether we be middle class, rich or poor, who complain about big government and taxes, were suddenly asking for more government services for ourselves, our businesses, our loved ones.

We wanted compassion and help and understanding and were reminded that government is not supposed to be some body else, but all of us acting together to make a fairer and more humane society.

Together we knew again how much of the earth we all are. Although at first one could understandably feel anger and alienation from the land that could strike so suddenly and fiercely, one also knew that this dynamic movement had formed the beauty of hills, valley and mountains. It is all the structures of our civilization that are in so many ways the intrusion. Were we still living in tents, earthquakes would not have such effects for us.

Yet, of course, this is the way we will go on living—with buildings and highways and gas, water, fuel and electric lines. What is probably most remarkable is that our earth, with all its tremors and storms, is still so benign and nurturing a home for us. But we need to learn how more safely and wisely to build and live on it.

And as important as stronger repaired roads and new buildings are, we also need to make investments in human capital through education, the strengthening of families, job training and community organization. Now can be a time to plan for such things as smaller, more local schools, more child care, and to rebuild our apartments and other housing in more affordable and livable ways.

In days past we have again learned much about self-reliance and about interdependence and cooperation. We have stories of courage and sharing to tell, stories of helping the injured, counseling the frightened, donating services, bringing food, helping a neighbor, doing our work more carefully, being tender to one another. Despite all the wrongs and selfishness we know are in our world, we can marvel, too, at the kindness and willingness to sacrifice. We can wonder where they come from and how we can make them more a part of the human adventure.

As always in such disasters, some will ask, where was God in the time of terror and destruction? For people of faith there remains the profound

21

awareness that God is never apart. We and the whole creation are of God. What happens to us happens also to God. And, whatever happens, God remains our ultimate trust and the ground of our hope and courage. "Therefore we will not fear, though the earth be moved...God alone is my rock and salvation, my stronghold, so that I shall not greatly be shaken" (Psalms 46:2; 62:2).

> Shattering sleep and fear
> In an uproar of heaving
> Heart and land and the falling
> Glass in darkness everywhere,
>
> I cling to you and bed,
> Silent in the awesomeness,
> Desperate for the violence
> To stop, ending the dread,
>
> So that living we can
> Creep caring in the fallen,
> Find our dog and try calling
> Friends and churches in the dawn.

For Freedom For?

The collapse of communism in the Soviet Union leaves the United States with a great opportunity and challenge.

For more than my entire adult life the United States has seen itself locked in a form of mortal combat with world communism. Terrible wars have been fought. Enormous expenses have been given over to armies and armaments, including weapons capable of destroying the whole world's population. Perhaps even more significantly, much of our nation's political and spiritual energy has been devoted to this struggle. We often identified ourselves in terms of what we were against—communist totalitarianism. We, by contrast, were for freedom.

Yet that part of the struggle may in many ways have been all too easy. Communism claimed to be able to free people from poverty and lack of opportunity. Since it very often clearly did not accomplish these goals, and instead locked its people into compliance by fear and force, it was easy to see ourselves as for freedom defined largely over against the lack of freedom in communist countries.

That was, however, mostly a negative way of understanding freedom. It was freedom *from* such forced compliance—being told where to live and work, accepting regulation of the media and the arts, and being excluded from any meaningful political process. But what happens when one *has* these freedoms? It is a question people are, of course, now beginning to ask in formerly totalitarian countries.

Are these freedoms goals in themselves? Is freedom primarily a matter of each individual doing what he or she chooses?

The United States greatly prizes individualism. Although both the political left and right in our country have communal values and their heritages, their political rhetoric and actions in recent decades strongly favor individual liberties—the left more as individual rights in terms of law, the right often now from a populist economic perspective. In some people's minds, such individualism may even seem to be the simple opposite of communism.

Yet most thoughtful people also recognize, if only on the basis of a wiser self-interest, the dangers of unguided and unlimited individualism. The environment is an obvious example. If freedom only means each individual or family exercising the right to do what one wants to do, will not our environment become uninhabitable or, at the least, much less pleasant for everyone?

Is it not also in some sense in everyone's interest to see that the young are well-educated, that everyone has food and shelter and access to decent medical attention? For years the threat of communism has meant, at least to many, that these questions had to wait—that there was not enough time or money or political will. What happens when they no longer need to wait?

And going beyond self-interest, does the human adventure—especially seen in moral terms—offer opportunity not only for individual accomplishment but for what humans can do together?

Cynics will say that many people find such questions too threatening. Soon a new enemy will be found. Instead of our being for freedom *for* what we can do for the larger community as well as for selves and family, we will find in that new enemy an excuse to think primarily in terms of freedom *from* the threats of others.

I have a different vision. At the least there is a greater opportunity to use our liberties for the benefit of others as well as ourselves. The Christian faith, which sees each individual as precious in the eyes of God while finding fullness of life in community and in self-giving and sharing, has much to bring to this opportunity. We shall do that best, not in our words, but by being willing to share of ourselves to help build communities of mutual care and responsibility in which there is respect for the dignity of every human being.

AIDS

My phone rang. It was a friend, four years younger than I, from my hometown. He had followed me into ordination in the Episcopal Church. He was in ways like a younger brother. He was a good priest—a kind and gentle human being. He told me he had AIDS. The reaction of his rather hysterical congregation was that he had to leave his ministry and livelihood.

This was some years ago. Then I didn't know AIDS was inevitably fatal. He had to explain that to me. A year later he was dead.

To those from my hometown who seemed to want to understand, I tried to explain. I tried to talk with his mother and father. But from the perspective of my understanding of God's love, there was no easy explanation. I prayed to God. I prayed against AIDS, but there were and are no easy words.

My phone has rung more times since then. Former students—friends. I prayed with them and for them, but there were and are no easy words.

Just a few days ago, I heard on the radio the story of a nine-year-old boy, a hemophiliac, who had died of AIDS. I thought of the agony for his family, the problems that he and his family had experienced...whether he could continue to go to school, play with his friends. I prayed for them, but there were no easy words.

The other day I visited in one of our hospitals. I talked with a young woman whose husband was a drug user. She had a darling little baby with her. They both had AIDS. There were no easy words. Sometimes there are no words at all.

I heard later that the landlord of this mother and child had had them evicted because he was afraid of how the other tenants would react.

A young couple in Zaire discover they both have AIDS. Their agony is fearfully multiplied because of their unborn child. We pray for them, but there are no easy words.

Andrew and John, two gay partners in Los Angeles, men who have cared deeply for each other over the years, find out that John is dying of AIDS.

There have been efforts in the past to find words for inexplicable

25

suffering. You and I remember Job, having lost his worldly goods and family, covered with loathsome sores from head to foot. "Curse God and die," his wife tells him. Give up, in other words, not only on the goodness and faithfulness of God, but on any meaning in life itself.

And then there are Job's friends with advice like, "You must have sinned, Job. If not you, then someone in your family. Who are you to question God? God cannot be unjust."

And today all these answers come back. AIDS is a result of sin. It is God's warning and punishment on the evil of homosexuality, of drug use. The words have come thundering down from some religious leaders to whom the words apparently come easily.

"Oh," might Job have responded sarcastically, "Oh, how wonderful it must be to read the natural world so clearly and to know God's will from it. How earnestly some will defend their view of God's ways—insisting on condemning suffering people as sinners in order to vindicate their view of morality. Forget the babies with AIDS. Forget the hemophiliacs and other recipients of infected transfusions—or the thousands of people in Africa and other poor lands. Those are the others, often poor, racially different—mainly people outside their congregations and view of morality—which make it possible to compound suffering by calling it God's judgment. One is not just saddened, we are ashamed and rightly angry.

And let me tell you about John and Andrew. I know John and Andrew. I know how much they have learned about love and compassion and profound caring for one another. I do not pretend to understand all the mysteries of life—certainly not of human sexuality—but neither do others. If there is one good thing that can come out of our AIDS crisis, possibly it is this: some moral and ethical humility.

John and Andrew, Bill and Mark, Ruth and Mary. I have seen their deep love and care. Everything I can discover about God's love and the love God would share with us tells me that much of their love is the love God wants us to have and learn and share with one another—caring, kindness, sacrifice, vulnerability, compassion.

But then the AIDS. Why the AIDS? Where is God in all this? With the Psalmist we cry out, "Why do you stand so far off, O Lord?" "The innocent are broken and humbled?" Why is it that these your children, already often troubled and afflicted by society, should suffer so? "Darkness," the Psalmist says in his despair, "is my only companion."

To our recent General Convention of the Church in Detroit there were brought the hundreds of memorial quilts made in memory of friends and loved ones who died of AIDS. They were laid out in the vast basement region of the Convention Center. That hushed room became like a great memorial. Occasionally one heard a sob, a cry as someone caught sight of the name of someone they knew, or perhaps was just overwhelmed by the loss of so many relatively young lives. Many faces leaked their tears.

One could feel just overwhelmed and despairing, but somehow there was also present in that great memorial room a sense of compassion, a sense of such profound caring that one sensed the love and the care of God.

One was reminded that we are all mortal—that, as the saying goes, none of us is going to get out of this world alive. We share that together. We need so much to care for one another. And somehow in that reaching out, somehow in the presence of all that love, the Spirit of God, strengthening our caring, caring with us—offering the hope of a love which transcends this life—that Spirit of God was present as well.

There are now so many individual stories of anguish—of changed lives—of caring and compassion. And there are and will be so many more. There are going to be so many challenges to us individually and together before medical science can offer us any hope of ending the disease.

There will be a continuing and growing burden on medical insurance systems, private and government supported, making it difficult for some people to have medical insurance. Will the business, government and insurance leaders have the compassion and courage to respond?

There will be a burden on our legal system. Many will contend that the community has a right to protect itself, but at what costs to individuals, to rights to privacy, and particularly to individuals who are members of certain groups. Will there be enough compassion?

Perhaps the biggest challenge will be fear. Despite all the evidence to the contrary, people can still be afraid that they will get AIDS from sneezes, doorknobs, toilet seats, hugs, a common communion cup. One cannot get AIDS that way, but how does one deal with fear, often irrational fear?

"Mature love casts out fear," the Bible tells us. Only compassion, only great love will give us the courage to stand up to the fear that may be in us, and especially before the fear of others. Only such love may begin to help us transcend our tragedy, and make it into one of humanity's great seasons of caring and sharing.

But before many can do that, they may also have to work to overcome their fear of those who are oriented to the same gender in their sexuality. That can go against a lot of upbringing and training, but now can be a time of new learning for us all. Indeed, it may be a time for us all to confront the trivialization of sexuality that has run through much of our society in recent years, separating it from sacrificial, vulnerable, committed love. Now can be a time for us all to again offer our total lives to God and to make our sexuality truly human.

There are then many things we can do. The Presiding Bishop has challenged each of the bishops to join him in entering into a pastoral relationship with someone dying of AIDS. I invite each of our clergy also to join us in that opportunity. Many others of you may also become a buddy with someone through such a relationship.

Maybe your congregation can be involved in a hospice or in support of some ministry to those with AIDS. Maybe you can give financial or other encouragement to a hospital to have an AIDS ward. Maybe you can speak up when someone makes a comment out of fear or a discriminating remark. You can give to medical research, and try to help our governmental leaders to give more resources and turn away from discriminatory legislation.

Dr. Jonathan Mann, Director of the Global Program on AIDS for the World Health Organization, has said, "we have seen all over the world that as people are informed about AIDS, panic and groundless fears recede; and as leaders speak knowledgeably and clearly about AIDS, public confidence and commitment increase and illusory and simplistic solutions to the problems of AIDS are rejected." Dr. Mann has also said that the churches are the places many people look to—not to be places of fear and isolation during this time of crisis—but to be centers of compassion, of reaching out and new understanding. That is also my hope and prayer to God for each congregation in this diocese. May we be drawn together in compassion, realizing that it is only our love for one another—the love of God among us—that can change our fear and alter our pain.

We are reminded once more of the fragility of life, that we all are animals, that all of us will die. Our deepest and ultimate hope is not in our longevity, not good medicine, not good health. Yes, we want these things; they are important, but what is of much more importance to us finally is our care for one another...never letting each other go.

Still, there are no easy words. We pray for an end to this plague. We pray for the healing of those whom we love—for all who are bereaved. But above all, we pray for compassion, to overcome fears—to enable us to reach out, to hold and care for one another.

We pray in the name of the one who was and is one with us, whom we remember reaching out to those with leprosy, who by faith we believe to be among us reaching out to those with AIDS, offering a way to begin to transform suffering and evil. Our words falter. Heal us. In the name of Jesus we pray. Amen.

Reason to Use Our Franchise

Perhaps I should not have been surprised. Leaving early for work one morning in order to vote, I asked my 27-year-old nephew, who is living with us while attending graduate school, when he planned to go the polls. "That will be difficult," he quipped with only a trace of embarrassment, "since I'm not registered to vote."

The next evening I tried to probe that non-participatory stance of his. Here is a well-educated young man, who reads the newspaper and is far from uncaring about what happens in our society.

"Why bother?" he said. "Most politicians and a lot of people who work in government are in one way or another bought and paid for. Either subtly or obviously they are obligated to individuals or groups who finance their campaigns. Or else they are making extra money on the side in ways that are bound to influence how they make decisions. And, if they are not doing that, they are making deals and associations now so they can make money after leaving government service. Financial institutions, developers, contractors, rich individuals, unions, trade associations — they are the ones who do the real voting in this country with their bucks and influence. Why should I waste my time?"

I wanted to claim he was exaggerating, but on most days, all he would have to do is pick up the newspaper to prove his point. One could contend that investigative reporters are only telling us what has always been true in politics and government service. But there is certainly a strong and growing impression that the ethics of those in government service are a long way from what they should be. My nephew is far from alone.

There is a crisis of confidence in Los Angeles and throughout our country. Many people suspect, rightly or wrongly, that the breaches of trust disclosed in the past decade alone are just the tip of an iceberg of major and minor misuses of public office for ill-gotten gain. Some might argue that in the face of drug wars, severe problems with schools, housing and medical services and other societal concerns, this crisis is only a minor problem. Yet it is also arguable that a crisis in confidence in the character of governmental leadership is a major contributing factor to the other problems—a major reason why people believe there is no way community action through government can solve them.

The city of Los Angeles has a great opportunity not only to halt, but to reverse this sense that many government officials are on the make and take. Now before the City Council is a stringent and carefully drawn ethics code for our municipal government. It must be strong. There is nothing else that will do now. It could become a model for other governmental bodies throughout our state and country.

There may be some minor adjustments that can be offered to make the code more equitable, but any major weakening will be an enormous step backward. Council members may be able to get themselves reelected if they do not pass a strong code, but they will have contributed to the crisis in confidence that will increasingly make it difficult for government to work on the real problems of society.

The one excuse, above all, we do not want to hear is how government officials need outside income to make their livings. I certainly want our officials to be given good wages. But if they feel that they must continue to take money from sources who call into question even the slightest possibility of conflict of interest, let them be thanked for their service and then step aside. Other fine people can be found.

How proud we will be if our mayor, who already backs the code, and our council members give us new confidence in our city government by approving this ethics proposal. I would so like to pick up the paper the next morning and say to my nephew, "Look what our leaders have done. Now go register to vote."

Government and Us

"If God wanted us to vote, God would have given us candidates." So read a bumper sticker I saw the other day. It no doubt reflects the cynicism a lot of people are feeling these days. Perhaps many of them won't vote.

That is tragic, and for those who are disciples, a dereliction of Christian responsibility. I happen to be one of those more sunny and optimistic individuals who see more good and caring people in political life than do some others. But, however we judge and appraise politicians, our failure to make ourselves heard can only make matters worse. Those who think that not voting is a form of protest are only kidding themselves. Few are the politicians who will hear that message.

Almost all political representatives are followers, not leaders. I do not mean that critically, but rather to state an important truth. Many people who do not vote complain that elected officials do not provide enough or the right kind of leadership. I could join in that complaint, but the fact of the matter is that most politicians do not so much lead as react to the mood and concerns of the electorate, which they are constantly checking.

Important changes in the United States rarely happen from the top down. The end of desegregation, the end of the Vietnam War, and the new concern for the environment are examples of changes that have taken place not because of political leadership but because of changes that happened at the grass roots. Christian citizens and Christian communities have played and continue to play important roles in these changes.

Yes, we have tremendous problems in our nation with the manipulation of the media, with PAC money and money from lobbies. These, too, are things only voters can change. In the meantime, you and I have before us not only candidates but other vital issues. We have opportunities to let our representatives know that we really do care about all our children, and their welfare and their education. We can send clear messages that we are a generous and caring people who are not just selfishly concerned with our pocketbooks.

Our Bible is quite radical in telling us not to place money first in our lives, and to care, because God cares, for the orphans, widows, strangers and the poor—that is, the most disadvantaged and powerless in our midst. Whatever our politics, we are Christians first, and we have a number of opportunities to make our voices heard on issues affecting children, especially those in poverty, and those others who need our support. Believe me, the politicians will listen if they know enough of us are making that a priority.

St. Paul can seem pretty conservative when it comes to our relationship with government: "Let every person be subject to the governing authorities" (Romans 13:1). We are not to be off thumbing our nose at government. In a democratic society that teaching could well translate into a mandate for every Christian citizen, a call to all of us to participate as fully as possible in the governance of our communities and country.

One could probably still get some good debates going with regard to questions about churches' participation in political life. In the past some have argued—particularly more conservative evangelical denominations— that churches ought not to become involved with governmental or political issues. Many of those faith groups have, however, in recent years changed their tune. Probably most Christians, even if they do not agree on particular issues, would agree that Christians in every aspect of their lives must show care and concern for that which God cares about. Churches have a responsibility to help people understand the moral and ethical principles that will help to guide them as they vote.

Many of us remember the famous line from the comic strip Pogo: "We have met the enemy and it is us." It's no good to sit back and be cynical about politicians. We have met the government and it is us.

Our Fragile Island Home

Paper clips, burger boxes, chemical waste, pesticides, auto emissions, Styrofoam, plastic forks, and on and on. Mountains of garbage, smog and polluted air. When will it end? Or will it be our end?

Many of us are so accustomed at least to giving lip service to environmental causes that we may be surprised when we realize that not all environmentalists consider Christians to be their allies. We can point to phrases in the prayers and litanies of our Prayer Book, resolutions from our General and Diocesan Conventions, and sermons we have given or heard. But what, others may ask, are you actually doing in response?

Moreover, Christianity (or at least branches thereof) has long been suspect in the eyes of a number of environmentalists for teachings and attitudes which could encourage an indifference to environmental concerns. Scriptural language bids humans to "fill the earth and subdue it; and have dominion over the fish of the sea and over the birds of the air and over every living thing that moves upon the earth... I have given you every plant... every tree" (Genesis 1:28-29). Such language could be understood to give humanity the sense that it is the only species with rights on this planet. It might seem to grant license to do whatever humans want with other life, the air, earth and water.

The belief that this world is to come to an end before long can encourage a disposable attitude: "'Why not use it up, since it all is going to pass away in any case?" This view of things is given a further boost by a spirituality which separates the spiritual and material spheres. Since saved Christians belong primarily to the former, why be much concerned about the latter?

Many of us will wish to respond that these are the views of a gnostic rather than of orthodox Christianity. Better Christian and biblical teaching holds that God's creation is good and that the time of its transformation in the new age is not known. As creatures, humans are fully a part of this world; their "dominion" is to be understood as one of great responsibility and stewardship for all living things and the common environment. While the environment is not to be worshipped, nor environmentalism made into a religion, the created world is a source of revelation to be revered, respected, fiercely protected.

Yet, while a sound environmental theology is of critical importance to Christian living, non-Christians as well as many of us will also want to say "By their fruits you shall know them." Sound belief ought to manifest itself in practice.

How well do church offices and meetings practice and witness to sound environmental guidelines? How many individual Christians take the care of the environment to heart and make sacrifices for the sake of those around them and those who are yet to come?

Perhaps the greatest enemy is apathy: a sense of "what difference can I and my friends make?" It is so much easier to blame the "they" and to forget that care and sacrifice has to begin somewhere.

There are many little things we all can do which cumulatively can make an enormous difference. A friend of mine once estimated that by leaving the tap running while brushing one's teeth, one lets a gallon and a half of water run down the drain. Try multiplying that gallon-and-a-half by even a few hundred Christians, three times a day over a couple of years. Many environmentalists consider the quality of human life to be in far more danger from a shortage of good water than of gas and oil.

Meanwhile, vehicles burning stupendous quantities of fossil fuels daily pollute and are very likely cooking us in our atmospheric envelope. Intelligent and caring people save energy—at home and at work—in every way they can.

Eliminating or just cutting down on the consumption of red meat can conserve great amounts of water and help to preserve depleted top soil and rain forests. Car-pooling to meetings and work can help save the air.

One doesn't have to give in to an overblown consumerism. We can hand back these unnecessary packages and wrappings. We can insist on recycling and protect the use of non-biodegradable materials.

As individuals and congregations we can let our elected officials know not only that we care, but that we are willing to pay the taxes and make the sacrifices to protect and preserve our common habitation.

As citizens and with our government we can work together with business in the free enterprise system to provide the pricing and other incentives for recycling and sound environmental practices. Controversial as it may be, let us also be wise enough to support policies which recognize that the world's resources are limited and that we cannot overpopulate without bringing it and us to disaster. We need to revise our ideas of growth and progress and what it means to achieve as individuals and to succeed as communities. Our new sense of progress must include progress for our environment.

"All that is is alive with his life," the gospel writer tells us (John 1:4). All that is is a result of untold eons of interstellar creativity and evolutionary formations. So, "give us all a reverence for the earth as your own creation, that we may use its resources rightly in the service of others and to your honor and glory."

April 22 is to be observed over the world and in many of our houses of worship as Earth Day. I hope that all of the churches in our diocese will find their ways of offering this reverence and of making renewed commitments, as individuals and communities to the care of this fragile earth, our island home.

Environmental Economy

Ten thousand species of plants and animals become extinct each year. That is an estimate. No one knows for sure.

Global warming, due largely to the burning of fossil fuels and fewer rain forests, creeps up on us. Atmospheric carbon dioxide is increasing at a historically unprecedented rate, along with methane, nitrous oxides and chlorofluorocarbons.

World population grows at the rate of a hundred million people a year. Soil erosion, desertification, over-fishing, air and water pollution, and waste disposal problems are increasing concerns in many parts of the world.

Although environmentalists are sometimes accused of using scare tactics, there is a lot about which to be very concerned.

We tend to think that the problems will at least develop only slowly and incrementally. That may be true in one sense, but problems also have a way of suddenly manifesting themselves. It can be a bit like the smoker who only has a nagging cough and a little shortness of breath. Then one day there is the spot on the lung.

We do tend as a race to hide from serious challenges. "In the shadow of the hawk," wrote the poet Edna St. Vincent Millay, "we feather our nests." Probably our favorite "out" in the face of environmental distress is our belief that science and technology will somehow rescue us. There will be, we want to believe, a spray or a chemical or cold fusion or some technology that will put everything right—perhaps just in the nick of time.

"Mommy," the seven-year-old girl asked, "can the hole in the ozone layer be fixed?"

Mommy doesn't know and scientists do not know either.

It is, of course, also an economic problem. That is among the reasons why present forms of government have such a difficult time doing anything serious and comprehensive in response to the concerns. Eighty percent of U. S. voters when polled say "environmental standards cannot be too high" and that improvement must be made "regardless of cost." Yet, because care for the environment seems to conflict with our short-term economic interests and because special interests are often more directly affected by particular actions than is the general public good, the environment continues to get much more lip service than actual help.

Yet, if the bottom line is not green, can it ever really be black? Many business executives know in their hearts that they and we are storing up deferred problems which will in time be very costly or impossible to fix. In the long run they may well put them out of business.

But maybe the "market," economists tell us, will eventually take care of our problems as water, land and food come in to shorter and shorter supply. The quality of life will go down and everything may be rationed, but cost will finally make people careful.

Yet, we have to recognize that the market economy often waits until things get very serious before it reacts. Putting things off in this manner seems rather like waiting to have a heart attack before engaging in health maintenance.

But if scientists, government, business or the market cannot save us from ourselves, who can? Many had hoped that maybe the "enlightenment" could—that the answers lay in education and progress.

Education can often be helpful, but it is becoming increasingly clear that the emphases on individual rights and achievement (particularly when the individual is viewed largely as consumer) and on progress as unlimited growth are a major part of our problem. The so-called enlightenment has not been able to bring about a sense of community, of living togetherness and belonging in the world and to each other.

What is enough for our human needs? How might we live more simply with a sense of sufficiency? Can we find other ways of using than using up? Can we lift the common good and longer term interests over narrower views? How can we see our economy (our oikonomia—living together) as more than money and goods? Can other aspects of life (such as relationships) matter more than what we can buy?

These questions go to the heart of what human life and responsibility are all about. They are, in the largest sense, spiritual questions and issues.

"The Creation," writes Wendell Berry, "is not in any sense independent of the Creator, the result of a primeval creation long over and done with, but is the continuous, constant participation of all creatures in the being of God."[1] All that is shares in the sacred.

"To till and to keep" is what Adam is called to do in the first garden (Genesis 2:15). Noah is commissioned to "bring two of every kind into the ark, to keep them alive with you" (Genesis 6:19).

To use but to *keep* is the kind of stewardship to which we as responsible creatures are called. We should do this keeping if only in our own self-interest.

It would be a major step forward if we could do this collectively, caring for forests and streams, oceans, wetlands and plains because we need them. We can understand them as not only necessary for food and clothing, but for the beauty and restorative power of nature, as places for recreation and contemplation, and for learning from natural history and nature's balance and sense of proportion.

We could take a greater step and see ecological sustainability as what we are also called to do for others—our children and theirs, those of other nations, the poor and less advantaged.

What may finally be required, however, is a still greater vision of ourselves as part of the larger economy/oikonomia of the world and life where we are responsible to and for all of creation.

What an irony it would be, notes Holmes Rolston III, if, with its intelligence and awareness, "the sole moral species acts only in its collective self interest toward all the rest." A human being may be of more value than a whooping crane, but what do we say when we are six billion humans and only one hundred whooping cranes? "Ought not this sole moral species do something less self-interested than count all the products of an evolutionary eco-system as rivets in their spaceship, resources in their larder, laboratory materials, recreation for their ride?"[2]

Max Oelschlaeger would describe himself as a convert to the conviction that it is only the faith communities—holding to moral and community values that lie outside the dominant economic paradigm—that can provide the will and leadership to move our society to ecological balance and sustainability. They are the grassroots groups who can all become environmentalists and join with others to help us find and hold the larger vision necessary for this conversion.[3]

Notes

1. Wendell Berry, *Sex, Economy, Freedom and Community* (New York: Random House, 1993), 97.

2. Holmes Rolston III, *Environmental Ethics: Duties to and Values in the Natural World* (Philadelphia: Temple University Press, 1988), 144, 157, 159.

3. Max Oelschlaeger, *Caring for Creation: An Ecumenical Approach to the Environmental Crisis* (New Haven: Yale University Press, 1994). See pp. 207-11 for church-related educational activities for youth, teenagers, and adults; and *Keeping and Healing the Creation* (with study guide), a Resource Paper of the Presbyterian Eco-Justice Task Force. See also Dieter T. Hessel, ed., *After Nature's Revolt: Eco-Justice and Theology* (Minneapolis: Fortress Press, 1992).

Helping the Homeless

Homeless. Most of us have probably never had to worry about not having a place to sleep, a kitchen to cook in, access to a sink and a toilet. Even if for a time we have been without a home of our own, we probably were able to move in with a friend or a relative for a while.

But what if we had no friend or relative with room for us? What if we also had children? What if we were sick?

What causes homelessness? Some people have mental disorders, and it is one of the tragedies of our country that so many mentally disturbed or deficient people live on our streets, subject to hunger and crime.

In more and more cases, it is a string of bad luck—an illness leading to a lost job. Or perhaps just not being able to find work paying above minimum wage when housing is so expensive. To give an example: a year's income at minimum wage is $7,904. A small one-bedroom apartment in Los Angeles' worst neighborhoods runs on the average of $5,700 a year, leaving $2,204 for all other expenses, or $183 a month for food, clothing, utilities and transportation. A surprising number of people use as much as 70 percent of their income in rent. It does not take much to tip them into homelessness.

No one knows for sure how many people are homeless. Perhaps there are as many as several million nationwide, probably more than 40,000 in the Los Angeles area. An additional 40,000 families live in garages here—many of them newcomers to our city.

What is our responsibility for the homeless of our region?

Through the prophet, the Lord questions the ritual fasting of the people and all mere outward forms of religion: "Is not this the fast that I choose...to share your bread with the hungry, and bring the homeless poor into your house...and not to hide yourself from your own flesh? Then your light break forth like the dawn...your vindication shall go before you" (Isaiah 58:6-8).

The Bible is full of admonitions and invitations to help those in great need, and few are more in need of help than the homeless. Jesus tells his disciples, "When the Son of man comes in his glory...he will say to those on his right hand, 'When I was a stranger you welcomed me'" (Matthew 25:31-36).

Perhaps few of us feel we can take the homeless into our own homes, but many of us are in positions to help. These are some of the things your church is doing:

The Church-Temple Housing Corp., established by All Saints Church, Pasadena, and Leo Baeck Temple, West Los Angeles, with the Skid Row Housing Trust has just dedicated its second completely rebuilt and refurnished single-room occupancy hotel. The hotels have been rescued from demolition that would have left many people on social security and low wages with no place to live. Residents of the hotels are offered counseling to help with personal problems and in finding work. Others of our churches are now joining this program. There are 63 more hotels to save!

The diocese has come together with other churches and neighborhood organizations to build Nehemiah-West, which will enable people with moderate incomes to own their own homes and shape a neighborhood and community in South Central Los Angeles where none now exists.

Housing is planned for people with AIDS and other difficulties who have been evicted from their apartments or cannot afford high rents. Others of our churches have built apartments for the elderly. We are working with a neighborhood in the Central City area of Los Angeles to build more low-cost housing. St. Luke's in Long Beach is planning an intergenerational housing venture. Congregations in Orange County work through the Episcopal Service Alliance to assist the homeless. St. Michael's in Isla Vista aids the homeless through an ecumenical project. St. Marks in Upland has a shelter for families without homes.

This list is not exhaustive. There are more stories to tell.

And there are other ways we all can help. We can be aware that during the last decade there has been an 80 percent reduction in federal government funding to help build low-cost housing. There just is not enough housing to go around. We can tell our governmental representatives that we are willing to make the sacrifices in order to see that we do much more as communities and as a society to provide housing for all our people. We can work for alliances between the public and private sector to meet these needs.

We can ask what each of our congregations is able to do. Every congregation can do something. We can offer our services and our financial support to our Commission on the Homeless or to other diocesan programs.

The spiritual danger would be to let ourselves become paralyzed by the dimensions of the problem or to believe we have too few resources to make a difference. God does not expect us fully to solve every problem, but God does call us to do what we can as individuals and as a Church and to try to set for others an example of service and encouragement.

The Nehemiah West Homes

We are here today to announce the Episcopal Church's participation in the Nehemiah West Housing program.[1] This is not a pilot venture, but a proven program in New York where the Episcopal Church was one of the major partners in a venture in which over 1,600 homes have been built. Not only are working people now able to afford homes of their own in that area, but the character of the neighborhood has changed for the better.

We are pleased to be able to participate again in such a program here in Los Angeles. We are pledging at least a half-million dollars for a revolving loan fund, and we are providing development support of $2,000 per month.

The Bible helps us to understand that human beings are not just a collection of individuals, but people meant to live in community, sharing and caring for one another, seeking to love their neighbors as themselves. We are taught of God's concern for those who are less advantaged in society. These understandings guide us to seek opportunities to see how we might be of assistance in various areas of social need.

The Episcopal Church at every level has a deep and abiding concern for affordable housing. Our national office has pledged to raise $9 million for a nation-wide economic justice program, the main component of which is making housing available for all people.

The housing problem is particularly acute in Southern California. It is at the crux of many of our social ills. Whether one talks about refugees, homelessness, AIDS, young families, single people, blue-collar workers, problems of the city, a major issue that continues to present itself is affordable housing. It is estimated that as many as 40,000 people in our cities live on the streets. A like number of families live in garages. Our city grows by about 25,000 households each year, yet at the same time we are demolishing 4,000 units of housing every year.

The Episcopal Church is involved in housing in Los Angeles on several fronts. Through the Church/Temple Housing Corporation we are undertaking the renovation and operation of a number of single-room occupancy hotels in the poorer sections of our city's core. Through our churches we are providing the foundation for housing for the elderly in retirement homes we have constructed. Some of our churches have built transitional living facilities to help those who have no home. We are working with community groups to build low-cost housing in neighborhoods near downtown Los Angeles. Through the Parish of St. Athanasius and St. Paul, we are hoping to develop a strong replacement housing policy in the City West development area. With the Nehemiah Project, we are entering a new phase of housing development and reaffirming our commitment to the central area of the city.

Nehemiah West is not just a plan to build houses but rather a strategy to create a community. A viable alternative to gentrification of poor areas is to provide a livable community for those who live there. The Nehemiah venture is based on the concept that people can improve their own lives and take a greater responsibility for themselves and their neighbors if they are given a chance. This program will give people in the low to moderate income range an opportunity to build equity, to plan for their future, and to create a secure and stable neighborhood in which to live.

Note

1. The first community of Nehemiah West homes, Viñas la Campana, built in conjunction with the Roman Catholic Church and the Industrial Areas Foundation organizations, was completed in the spring of 1995.

How Are the Young People Doing?

The Bible gives a central role to children. They are offered as a promise and a gift of hope for our future and our future with God. The birth of a baby brings new hope and promise.

At the same time the Bible recognizes the need and vulnerability of children. How easily they are injured and deprived. How easily even the disciples can push them aside. But when Jesus saw this, he was indignant and said to them, "Let the children come to me. Do not hinder them; for to such as these belongs the kingdom of God."

"How are the young people doing?"

In almost every congregation I visit, that question can begin a lively conversation. Obviously people care and, just as obviously, they are concerned. Often they wish that their church could do more to teach their children and teenagers the Christian faith, that the church and the home could do more to help impart the virtues of honesty, caring for others, sympathy, self-control, a willingness to share and sacrifice, postponing gratification, hard work, keeping promises, courage, leadership.

They are concerned that the church help families—all kinds of families, with single parents and two parents—to be stronger, to stay together, to be more supportive of each other, to share in faith and caring.

They worry that the church is not devoting enough resources, energy and intelligence to support the moral, intellectual and faith development of their youth. They worry about their own willingness to give time, money and energy for this support.

When it extends out to the wider society, the conversation becomes yet more concerned—even alarmist. While rates are up for drug use, gangs, teen suicide and child abuse, overall achievement scores are dropping and young people are dropping out of school. The public schools are hard pressed to do their job well. TV and movies seem to dominate attention and set values.

A number of people are aware that more than 20 percent of our nation's children now live below the poverty line. That is a shocking figure in a land with so much relative wealth and so many resources. But children, as is well known, are not a constituency. They do not vote or organize to become a special interest group.

Recently I heard a nine-year-old describe how his stomach hurt when he went to bed hungry. I saw the tears of a 10-year-old whose family was living in a garage. He grimaced and said he didn't want to go on living like this.

Perhaps all this is a sign that we as a nation do not plan very far ahead. We are not educating people well for the future job market. So many young people receive inadequate medical care. More than 25 percent are not covered by medical insurance. In the state of California fewer than half the state's two-year-olds have had the basic immunizations.

Some people throw up their hands. But that is not our Christian response.

I have challenged the Diocesan Council, and I want to challenge every congregation and group in the diocese to think with me in the months ahead. I have asked John Hitchcock to chair a special Task Force to help us all do this. What can we do as a church to help support and develop hope and strength in our young people? What can we do to encourage our society—to encourage all of us—to love and educate and care for our young, to provide them with a safer and more hope-filled environment?

There is much we are already doing through our congregations; youth and camping programs; the training of youth leaders; several of our vital institutions, particularly the Hillsides Home and the Neighborhood Youth Assn.; our parochial and diocesan schools; and our educational and other diocesan programs. We are doing some useful planning and work ecumenically and with community organizations. As nurses, doctors, teachers and in a number of other ways, many of our people have important ministries with youth.

But there is surely much more that we can do as disciples and as Christian citizens! And let us not fool ourselves with mere sentiment. If we genuinely care, we are going to be involved with politics, taxes and controversy. But where else would Jesus have us be for the sake of the children?

What programs, we can also ask, are working especially well in our congregations or elsewhere that others can copy? Who can we learn more from? What should be our priorities?

Let's think and pray and work and plan together. Let's start some new initiatives. Then let's bring all this to our Diocesan Convention at the end of the year and devote much of our time there to seeing what we have learned and done and to setting a course for future work and service. What could be more important?

For Desmond Tutu and South Africa

This statement was made in September of 1989.

I am here to join this protest in behalf of my friend and brother, Archbishop Desmond Tutu, one of the bravest, most deeply Christian men I know and for whom I speak as a fellow Anglican bishop. Desmond Tutu has been a voice of reconciliation and hope in the midst of anger and fear and increasing violence in South Africa. He has consistently denounced violence, whether by those in the government upholding the system of apartheid or by those who seek to overcome it.

Yet this peaceful and peace-loving man was arrested twice in one week by South African police—once as he took part in a peaceful attempt to use a public beach near Cape Town that is designated for whites only, and again as he challenged the blockading of a church with an armored police vehicle. On another occasion he was teargassed as he left a church where he had gone to dissuade a group of school youngsters from engaging in a demonstration. The police also threw tear-gas canisters at the youngsters. Another day police marched into his cathedral, carrying firearms and whips, so desecrating that building he felt that it had to be reconsecrated as a holy place.

Outside the cathedral, police beat peaceful protestors including middle-aged women who were already lying on the pavement when the beatings started.

Again and again we hear of men, women and children being beaten, bombarded with water cannon, teargassed. By every human rights standard and democratic value that citizens in this country hold dear, what happens on a regular day-to-day basis to black people in South Africa is like some terrible obscenity.

Today there are signs of new hope. The acknowledgment by the South African government of responsibility for the violence surrounding the elections, and the permission for yesterday's peaceful protest march makes us want to believe that a new day has come. We must not forget, however, that the reason for yesterday's march was to remember the some twenty-three people who were killed as a result of recent police action and to protest the fact that all the basic foundation blocks of apartheid life in South Africa remain in place. Black people still have no vote, and in education, medical treatment, housing and jobs they continue to suffer severe discrimination. Now is not the time to relax the international pressure and concern which has given at least some help to Desmond Tutu and other leaders for peaceful change. Now is the time to find ways to help change take place.

The South African government cares about world opinion and economic action. If they didn't care, they would not spend so much money and effort trying to influence it. That is why I am glad you all are here today.

Cape Town, South Africa, is 10,000 miles from Los Angeles, but in today's global village in which all of us reside, it is really next door. What happens there is our concern, too. When human rights and human dignity are violated there, they are threatened everywhere. If you care about racism and discrimination here, you are bound to care about it in South Africa, too. We are joined to the people of South Africa by bonds of concern and care, of prayer and mutual support.

We pray for our brothers and sisters, black and white and colored, in that troubled land. We urge the South African government to end the oppression of apartheid and to restore to South Africa's majority people the dignity granted to each person by God.

Iraq: What to Do? What to Learn?

*This commentary and the two that follow were written,
respectively, before, during and after the Gulf War with Iraq.*

"Heads I win, tails you lose." That's the bet with which a 9-year-old tries to trick a 5-year-old brother or sister. I fear we are like that 5-year-old in our involvement in Iraq, in a situation where any outcome may be a way of losing.

Clearly it is a very tough set of circumstances for us and many others. Saddam Hussein is a ruthless dictator. His war with Iran, his attacks on his country's Kurdish population, his murder of compatriots, his use of poison gas, these and other actions point to a complex and cruel man. Giving every allowance for the grievances of many peoples of that area and their past sense of powerlessness to control their own destinies, it still is not a compliment to human nature to see the readiness of many there to praise Hussein as their champion.

More important than Hussein is the concern for world order. In the post-Cold War era, this concern is what has led so many countries to act with an unprecedented show of unity through the United Nations Security Council to condemn Hussein's aggression.

If nothing is done now, it may embolden him, and others after him, to swallow their neighbors. And what of the day when Hussein may have nuclear weapons?

Yet what would constitute a victory for the United States under present circumstances? Of one thing we probably can be sure in the complex and volatile politics and cultural conditions of the Middle East: the results will be different from what our planners plan. Certainly that has been true in that region throughout the last half-century. Alliances shift even as I write. There are more than 100,000 destitute refugees. Our actions have helped to double the price of oil. The pressures on our own economy grow. It would be, at the least, ironic if in seeking to keep our economic lifestyle, we should lose it.

If by design or miscalculation, war breaks out, we could lose many American lives and surely the lives of thousands of Iraqis, soldiers and

48

civilians, and of others, among them the hostages whom we must keep in our prayers and concern. Costs will escalate. Our sad tendency here in the United States to lump all Arab peoples together and to discriminate would doubtless be further fueled.

Even if by means of embargo and firm diplomacy Hussein should be made to withdraw from Kuwait, or we help force his ouster, the United States will be seen as the western power that has again enforced its will on the region for its own benefit. We will have supported feudal rulers and, at a time when we had just begun to play a more even-handed role in the area, tied ourselves more firmly to right-wing policies in Israel. We may win a war of a kind but further lose in the battle for the future of the Middle East. Our standing will suffer even more if our victory is accomplished at the cost of starvation and disease among the Iraqi peoples.

As Samir Kafity, the Anglican Bishop in Jerusalem, has reminded us, what is happening today must be seen in the larger context of generations of disputes still to be resolved throughout the Middle East. Our choices are now far from easy, but our goal should be more clear: to help as best we can the nations and peoples of the area to find solutions that are in their own interest to this and other problems. In whatever we do we would be wise to stay within the mandates and consensus of the world community as expressed through the United Nations.

I find myself in some agreement with a number of the more conservative politicians and analysts in this country who hold that it may be in our interests to be less directly involved. No matter our intentions, our long-term military presence may make matters worse for everyone but a few oligarchies that do not exactly represent American ideas of democracy.

When a semblance of stability returns to the area, the price of oil will find some level again. It is, after all, in the interests of the oil-producing countries to find a price that will keep the western industrial countries and Japan "hooked on" oil. We may also remember that it was only in 1986 that then Vice President Bush went to the Middle East to try to raise the price of oil!

But there are also moral reasons to look very carefully at the degree of our recent engagement in the region. It is not just pious to ask that we only involve ourselves in such complex geo-political situations with cleaner hearts. We must try to love our neighbors, in part so that we can understand them. One of the reasons we erred so badly with Iran in the 1970s is that we failed to understand the spiritual, economic and cultural aspirations of the people.

We blind ourselves to our own long-range interests when we do not take carefully into consideration the interests of all the peoples of the area, many of them poor and struggling. With that care in mind we would likely not have been so eager to tilt toward Hussein and help build him up during his war with Iran.

President Bush has appealed to our need to preserve the American way of life. It would be a good time to ask ourselves, what is essential to our way of life? What kind of people do we want to be?

Surely economic welfare is important, but I would like to believe that most Americans would find that there are still more significant underlying values—among them caring not only for our way of life but the ways of life of other peoples.

A part of our care for ourselves and others is a concern for the total environment and future generations. For much of this century the United States has not been careful with energy resources. We continue to consume vast amounts of the world's oil, much more than we really need for decent and productive lives. We pollute our air and skew our own economy. The greenhouse effect is probably already upon us.

Even if we just followed the basic conservation and energy practices of western Europe, we wouldn't feel such a sense of dependency and need to assert our interests with every change in Middle Eastern politics.

Some good news is that, with very little change in our lifestyles, we have made progress in energy conservation over the last 10 years. The further good news is that, with comparatively small sacrifices, we could make considerably greater savings.

There are, then, spiritual and moral as well as economic and political lessons to be learned from these current events. Among the most important of these for Christians, Jews and Muslims is the necessity of dialogue and understanding if religion is to become a way toward peace rather than a means of strengthening prejudice and division.

Present choices remain very difficult, but such learning may help us to avoid lose-lose situations in the future and to see more clearly what is in our true best interests now.

The Gulf War
A Letter to the Clergy

Dear friends,

That which we have feared has come to pass. No matter how we view and understand what is now taking place in the Middle East, each and everyone of us is full, I am sure, of a host of emotions sometimes competing with each other.

At this time only one response is sure and clear—let us pray:

For those who serve in the military forces, for those who wait
at home, and for all the innocent caught up in the conflict;
LORD, HEAR OUR PRAYER

that the conflict may come to a speedy end, and that those at risk
may be safely delivered;
LORD, HEAR OUR PRAYER

that weapons of mass destruction not be used;
LORD, HEAR OUR PRAYER

that our spirits not be inflamed by hatred;
LORD, HEAR OUR PRAYER

that we may be granted the spirit of repentance and reconciliation;
LORD, HEAR OUR PRAYER

that our President, George, be upheld by our prayers and that he
and Saddam Hussein and the leaders of all the nations be guided
by your Spirit of mercy and peace;
LORD, HEAR OUR PRAYER

that refugees may find safe haven;
LORD, HEAR OUR PRAYER

that international humanitarian law be strictly applied and
adhered to;
LORD, HEAR OUR PRAYER

AND LET OUR CRY COME UNTO YOU.

Many of these words come from Presiding Bishop Browning who has
also asked me to tell you that the Presiding Bishop's Fund will provide
assistance in the area through local bishops, where possible, and by joining
with other ecumenical agencies. The need for medicines, food and shelter is
enormous.

He has also instructed the Fund to provide immediate assistance to
dependent families of members of the armed forces, when no other aid is
immediately available. This assistance will be granted through the Bishop of
the Armed Forces, or through the Bishop of the Convocation of American
Churches in Europe.

Please ask your people to give generously and immediately to the
Presiding Bishop's Fund, noting on checks "Persian Gulf Relief."

For the intense pastoral needs of military personnel, their dependents,
and our chaplains serving in Desert Storm, to provide the best pastoral
response to these persons, the following plan has been established in Bishop
Keyser's office at the Episcopal Church Center:

1. A 24–hour phone has been established. The office of the Bishop for
the Armed Forces will act as a clearing center for information which
will be appropriately relayed to bishops, clergy and families.

2. Bishops Keyser, Craig Anderson, John Ashby, Maurice Benitez,
Herbert Donovan, Harold Hopkins, Calvin Schofield, and Robert
Witcher are prepared to travel to areas of high pastoral need in
the United States or overseas.

3. Reserve, active duty and retired chaplains in all areas of the country
will be available through the 24–hour line to assist with pastoral care
in locations near their homes.

4. Follow–up pastoral contact will be coordinated through the office
of the Bishop for the Armed Forces.

In his communication, the Presiding Bishop continues: "I must emphasize here that many thousands of faithful people in the country and abroad
have prayed and marched for a peaceful resolution of the Gulf crisis. Some,
myself included, have long believed that war was uncalled for, that options
short of war were far from being exhausted. It is now left for us to continue
to pray and work for peace. I am heartened that people around our Church

are doing just that. Even in the heat of battle let us not forget that the call to peacemaking is an imperative for Christians.

"I will continue my peacemaking efforts in cooperation with other religious leaders. Strategies for peacemaking will develop as events unfold and I will share them with you. Such efforts must continue in strength, and be guided by repentance rather than righteousness.

"My dear friends, in closing I want to tell you that I know that we are fearful. Let us acknowledge our fears before God and ask that we may feel the sheltering arms of Jesus Christ. Our fear, our anguish, our grief is part of our humanity. We could not be alive to our world's realities and remain untouched by its pain, nor would we not want to be untouched. As we follow in the path of Christ, we mold ours into compassionate hearts and we open ourselves, as he did, to the wounds that come from loving. Let us make ourselves vulnerable in this way, knowing that Christ will take our pain and transform us."

You may be interested in one story that Ed Browning shared personally with me. At 9 am on the morning the war was to begin the Presiding Bishop received a telephone call from Secretary of State James Baker, a member of our Church. Secretary Baker asked the Presiding Bishop to pray with him over the telephone.

In the days and weeks ahead many people will be asking you to pray with them. Your own resources may be exhausted. It will be a time to use the pastoral skills and ministries of many others in your congregation. Please be, as I know you will be, extra alert to the needs of your people, especially those with family members in the military.

Ed Browning tells me that with Secretary Baker he used the prayers for "In Times of Conflict" (Book of Common Prayer, p. 824), and "For Peace Among the Nations" (Book of Common Prayer, p. 816). There are many other fine prayers in our tradition available for use; for example, the Prayer Attributed to St. Francis on p. 833, the prayers for the nation and for peace on p. 258, and, of course, The Great Litany and The Supplication.

Lord, have mercy. Christ, have mercy. Lord, have mercy.

The Weakness of Violence

A father, seeing his son hit his little sister, grabs the son's arm and slaps him soundly. "Don't you ever, ever do that again!"

A lesson has been learned, we might like to believe. Or has, in fact, something else been taught? That hitting is the legitimate response to hitting? That, when the cause is just, violence is a proper response to violence?

President Bush and many others sincerely believed that the rightful response to the aggression and atrocities of Saddam Hussein was even greater violence and death. They were wise enough to recognize that they had other motives—that geopolitics and economics were also involved. Still, their main concern was to establish a world order in which violence like Hussein's would not be rewarded. Only so would future dictators and tyrants see what violence leads to and be deterred.

In fact, of course, armies and countries claim to have been trying to teach this lesson over generations. In this war-addicted century, world wars and dozens of other terrible wars have been fought with this justification as one of the stated purpose.

"The ultimate weakness of violence," said Martin Luther King Jr., "is that it is a descending spiral— begetting the very thing it seeks to destroy. Instead of diminishing evil, it multiplies it. Through violence you may murder the liar, but you cannot murder the lie or establish the truth. Through violence you murder the hater, but you do not murder hate... Returning violence for violence multiplies violence, adding deeper darkness to a night already devoid of stars. Darkness cannot drive out darkness; only light can do that. Hate cannot drive out hate; only love can do that."

Some will no doubt hear these words of Dr. King as weak words in the real world of Saddam Hussein. They are, in fact, prophetic, strong and profoundly realistic words. It takes great strength to seek to care for and understand one's enemy and to seek ways to resist and overcome evil and violence without resorting to even greater violence.

Many people were hopeful in the fall of last year that we were, indeed, on the way to a new sense of world order. We hoped that the coming together of so many countries under the United Nations to condemn and resist the wrongful acts of Hussein would mean that the world was struggling forward toward strong new ways to deal with such crimes.

Our fear now is that, however successful and popular this war may be deemed to be for the time being, still greater violence has once more been held up as the rightful response when future governments feel their cause is sufficiently just. The man of violence has again set the terms for all of us.

Whatever the outcome of the war, it is the way of violence that has won. Tens of thousands of people have died in Kuwait and elsewhere in the Middle East. As usual in war, many refugees, the elderly, women and children will in the end suffer the most. Iraq has been dealt a humiliating defeat. The humiliation is felt in other parts of the Arab world. Five or fifteen or even fifty years from now history may teach again the results of such a humiliation.

While we can be proud of our military men and women, their very skills and bravery, along with the skillful management of the news which largely masked the horrors of war, may seem to make war seem an increasingly acceptable option to diplomacy. We know, too, that our soldiers and sailors have been made to kill other human beings—an awareness they will carry with them all their lives. After some past wars violence abroad has contributed to a more violent society at home.

What can we do now?

As Christians, we can begin by looking more closely at ourselves and our own communities. How do we respond to Jesus' words "Blessed are the peacemakers"? How can we live more peacefully among ourselves and with others?

Christians are meant to be a different kind of people. Since 1930, the Lambeth Conference and General Convention of our Church have affirmed "that war as a method of settling international disputes is incompatible with the teaching and example of our Lord Jesus Christ." Can we follow Jesus' "third way" of active non-violence in respond to injustice and wrongs?

Can we ourselves better realize that loving those who may be seen as enemies is the first step to a better foreign policy—that if we seek to love those of different religions and cultures, we shall be better able to understand them, their values and their motivations?

One of the possible benefits to have come from this war is the meetings and shared prayers that have taken place among Muslims, Jews and Christians in the United States and in other parts of the world. Can we now learn to develop greater dialogue and understanding among people of faith?

For Christians, responding to such questions and concerns may be the highest form of patriotism—the best way we can continue to strengthen the values of our nation. It may be the best way we can support our military—among whom my son is one.

We may respond, now that so much environmental damage has been done, by determining to take much better care of our earth—to volunteer, as individuals and communities, to lead simpler lives, especially to conserve fossil fuels.

We may resolve that as a nation we will contribute more forthrightly and fairly to the settlement of all regional disputes in the Middle East—particularly toward finding a more just and safe way forward for Israelis and Palestinians. We may look again to what our weapons are doing to El Salvador.

We may resist once more making the mistake of believing that the way to peace is to arm nations with more and more modern weapons. Those weapons, this war has again taught, will sooner or later be used by all sides.

Such weaponry, we must not forget, is also a very lucrative business to individuals and nations. Limiting their manufacture and sale will be a worthy new challenge for our country and for the United Nations—surely a way toward a new world order.

Might we also hope and ask that the ingenuity that has made bombs so "smart" that they can practically go in the side door, slip down the hall and into the kitchen before exploding, be devoted more and more to cures for disease, better medical care, better education and housing.

Before the war many without adequate housing, education and medical care in our nations were told that there just was not enough money to help them. "We have the will but not the wallet" was the phrase.

It turned out there was the wallet to fight a very costly war. Now the poor and many of the rest of us want to ask whether there is the will to try to build societies where the causes of strife and war may be dealt with first, and where we will recognize that violence is not strong enough to do other than multiply violence.

We Do Have Power
to End the Madness

Throughout history there have been religious and philosophical groups that have, for one set of reasons or another, withdrawn from society and established their own communities. Many of these groups have been peaceful, though some have veered toward more paranoid attitudes and, at times, behavior dangerous to some of their members. They have, however, rarely posed much of a threat to society at large, and the more dangerous forms of behavior could often be ameliorated or regulated by outside influences.

The major difference with a group like the Branch Davidians is that they were armed to the teeth.

When the rest of the more civilized world (in whose countries deaths by gunshot are but a small fraction compared with ours) looks at the United States, it is not the existence of the Branch Davidians and other groups that surprises them. It is the fact that we blithely allow them to load up with all manner of armaments. The weapons are used to control behavior within the group and, when finally perceived to be a danger to society, bring about a heavily armed response in which lives are lost on all sides.

In the five years that I have lived in Los Angeles, I have watched this region become increasingly more armed, both by people who may be prone to crime and by a frightened citizenry. Every thoughtful person knows that some of these guns will be stolen and used for criminal purposes, used to settle domestic disputes, found and played with in deadly games by little children, and accidentally used to wound or kill friends or family members mistaken for intruders. In a few cases, they may actually be used to prevent a crime, although sometimes with unnecessary deadly force.

My father was a duck hunter, and I know what pleasure he took from that activity. I and many other Americans are not opposed to guns for hunting and target practice, but there are ways of making those guns available to people with licenses for their specific and temporary use. We can also easily make provision for those who like to collect antique guns rendered inoperable.

Some critics will tell us that it is too late. Criminals and other dangerous people are already so well armed that we can only respond with more police firepower and guns of our own. But, as we see in Los Angeles, there is no end to that spiral. If we do not start to severely limit the sale of ammunition and guns and to confiscate all the ones we can, the spiral of violence and fear will grow.

A strong majority of our citizens have said that they favor better gun control. Police departments have urged such efforts. But a smaller group is holding the rest of us hostage—the gun lobby and those who make considerable money from the manufacture and sale of weapons. They tell of a constitutional right to bear arms—a provision that surely was never intended to lead to our present crises.

What of the constitutional rights of the rest of us not to be afraid when we pull our car up to a stop sign, or withdraw money from ATM machines, or knock on a neighbor's door or hear another sect has been taken over by a psychopath?

No doubt many people feel it is too late to do much of anything. The gun lobby may seem too powerful, politicians too pliant. The gun lobby will try to focus our attention on criminals and the need to protect ourselves. But the only group that has a chance to change the madness is an aroused citizenry that will speak out and insist that we will not take it anymore.

The Cost of Guns

FOURTEEN-YEAR-OLD BOY KILLS MOM. Just before I sat down to write this commentary I heard the news on the radio. I could see tomorrow's headline. Or will it even make the headlines? The tragedies are now so frequent.

In this case the boy was waving around a handgun he was told was unloaded because the magazine had been removed. But there was still a bullet in the chamber. The gun went off. A mother is dead. A boy's life is ruined. A family is in tatters.

Three young boys are killed in Pasadena on Halloween when they are mistaken for gang members.

It happens over and over again: handgun crimes, accidents, the angry grabbing of a gun in a family dispute, suicides. And then six are killed in an unemployment office, thirteen in a post office, others in a law office, on a train, in a fast food restaurant, in a school yard, in a park. More and more people are afraid to go out at night or even to go into the city, or for that matter to shop in their towns. Long Beach had more than 130 homicides last year, most of them by guns.

Guns give a sense of power. Guns give criminals an enormous power. They can kill at a distance. One can kill people anonymously—without even touching them. There can't be drive-by knifings or strangulations. There are hundreds of drive-by shootings.

We still weep over the tragedy and loss of life in Vietnam. In less than eighteen months there are more gun deaths in this country—in our towns and streets and homes—than deaths of U.S. soldiers in all the Vietnam War. Right here! Among us!

Many of them are accidents. Many are suicides. Every six hours a youth age 10 to 19 commits suicide with a gun.

Last year more than seventy law enforcement officers were killed with guns, many of them handguns; in some cases assault weapons. No wonder so many police chiefs want much stricter gun control. Meanwhile it is incredible what we are doing to our children, allowing their schools to become fighting places because of guns.

The economic costs to society are enormous too. It is estimated that each gun death or injury costs us over $300,000. Total costs are at least $20 billion a year.

But that's only part of it. If one adds up all the police, private security and other costs, the costs are surely over a $100 billion to protect ourselves from people with guns.

So let's put more of these people into prison for much longer periods. Fine. But reckon that this costs more than $25,000 per person per year. (It would be cheaper to send them to a top-rated college!) As guns proliferate, the number of crimes grows.

Many of us have heard the arguments against gun control over and again. Guns don't kill, people do. Guns in the hands of private citizens deter crime.

But only 200 or so of the gun related deaths in 1992 were the result of such defensive actions. At least as many deaths were those of innocent people thought to be criminals, and the figures for defensive shootings pale beside the more than 15,000 firearm homicides and the even greater number of accidental deaths and suicides by guns.

If not a matter of practicality, it is said by some to be a matter of principle. The second amendment guarantees the right to bear arms, they claim. Yet it has been shown over and over again that the second amendment was concerned with the right of the states to be free from federal interference, to have a well-regulated militia—in other words the equivalent of a national guard. And note the words "well regulated."

But then we are told that we are a country with a violent past where the toting of guns has a certain mystique—as if this justified continued violence. Whether true or not about our past, enough is enough! Let us join the rest of the civilized world where assault weapons and handguns are severely regulated or banned altogether. In these countries deaths by guns are but a fraction of the deaths in the United States, and, even in those countries with relatively high crime rates, it is still a lot safer to go out at night.

The peoples of the biblical faith have no monopoly of virtue on this issue, but the Bible tells us "Thou shalt not kill." The commandment especially means not to murder and certainly can be understood not to allow murders that could be prevented. While some murders may be deterred by the widespread ownership of guns, many more result from the fact that there are now over 200 million firearms in the United States. As a society we together are responsible and accountable to God for so many tragic deaths.

Some voices of despair will say it is too late. There are already too many guns, they say. But we've got to start somewhere, and even beginning efforts would go a long way toward getting handguns and assault weapons out of the hands of teenagers and out of our schools.

It would be cheap at the price to buy up a lot of guns.

No doubt there would be some kind of black market. But let's make it a black market. Let's make such guns much more expensive. And let's see if we cannot at least approach the success of other civilized countries where there are so many fewer guns.

Many more things need to be done. We need to prevent criminals. We need further to develop our ambitious Hope in Youth Program. We need to create opportunities for many more jobs. But these things, too, can be much better done without guns. Meanwhile, it is our poorest communities that suffer the most from gun fear and violence.

Please join me in speaking out and writing to our political representatives—especially those in Congress. Political representatives have been cowed over this issue in the past. A number of them will tell you that privately. They know that the great majority of the citizens want tougher gun control, but they also know that there is a lot of fear out there that can be manipulated. And there is a continuing mystique among a number of people about guns. There is, too, a lot of money—most of it from the industry that sells and manufactures guns and bullets.

So our representatives need our courage, our strength and our support. People of faith are the largest grassroots organization in the world. Let's start our letter writing campaign. We've had more than enough of guns. The legitimate rights of hunters and sports enthusiasts can readily be preserved. Otherwise let us leave guns in the hands of the police to protect us. Let us join together in offering our support and in writing letters like the sample letter I have provided.

SAMPLE LETTER ON GUN CONTROL

Dear Representative _____ / Senator _____,

I write to offer my support to you in creating much tougher gun control for our people. I know you have pressures on the other side, but there are many more of us who want to see all assault weapons banned and, at the least, a far tougher control of handguns. Many of us find no reason why handguns, too, could not be outlawed as in other civilized countries.

I am enclosing an editorial by my Bishop on the subject. We are prepared to support you on this issue. We know it will require your courage. We greatly need that courage and leadership, and we will stand with you and support you as you exercise them.

Please help us to make our schools, streets and homes much safer.

Yours sincerely,

Illegal Immigration

The passage of the Proposition 187, attempting to affect illegal immigration in our region, continues to cause further concern and ethical reflection. It would seem fairly clear from the results of the exit polls that Bishop Talton and I and your Diocesan Council among others are probably in disagreement with the majority of the members of our Church who voted with respect to the specific steps set forward in Proposition 187.

At least this resulted in a lot of mail for me. Mine is one of those jobs where you can benefit from an abundance of free advice, freely given. A number of my letters were courteous and thoughtful. Some, however, were angry and seemingly fearful. I understand anger and fear, but I do not find them the best emotions to motivate us. And I continue to believe, that, if we are to be serious about problems regarding illegal immigration in this state and country, there are more astute, forthright and compassionate ways to approach the issues than to make life difficult for children and their families and those who need medical care. I still find something ethically remarkable about our evident willingness as a society to employ or otherwise benefit from the inexpensive labor of those who clean many of our houses and businesses, help bring agricultural products to us, tend gardens, care for children and wash dishes in our restaurants, if we are not concerned about the education of their children, many of whom surely will become permanent residents of our communities.

With many of you I am also aware that anti-immigrant feelings have gone in cycles in the United States. Shortly before the Civil War, for instance, it was the Irish and the Germans whom citizens feared were taking their jobs and overusing government services. This was also a time of recession and, when the economy improved, the anti-immigrant sentiments largely disappeared. Similarly, one can point out that there was evidently more illegal immigration in California 10 years ago than there is now, but there was considerably less concern then, probably because the economy was stronger and it was not as easy to stress concerns and fears.

In all this we must remember how much God who speaks through the Bible cares about all our lives, how we pray, spend our money, vote, and treat and care for one another. Particularly we know of God's special calling to care for "the widows and orphans, the poor, and the stranger in your midst," that is, especially for the defenseless in society. Surely we can agree that this God will not let us separate our spiritual, political and material lives and so not discuss difficult ethical issues because they also have political ramifications. The separation of Church and State in our Bill of Rights was not meant to inhibit the free exercise of religion in this country, nor to keep people of faith, individually and collectively, from practicing their faith and speaking publicly to themselves and to the body politic with respect to things they believe matter to God. I am proud to be part of a church which can do this while listening to and respecting the dignity of every human being.

Obviously more education about the issues and thoughtful prayer would be helpful to those of us on various sides of the issues. We would also be wise, before we are presented with other propositions or laws on these matters, to study alternative approaches with respect to what we can do together about such serious issues—approaches dealing, for example, with employment and borders.

To this end, I want to help form, in conjunction with other faith groups, a task force to study issues and alternatives and to bring their considerations and recommendations to us, and to our congregations and political representatives for further reflection and action. Here again I do believe that we have a Gospel that is more than strong enough to teach and enlighten us, to arouse our understanding and compassion, to help overcome fear and anger, and to be a well-spring of new hope and courage. How greatly that is needed.

Affirmative Action Christians

Political correctness? Social engineering? Some might get the impression from the current political debates that a concern for multiculturalism and for more equal access to the full life of the community for all was a fairly recent liberal invention. Such a vision, however, has been at the heart of Christianity from the beginning.

On the first Pentecost, fifty days after Jesus' resurrection, we are told that people from Galilee and Parthians, Medes, Elamites, residents of Mesopotamia, Judea and Cappadocia, Pontus and Asia, Phrygia and Pamphilia, Egypt and the parts of Libya belonging to Cyrene, and visitors from Rome, both Jews and proselytes, Cretans and Arabs (in other words, people gathered from all over the then known world) found themselves drawn into a new community of hope and understanding by God's Spirit. Paul was soon to insist on what this meant in Christians' relationships before God and with one another. "There is no longer Jew or Greek, there is no longer slave or free, there is no longer male or female; for all of you are one in Christ Jesus."

Differences, of course, continue to exist, and are vital to life and the society, but race and ethnicity, gender and class are not to give one advantage in the new community. Indeed, Christians are to be willing to give up privilege for the sake of one another. When joined with the biblical call for compassion and justice, especially for those who would otherwise be easily pushed aside in society, and, when one considers the richness of the resulting community and the greater understanding of the God of all people that can come from such richness, one can sense the power of the vision for inclusion and the exhilaration in some of those first Christian churches.

The vision has, however, been exceedingly difficult to put consistently into practice. From the beginning resistance was manifest, and there would seem to be abundant evidence that such inclusiveness goes against natural inclinations. In nature, whatever competition or cooperation there may be within a group, like generally prefers like - which is essentially true among humans as well with regard to race, ethnicity, language, religion and clan. Such preference can become very exclusive. Recent history has borne this out, sometime in rather terrifying ways, particularly in Rwanda and the former Yugoslavia. But they are far from alone in their strife and horror.

Because of this preference for the known and familiar, and due to the relative geographical separation of ethnic groups during its first nineteen hundred years, Christianity has developed a number of distinctive forms. These ethnic and religious identities have been a strength for many peoples, particularly in times of challenge and distress, but they have also led to exclusiveness, discrimination and persecution. Imported to the United States by immigration, this has meant that Christian English and Germans, Irish and Italians, Koreans and Japanese, and so forth, have found difficulty in fully accepting and supporting one another in equal access to the opportunities and benefits of the common faith and their society. Historically, and to this day, this has been especially true in the treatment of American Blacks, and all is further complicated by continuing gender discrimination and large economic disparities, now growing again.

The leaven, however, remains working in the dough. If not by nature then by grace Christians believe that different peoples can and should live in more sharing and affirmative ways - that seeking love's justice for one's neighbor means all one's neighbors, including those who might otherwise be regarded as strangers or "the alien who resides among you." While they cannot impose their vision on society, Christians can work with other like-minded persons at least to ameliorate the effects of discrimination and toward the implementation of this vision for humanity with peoples of all backgrounds and religions.

The first place to begin, of course, is at home—within the household of faith. Here there is much to do. Sunday morning may well remain the most segregated time of the week in America, which would not be quite so objectionable if it was not so often based on privilege in terms of housing of one kind or another. Employment and other church positions are still too regularly subject to various forms of discrimination. These are among the reasons why we have developed our own diocesan standards and policies with respect to non-discrimination and affirmative action.

Our further responsibility is to do what we can, as Christian citizens and voters, to share this sense of fundamental equality of opportunity with others. We can do this both through our own attitudes and actions and by doing what we are able to see that, as a people acting together, we are setting standards and guidelines to help overcome the effects of discrimination and racism.

While we once had a broader social consensus in support of such policies, they are now also under considerable critique by those who believe that such standards, when legislated, can lead to reverse discrimination in individual cases and that contemporary society already is becoming or ought to be "color blind" with regard to various forms of discrimination.

The belief that we should try to be a color blind society could certainly form a common basis for all people working together, but the experience of Christians suggests that we do not get there by wishful thinking or on the basis of our natural inclinations. Meanwhile the fact that the reality and effects of discrimination are still potent in our society should be obvious to all those who have not experienced another form of blindness usually associated with ostriches.

One can agree, however, that affirmative action standards could from time to time lead to certain other unfairnesses—particularly when economic status is taken into account. Affirmative action guidelines have done all too little to benefit the poorest members of various groups and may at times undercut what has tended to be the privilege of middle class whites in certain professions and educational opportunities.

The appearance if not the reality of such reverse discrimination needs also be guarded against, not least because it can be used by those who are so-minded to promote hostility between groups. It is important in these circumstances to look at real numbers and situations, rather than those that are imagined, and to continue to remember that it is standards and policies that are being set forth rather than quotas. It is important as well to rehearse for ourselves the goods which have been achieved by affirmative action laws and practices—both in terms of opportunity and for the benefit of the workplace and educational institutions. The best way that such opportunities and benefits can be further developed is to increase our involvement and support of education, family life and basic nutrition and health services for all young people so that they will be prepared to improve their own lives and strengthen the whole society.

For those of us who have the Christian faith it is most important to keep before us the vision of fundamental equality of opportunity for all God's people in which we are invited to share and to share with others. In the get and give of everyday life it will always be easier to prefer the similar rather than seeking to extend the care of God for all persons, but this is part of the challenge of being affirmative action Christians.

Remembering the Savior: Remembering El Salvador

We flew overnight—a small group of people of different backgrounds— from Los Angeles. We were going to see and to hear, to learn and to share with some of those oppressed and lacking basic human rights in El Salvador.

Just after dawn our plane banked over the Pacific and descended toward the airport. Dark volcanic mountains, each crested with its own white cloud, rose from the green, lush land. The sun streamed from the east while a rainbow arch seemed magically to greet us from the west.

We were met by Carolina and Isabel, our two Salvadoran trip organizers from Los Angeles, and were driven by van to San Salvador.

There was much to do, and time was precious. If we were to see one of the recently repopulated villages several hours from the city, we needed to get started immediately.

Forms had already been submitted for our safe conduct papers. Still we had to spend several bureaucratic hours filling out more forms and being interviewed. In the tiny office, the entire wall behind our interrogator was a mirror. We surmised that through it we were being watched—the beginning of our surveillance.

El Salvador is about the size of New Jersey. Despite the condition of the roads, the trip north to the village in Chalatenango province need take only three hours. We were expected for a religious service and supper. We did not make it.

At each of three military checkpoints we were detained and questioned by young men—who are often little more than boys conscripted into the army—with M-16s slung over their shoulders and grenades on their belts. Once the detention lasted more than an hour and a half. I was told that my being a bishop would help give us safe passage. I began to believe that it was also bringing us extra attention.

One had the feeling that the harassment was being masterminded from somewhere. Suddenly and frighteningly we found out by whom. A jeep and two pick-up trucks with machine guns mounted on their beds raced up from behind and forced our van to the side of the road. One truck assumed a position behind us—the other ahead. The forward machine gun swung to point into the van.

I recalled my wife's questions about my going on this trip. I said to myself, Barbara's going to be really ticked off if this guy pulls that trigger.

An Episcopal missionary who had joined us whispered to me that we were in the hands of a notorious colonel—who, the week before, had hit a North American woman in the face with his rifle butt and told another woman that he wouldn't hesitate to shoot her just because she was pregnant.

He didn't keep us long there on the road. He had accomplished his purpose. We remembered other Americans who had been killed on the roads in El Salvador. And, besides, he had a last detention in mind for us further up the way.

This time we were taken well inside the military compound where, after an hour, we again met the colonel, who was obviously enjoying himself. One had to wonder what kind of a war the Salvadoran army was fighting if the head of the Fourth Brigade had time for all this.

We were told the checks were being done for our safety—to protect us from the guerrillas. That was hard to believe when it was night when we finally resumed our journey.

Unable to reach our destination because of the darkness and condition of the roads, we sought haven in the church in the city of Chalatenango. There, Rafael, a strong young lay worker who had given up his banking career for the work of the Church, welcomed us generously. We were served papusas—pockets of tortillas filled with beans and cheeses, so popular in El Salvador.

For several hours we talked, Rafael telling us of the missionary and social service work done in the province with the people. Then mats were found, and we had our own little slumber party on the floor of the church hall.

Up before dawn, we hoped that we might pass our last checkpoint while the soldiers, themselves fearful at night, still slept. We didn't make it.

More questioning. I'm sure they thought we were carrying weapons or other contraband to the guerrillas. This is what the young soldiers are taught. Instead, our boxes were filled with crayons, paper and clothes brought from Los Angeles.

We were sent back to Chalatenango to have our self conduct form stamped for the fourth or fifth time. Then back to the checkpoint for a few more questions.

Five miles or so of torturous road conditions later we arrived at our destination. The people were glad and relieved to see us. Food was presented, and we sat down to hear their story.

A little history of El Salvador is important here. Early in the century most of the land, formerly lived on and farmed by the people of the country, was expropriated by a few families and made into large plantations for the growing of coffee and cotton for export.

In the early 1930s an army was established to keep peace in the land and to secure the property holdings. The United States, the dominant foreign power in the region, found it convenient for economic and political reasons to side with the oligarchic families and their army.

There were various troubles and several massacres in the succeeding decades. Problems arose again for the ruling forces in the mid-1970s when the poor and landless began to ask for rights and to come together to form committees for self-help and political action. A number of groups joined in opposition to the government and the army. Some took up weapons. The main armed opposition grouping became known by its initials as the FMLN.

While some of these groups adapted their versions of Marxist ideology, the ruling forces labeled almost every effort on behalf of the poor as communist and undertook a series of repressive acts.

When, in the early 1980s, the U.S. government signalled its support of these anti-communist activities and began to pour well over $1 million a day into El Salvador in support of the military, the repression became more earnest. In Chalatenango province much of the population was forced out. All were regarded as supporters of the guerrillas and treated accordingly. Village populations fled to Honduras, Nicaragua and some to the United States. Throughout El Salvador tens of thousands of civilians were killed.

I am sometimes asked why I, as the Episcopal Bishop in Los Angeles, should have concern for the situation in El Salvador. My first response is that there are now more than 400,000 refugees from El Salvador living in Los Angeles. A number of them have become Episcopalians.

Last year, emboldened by international support and pressure, the remaining people of the village of Corral de Piedra decided to try to return from their settlement camp in Honduras to their home. A trip that should have taken two days lasted ten due to problems with the Honduran military and harassment in El Salvador.

Now they try to make a life again. They have beautiful children. Their government gives them nothing, still regarding them as a kind of enemy and severely restricting any movement or even basic supplies in or out. With the help of the International Red Cross, pipes have been brought in so that the village—now renamed Ignacio Ellacuria after one of the murdered Jesuit priests—has a water supply. The people have organized themselves into directorates or teams for health work, education, agriculture and so forth.

From time to time the army occupies the village demanding food and other assistance. Several times they have lobbed mortars into the village. This past February the village was strafed from helicopters and a rocket was fired into one of the buildings. Four children were killed along with the father of two children. Sixteen people were wounded.

The army at first blamed the guerrillas until international groups pointed out that the guerrillas have no way to shoot people from the air. Then, in response to requests that there be an investigation, the army dismissed the incident as of minor significance.

This is the story of one village.

There are no doubt guerrillas in the countryside outside Ignacio Ellacuria. We saw two of them. I know they can also do terrible things in the name of their cause, but somehow I felt safer with them than the El Salvadoran army.

I am convinced that the people of the village only want peace and to be left alone. They proudly showed us the buildings they had built, the fields they had planted, the embroidery they were doing, where they taught their children.

At noon we held a worship service with these deeply Christian people, left them gifts of money we had brought from our churches and other organizations to help them rebuild, and promised to tell their story. The faith, willingness to sacrifice for each other, and readiness to forgive from a people who have suffered so much are beyond my powers of description. In North America, God often seems distant to us—partially hidden by our surfeit of things. To the people of Ignacio Ellacuria, the presence of God is, as some of them would say, thick among them.

Our return trip was, in comparison, much less eventful. We had squeezed in a couple of extra passengers from one of the neighboring villages and now the heavy pounding from the rugged road finally took its toll. Our van broke down, and we hiked under the hot Salvadoran sun into the next village of Guarjila.

The breakdown turned out to be a blessing as we were there able to meet with the pastor in that area, Father Jon Cortina. Jon is an unassuming individual, a Jesuit engineering professor who is the pastor to these villages. One senses a man who might rather spend his time in the classroom and library, but the needs of a people so poor and oppressed have given him another calling. I had first met him in Los Angeles where he had come, after the murder of his six Jesuit brothers, to tell the story of El Salvador. In

August he and another priest were shot at several times. The car has a bullet hole in it inches from where the driver's head would be. Two weeks later Jon received a death threat from the army.

Jon Cortina's gifts are many. He was able to help us with the repair of the van.

In four hours we were back in San Salvador, held up by only an additional hour of military checking. Evidently the military is glad to get any international witness out of the provinces.

We arrived back in time to join the candlelight march and the first of the services remembering the six Jesuits and two women who, a year ago, were dragged from their beds and murdered near the chapel of the Universidad de Centro America.

As a former university teacher, I was shocked that an army should invade and search and sometimes trash university buildings. The poor soldiers who did the killings had, no doubt, been told by their superiors that the six Jesuits were communist intellectuals who had been stirring up the masses.

The next day we met with a number of groups who described to us their struggles for the most basic human rights for the poor of El Salvador. Often they strive just to get the government to obey its own laws. We heard all too believable stories from brave men and women who had been imprisoned and sadistically tortured. We heard how often the United States Embassy takes the side of the government even when its officers would have to know better.

I visited our Episcopal Church of San Juan Evangelista in San Salvador. It is a beautiful church, but its membership is now greatly diminished. During the civil warfare of November 1989, when the Salvadoran government struck back at the guerrillas by bombing a number of the poorer areas of the city, the Red Cross brought many of the injured and homeless to the church. The government, having decided that support of the cause of the poor by the church meant siding with the FMLN, forced its way in and arrested many at the church, including all its clergy and lay leaders.

Only because of pressure from the Episcopal Church in the United States and from others were the leaders finally released. But the terrorizing and intimidation were successful and they continue. Some of the best lay leaders have had to leave the country and are now with us in Los Angeles. In San Salvador, many people are afraid to go to San Juan Evangelista.

It was especially moving to me to be able to have breakfast with Luis Serrano and Archdeacon Victoriano Jimeno. Luis, the priest of San Juan Evangelista, barely escaped after the 1989 assault. He had come to the

United States seeking help and I had met with him in Los Angeles. He returned to his people the following Easter, but he now must be very careful in his movements.

As with most human situations, the circumstances in El Salvador are complex. On this trip and at other times, I have also listened to groups who defend the policies of the government and the military. Indeed, there is a whole industry, led by individuals sponsored by our government, who write and compile defenses of the anti-communist efforts of the Salvadoran government. Much is made of the elections which chose President Cristiani.

I am unconvinced and sometimes surprised by the thinness of the argumentation. One must also say that it is very hard to have any kind of fair elections when a military of over 55,000 dominates in so small a country.

And they do dominate. Even many defenders of U.S. governmental policy admit that in essential matters, Cristiani is little more than a puppet. The military that was created to help the oligarchy rule now ironically tends to rule the oligarchy. More than $4 billion of U.S. aid has enabled the military hierarchy to become its own rich oligarchy. The money also is a corrupting influence at other levels of the society. Some among the wealthy and other business leaders, who wish to begin a process which will bring some form of peace to their country, find themselves opposed by the military.

A decade after our massive intervention began, it is not easy to find the basic argument for U.S. policy that continues to pour so much money into El Salvador for the support of its military. The support used to be based on the belief that we had to draw the line against international communism. Dramatic political changes throughout the world have finally, however, made it possible for Congress members, long fearful of being accused of being soft on communism, to cut some of the military aid to El Salvador. Yet all our aid really goes to help support the military government in one way or another. When U.S. money is spent on help to education or housing, the government simply switches other funds to support the enormously expensive and self-protective military.

One can understand the concerns of the military leaders, the oligarchical families and those whose jobs and security depend upon them. They are fearful that losing power would mean to share wealth and land—risking privilege and their way of life. Their concern is for their children, too. Some of the military are fearful they will be brought to justice.

Yet brave and thoughtful business leaders have begun to join with a new force in Salvadoran life, a coalition known as the Permanent Committee of the National Debate for Peace. Forming the coalition are members of business, labor and university groups, also of women's groups, of the displaced communities, of the churches and public workers. The radical and fundamental tenet of their program is the total demilitarization of their country—with no weapons or military assistance for anyone. In this manner El Salvador might become like Costa Rica.

One can both hope and pray that our United States government policy could change and support such a goal. One might hope and pray that we would then use our aid for the new development of El Salvador—for homes, education, and medical care for places like the village of Ignacio Ellacuria. Such purposes are so much more in keeping with the long range interests of the United States and, still more importantly, with what most of us have always understood to be the values of the people of the United States.

During my last evening in El Salvador, I went to the outdoor Mass where we remembered and gave thanks for the lives of the six Jesuits and their two women colleagues. We remembered, too, Archbishop Oscar Romero, the raped and murdered nuns, and the thousands known and unknown who have been martyred for faithfulness to God's call to be a help for those who need help.

The prayers of the people were led by various representatives of the newly repopulated communities and by those who had been political prisoners. Relatives of the martyrs were present as well as bishops and Jesuit leaders from around the world. There was sadness and pain—including pain that those who ordered the killings were little nearer to justice a year later.

There were also songs and words of faithfulness, of bravery, of forgiveness and of hope. I stood with a prolonged choke in my throat, only feet from the graves of the martyrs. I looked about at the thousands of people hearing again of Jesus' suffering, death and resurrection and holding onto him in faith.

In El Salvador, the country named for the Savior, there are so many people of faith and courage, willing in the face of such suffering and against human odds, to forgive—to forgive their own leaders and to forgive the United States, while determined to continue the struggle for a more fair and decent and peaceful El Salvador.

The Tough Get Generous

Although it is said that some of his worshipful fans and players thought he was Jesus Christ, it was not Jesus but Vince Lombardi who coined the saying, "When the going gets tough, the tough get going." Lombardi was the famed coach of the Green Bay Packers in their heydays, and I suppose his words have a macho ring to them. Yet I confess they have stood me in good stead a number of times in my life—on the athletic field, but also in situations which called for responses of extra courage and compassion.

Life has taught me too much to think I or anyone else can get through every situation just by taking another deep breath or holding that stiff upper lip. Sometimes we are just too tired or injured. We need the arms of others to lean upon and perhaps it is part of a true human toughness to recognize and know our limits.

Yet I believe it is also true that many of us have greater God-given resources than we sometimes realize and that it is times of challenge that call them forth. The Gospel message is often such a challenge—not only comfort and solace but a call to those who hunger and thirst for justice, to the makers of peace and those who will continue to show mercy and forgiveness, though that can, at times, be hard. Even Lombardi's words pale when set beside Jesus' challenge, "If any want to become my followers, let them deny themselves and take up their cross and follow me."

I was pondering some of these thoughts the other day when reading and reflecting upon the continuing economic problems of our region—of more people losing their jobs, and of services and help to the needy being cut further. These are indeed tough times and many people need assistance and compassion.

I was thinking of them, but I was thinking especially of the rest of us - people like myself who still have income, food and housing. Some of us had to take pay cuts this year, and there are many bills and taxes to be paid, but the saying came back to me in a different way: "When the going gets tough, the tough get generous."

No, that response isn't at all strange or unnatural. The needs are greater than ever. There are many important causes to support, and giving through the Church continues to present one of the most cost-effective ways to bring pastoral caring, faith and hope in God, and other forms of material assistance and encouragement directly to those with whom we can share and minister.

It makes sense, too, because in times like these my blessings stand out all the more obviously. I have much for which to be thankful. There is more opportunity for giving in thanksgiving.

When we tithe as a family—in times like this when we reach beyond tithing—we find the joy in having a not inconsiderable amount of our total income that we can share with others and put behind efforts where we are also investing our time and talents.

And, finally, it is tough, generous giving in thanksgiving which breaks the hold that anxiety's greed and self-centeredness can otherwise have on us. It allows a measure of simplicity to enter into our lives and helps us better to see what really matters. We discover again that what most counts is not what we have for our own but what we have shared with others.

When the going gets tough, the tough get generous. Maybe such an attitude does seem contrarian in a year when just about everyone is naturally concerned about national, state and personal economies, and when the body politic seems so worried about its own consumption that it is afraid to tax itself enough to invest in our youth and education and those with no medical services. But I think there are enough people of faith out there to keep a counter-movement going and to call for a different kind of response. That response after all is what Christianity is always meant to be: people who know that they are blessed and who want to give blessings in return— people of courage, made sufficiently strong and tough by their faith that, when the going gets tough, they pull up their socks and further open their hearts and wallets.

PART 2

Freedom and Form:
Things Theological
and Ethical

Freedom and Form

God does not play dice with the universe, Albert Einstein once insisted. To his death Einstein believed that the universe could finally be understood in terms of unifying principles. Against the evidence, he objected to the principle of indeterminacy which held that the mass and motion of sub-atomic features can never both be precisely known at the same time.

The electron, Einstein argued, must ultimately be viewed as a clumping of waves in a non-linear field theory. Others, like the great Ernest Rutherford, insisted that the electron had to be understood as a particle with a real physical existence.

When Niels Bohr introduced the idea of complementarity, neither Einstein or Rutherford—from their different perspectives—could accept it. Bohr held that an electron must be described in two complementary ways, emphasizing its particle and wave behaviors separately. In terms of human metaphorical description, an electron behaves like both a particle and a wave while from the one perspective or the other it is neither. It is Bohr's understanding that is now firmly established in the field of quantum mechanics.

In his book *Infinite in All Directions* Freeman Dyson suggests that scientists tend to belong to one of two camps. There are the unifiers and the diversifiers. The unifiers are always searching for the general principles which will explain everything. They tend to look inward and backward into the past for their understandings.

The diversifiers, on the other hand, look more outward and forward into the future. They see an evolving universe. They are not only tolerant of diversity and complexity; they believe it is of the essence of existence. They are excited rather than depressed that Kurt Gödel's theorem denies the possibility of a universal algorithm which will settle all questions, for this gives a guarantee that mathematics will never die.

Dyson takes his book's title from the prophetic words of Emil Wiechart, written in 1896:

The universe is infinite in all directions, not only above us in the large but also below us in the small. If we start from our human scale of existence and explore the content of the universe further and further, we finally arrive, both in the large and in the small, at misty distances where first our sense and then even our concepts fail us.

Dyson tends to side with those who subvert the efforts of the unifiers. One of his heroes is the physicist John Wheeler whose words sometimes seem more poetry than science. Anticipating the developing science of chaos, Wheeler speaks of "Events so numerous and uncoordinated that, flaunting their freedom from formula, they yet fabricate firm form."

It is, however, Dyson's thesis "that every science needs for its healthy growth a creative balance between unifiers and diversifiers." Later he continues, "Sometimes unity and abstract structure are over-emphasized. Then the universe is seen as the solution of a finite set of equations... Sometimes diversity and richness of detail are overemphasized. Then the universe is seen as infinite in all directions, but without any backbone of mathematical structure to give it coherence."

While not wishing to reduce the issues to psychology, one can see that the two views are to some degree matters of temperament. We are reminded again that scientists and all the rest of us live in a participatory universe. In important ways we "see" what we believe is there or ought to be there and then experiment and seek to correct and make sense in these terms.

These thoughts have been in my head as I have listened to some of the moral debate in the churches in the last few months. Although it is too simple a classification, it has occurred to me before that religious folk can also be divided into two groups. There are those who seem more insistent on universal laws and knowing what is right. Indeed, they may have a hard time seeing revelation as being about much else, and they can find it is as difficult to understand another approach as Einstein did in understanding Bohr's insight.

The other group not only enjoys diversity and mystery in their religion, they view the appreciation of them as necessary for an understanding of a creation and a God beyond all human comprehension. They are not only tolerant of not having answers, they tend to be suspicious of what they regard as the narrowness of those who have a need for them. They see themselves as inclusive and not exclusive. Sacrament, song and poetry, they believe, draw them nearer to the mystery and freedom of God than do carefully drawn moral principles and doctrines. They look less for answers than the direction in which they face to begin to find them.

Probably the two groups will never coexist comfortably. In an important sense, however, Anglicanism has developed on the trust that both groups cannot only live and worship together, but they need each other for a larger understanding of life and faith.

In the Bible God's holiness is realized as God's absolute justness and mercy. While human beings may have difficulty understanding how justice and mercy can at the same time be attributes of God, in biblical story God is somehow like both a stern and demanding judge and an incredibly compassionate parent. In literal terms God is, of course, neither while both analogies may be true as ways of helping to approach a larger awareness of God and how we may respond to the gift of life.

Freeman Dyson writes of the adventure and excitement of scientific exploration. There is also the great adventure of our spiritual and moral life, both as individuals and as a species. To paraphrase Dyson, it may be necessary for a healthy and robust religious faith to have both those who would emphasize principles and God's justness and those who would lay their stress on life's complexity and mystery and God's compassionate outreach.

> Both and either or,
> Waves and/or particles,
> Matter is and is not,
> Fleeing all directions,
> Still secret its articles
> Of that moment when
> All may or may not
> Have been one, blown
> To superstringed bubbles,
> Both chance and symmetry,
> Ruled indeterminacy,
> To be known and unknown.
> Novae and holes,
> Gluons and quarks
> Leaving their arcs
> Ending in ways to be born,
> "flaunting...freedom from formula
> They yet fabricate firm form."

Chaos and Creativity

The scientific study of complexity involves a sophisticated recognition of one of life's most basic and obvious realities. Many phenomena of life— from genetic patterns to national economies, and from insect populations to the neural patterns of the brain—are so extraordinarily complex that they can not only overwhelm powers of measurement but seem to have characteristics that are inherently unpredictable. Some observers may counter that this unpredictability exists more at the micro rather than the macro level of existence, but it is yet the power of little variations at the micro level to generate extraordinary and sometimes surprising differences at the macro level which make the study of, for example, the weather both so frustrating and so intriguing. We know there will be hurricanes, but the precise landfall and the intensity of hurricane Andrew were neither predicted nor predictable.

Partly because of the messiness of such areas of activity the sciences of the last two centuries have tended to study more discreet phenomena, where measurement and predictability are not so severely tested, and/or they have looked for mathematical models from which general rules could be derived and which would offer at least helpful degrees of predictability. Gradually, however, and now with increasing speed, the interests and the outlook of a number of scientists have begun to change. Computers have undoubtedly been vital to this shift. Scientists now have the capacity to compute and analyze vast amounts of data issuing from the non-linear behaviors of ocean waves, river flowage, cloud formations, biological population changes, subatomic particle activity, complex oscillations in bodily organ functions, the stock market, and all manner of other forms of turbulence in nature and society.

In his best-selling book *Chaos: Making a New Science* (1987) James Gleick chronicled this shift in scientific outlook and understanding. He and others suggest that twentieth century science will primarily be remembered for three great revolutions: "Relativity eliminated the Newtonian illusion of absolute space and time; quantum theory eliminated the Newtonian dream of a controllable measurement process; and chaos eliminated the Laplacian fantasy of deterministic predictability."[1]

The most fascinating insight of the study of chaotic phenomena is the awareness that there are forms of order within the vast disorder. If there were only disorder, entropy would eventually see to it that any and all things which happened to exist would be reduced to an undifferentiated virtual nothingness. What we instead see, however, is not only how closely the seeming orderliness of life borders on chaos but how mysteriously types of order lurk within the chaotic. Within the random and erratic of myriad real life behaviors there are deep patterns—often surprisingly kindred in shape—which evidently reflect some organizing principles of existence. Chaos and instability are fundamental to existence but so are intrinsic tendencies toward pattern, form and organization. Scientists who probe complexity now speak of "strange attractors" which somehow are the focal points for patterning and form within disorder. What is amazing are the capacities of these simple patterning factors to produce the extraordinary complexities of life. The analogy of the kaleidoscope is often used. A slight shake can bring about a vastly different reality.

What is still more wondrous and essential to the emergence of life is the capacity of these simple factors to link together and effect more complex organization. In his study *Complexity: The Emerging Science at the Edge of Order and Chaos* (1992), M. Mitchell Waldrop tells the story of how scientists, who were at first at the edges of their disciplines, have over the last twenty years gained insight into the processes of feedback and reinforcement which encourage organizations toward ever more complex forms. The study of chaos, or dynamical systems theory, leads not only to the awareness that simple rules of behavior can result in astonishingly complicated dynamics but that there are factors which reward the emergence of auto-catalytic behaviors leading to self-organizing activities and more and more complex organizations. "The gear wheels of both biological and social evolution," it has been said, "have a rachet."

Certainly a critical means of this "rewarding" is found through competition. Organisms (as well as other forms of organization) which are best adapted to their environment gather more food, live on and reproduce more successfully. Those which do not disappear. Generally speaking (though there can for a time be the exceptions of extraordinarily well-suited species) this survival calls for increasing adaptation and complexity. Here the variety of genetic combination and the accidents of abnormalities, which in some cases may turn out to be highly successful, play their roles. The trial and error of natural selection may seem messy and inefficient from one perspective, but, seen in another way, it may not only be the best nature can do, it is extraordinarily efficient, productive and creative—leading to the incredible variety in existence and, among other things, to sentient life.

Yet, if on the one hand, natural selection seems like a kind of evolutionary arms race (resulting in ever increasing complexity and specialization), there is also an important place in life not only for *detente* (live and let live), but also for cooperation and symbiosis. Not only species but species in relation to one another can learn mutually beneficial ways of living together. Species not only evolve, they also co-evolve in relation to others in an incredibly complex ecosystem which itself may be regarded as an ever-changing and adapting organization. And everything, from quarks to DNA, to the climate and the global economy, is interrelated within the system.

The evidence now suggests that, from the beginning until today, and in every form of organization, creativity takes place at the edges of order and chaos; that is, on that fine but extensive line where order is verging into chaos and where order is emerging from disorder. For organization and life to be there must be this dynamic and infinitely complex interplay between chaos and order.

> The ordered stage we were told to watch,
> With chance the outlaw actor,
> While now we see in every scene
> The accidental factor.
>
> Without random's role then stasis' rule
> Would have creation frozen;
> Yet as surely it's necessity
> Upholding all that's chosen.
>
> Not only once, but at every edge,
> As chaos threatens ever,
> Bits link, shape life, they end and eat
> Where strange attractors gather.
>
> There's tense interplay among the ways;
> In the flow to entropy
> Mere principles in subtle sets
> Gender vast complexity.
>
> And in the joining, in the struggle,
> As the smarter, stronger form,
> In the suffering, in the learning,
> Terrible beauty is born.

And how and where may we think of God in all this chaos and creativity?

When the first Russian cosmonaut returned from space, Nikita Kruschev, speaking for the official atheistic philosophy of communism, smugly noted that Yuri Gargarin had not seen God anywhere. It was easy then and now to smile at such superficiality. Yet there is also no doubt that Kruschev was at least raising a theological question which will not go away for many twentieth century people. Only a few generations earlier, when the universe seemed a somewhat cozier place, it was apparently not all that hard to imagine God up there somewhere. More than this, it was difficult not to explain otherwise inexplicable events as "acts of God." God could be seen as a kind of stage manager of much that took place in life, the good and the bad, and it could be a test of faith to hold this view in detail. Less than two hundred years ago Christians argued with one another about whether lightning rods should be put on churches. Opponents of the protectors referred to them as "heretic rods."

Christian theologians could be seen to have been fighting an increasingly rear guard action ever since. For some, their understanding of God's role has been described as the "God of the gaps." Wherever science has no full explanation for something, there is a place for God. Yet as scientists have come to explain more and more phenomena (from lightning and earthquakes to diseases, quasars and DNA) the gaps have grown fewer and narrower. As has been rightly noted, it is the business of scientists to fill in gaps, and they continue to do so.

Still, there has been one gap that has seemed the most important of all —what might be called "the creation of life gap." For many people there remains at least the suspicion that science can never fully explain the fullness of all the enormous complexity of life—how it first began and then developed into the intricate beauty of a goldfish, much less of a whale, and the magnificence of the human eye. Then, above all, there is the emergence of consciousness. How could a purposeless flow of energy bring reflective life and consciousness into the world? Some Christian theologians have quoted the apparent astronomical odds against any matter being able to come into existence and to sustain itself against anti-matter, and then to develop over fifteen or so billion years into the incredible array of galaxies and life on this earth.

The argument clearly has its force, but it may also leave a still deeper theological anxiety. The God glimpsed by such reflection may seem in many ways like the God of eighteenth century Deism, the magnificent clock maker, who set everything going so splendidly that this God is now more observer than participant in creation. Such a First Principle it is argued, is needed for the creation and to set the rules that keep it all going. Yet this deity does not seem much like the caring and robust God of the Bible. Moreover, given the reality that so much of natural life is motivated by a fierce competition for survival and a struggle to eat before being eaten, such a God may finally appear to be a kind of Darwinian evil genius who has scripted us all for but a few moments of pleasure and enlightenment before suffering and inevitable death.

There are, of course, more sophisticated ways of interpreting the script and God's role in it, and all of us, including theologians and scientists, must struggle with the limits of human thought, language and imagination. Yet we have also seen how a number of scientists now describe a creative universe in which a controlling principle or agent is not only unnecessary but would be itself more difficult to explain than a fully natural process which favors increasingly more complex phenomena. While the wondrously complex universe that now exists may lead us to awe and even a kind of reverence, it does not, from this perspective, require an arranger. Given the stuff of existence, enough time (billions of years), a relatively few rules of strong probability, together with accidents and trial and error, life as we know it, including our conscious reflection on it, has come into being. There is much to puzzle over, but no great God gap.

Some religious folk may not like this way of understanding, but they may, in fact, being done a favor. The God described by earlier quasi-scientific arguments has not won a lot of devotees. Increasingly the God imagined as acting on the universe from another part of or from outside the universe or from some other dimension grows harder for a more secular world to relate to. How is this God present to creation? What difference would this God make to daily human life?

There are, of course, the options of either ignoring or compartmentalizing scientific insights. Many religious people have and will continue to do so, but at a cost. While the natural sciences have limitations and can only help explain part of our reality, it is in this day and age a vital part, and those who keep the insights of science separate from their faith will have to live with certain inevitable contradictions.

There are, on the other hand, enormous opportunities for those who believe that their faith in God and the forms of truth which science can discover should not be in conflict. What may be most important for this integration is a profound awareness that God is so present and intimate to all that is that we might even speak of the world as God's body.

We are again deeply conscious of the limits of our understanding. This is not the only way to try to think of God, and we may be quick to add that God, to be God, is more than the creation. Here we might helpfully use the analogy (though it is only that) of the human person. We both are our bodies, and we are more than them. We have conscious and reflective life, grounded in our bodies, but which enables us also to transcend them—to think about our bodies and to relate to them. In addition to being our bodies we are present in relationship to our bodies. We rightly speak of the presence of a person which is more than their body. We would not, however, have a sense of that presence apart from the body.

Contemporary science looks upon the universe as much more like a vast, intricately connected and related organism than like a machine which would have an external maker. In essence composed of myriad relationships of energy, the substance and activity of the universe are more like software than hardware—related more to thought than mechanics.

Perhaps the oldest religious sensibility of all (alluded to in the biblical phrase "in God we live and move and have our being": Acts 17:28) offers this awareness of God's presence integrally related to every nook and cranny of existence. God will also be understood to transcend creation, and it will be dependent on God in ways different from our relationship to our bodies, but God is in all things and we are in God.

Such an awareness of God, which has been part of the faith of many men and women of prayer past and present, is mystical yet fully grounded in reality. There is no God of the gaps because there are no gaps which science should not, at least in principle, be able to explain. We do not need to send messages "somewhere else" when we pray because we are already part of God's life. Whether we live or die, we are never separate from God. This earth is our home, not a hotel we are visiting (which awareness has dynamic consequences for our ecological understanding and behavior and is a critique of various forms of spirit-matter dualism).[2]

Everything that happens to the universe—everything that happens to us—also happens to God. As the dramatic quest toward life in the universe requires imperfection, accident and suffering, then God suffers. Indeed, if it is characteristic of higher and higher forms of consciousness to be able to suffer more, then God suffers most. God is not apart. Ultimately God bears responsibility and care for all that happens in God's body. "I form light and create darkness, I make weal and create woe; I the Lord do all these things… I have made, and I will bear; I will carry and will save" (Isaiah 45:7, 46:4).

Christians, in the life, passion and death of Jesus, see the cruciform shape of creation in a human life. They see, too, the result of human sinning.

But they glimpse more. They perceive the power and purpose of God to transform—to imbue nature with grace, and to open new chapters in life's story which will value and include individuals and all those whom nature might seem to devalue and discard. They see the strong caring for the weaker. The queerness, the beauty and the tragedy of life are infused with God's caring for God's body—of which we are part, with the Spirit of God's presence working in and through conscious life to bring about opportunities for grace and growth.

Faithful people will not be fearful of any form of truth. They will not be afraid of the insights which science can offer. But they will also want to be in contact with all that is true, including aspects of truth which versions of science may leave out. This truth will include heartbreak and passion as well as creativity and color—and joy, sorrow, love, courage and a call to responsibility and care for God's body and for one another.

Notes

1. James Gleick, *Chaos: Making a New Science* (New York: Viking 1987), 6.
2. Those who wish to explore this model for theological reflection further may do so in Sallie McFague's *The Body of God: An Ecological Theology* (Minneapolis: Fortress Press, 1993).

Si Comprehendis, Non est Deus

We Can Never Comprehend God

If you think you comprehend, it is not God. If you think you comprehend God, whatever it is, it is not God.

Awareness of this warning comes at the beginning and remains at the heart of all thoughtful theology. It is a caution against every form of idolatry, especially the most subtle forms which uncritically shape our ideas of God to suit cultural mores and needs. J. B. Phillips put it more directly: "Your God is too small."

While powerfully telling of God's presence in the world, and revealing the character of the inbreaking reign of God's justice and mercy, the Bible repeatedly warns of the limitations of human understanding: "For as the heavens are higher than the earth, so are my ways higher than your ways and my thoughts than your thoughts" (Isaiah 55:9). We are to be firm in our faith, but all good theology has an appropriate modesty about it.

While, then, we are to love God with our minds as well as our hearts, we are also to be acutely aware that our creaturely comprehension will always be stretched even beyond our power of imagining, and certainly beyond the limitations of human language, metaphysical or otherwise. If we even begin to attempt to limit God to what fits into our brains, we can be sure we are missing the most important dimension of divine life.

All the great men and women of prayer have known this keenly. It is why they have always placed the love and adoration of God, which reaches out and opens the self to God, at the heart of their theology. Understanding follows.

It is also why the most sound and effective Christian theology is always Trinitarian. While inferior theologies, for sentimental or other reasons, misleadingly overlook or fasten upon certain aspects of the divine life, Trinitarian awareness helps us to glimpse and to worship God who is interrelational and relational. This is the God who transcends and participates, who judges in mercy, who forgives and challenges, who is of and beyond human life; God who suffers and who creates, sustains, redeems and inspires, who has particularly revealed God's self but does not discontinue revelation; who reigns, who is beyond, with and within, known and unknown, dwelling in light inaccessible and in whom we live and move and have our being; the God whose center, as Bonaventure put it, is everywhere but whose circumference is nowhere, whose evergiving and never ending love moves the sun and all other stars and moves also within human hearts, uniquely shown to us in the life, death and new life of Jesus.

In recent years I have found some of the most effective and renewing theology to have been written by women theologians. In part this is because they have reclaimed vital aspects of our tradition—particularly the revealed motherly and womanly attributes of God. In lifting to greater attention, for example, the ways of God's Sophia-Wisdom, they have helped to avoid the subordinationism (i.e., placing the first person of God above the others) of much popular theology and enabled many men and women to sense in new ways God's intimacy with creation. This perspective offers more opportunity for our reverence and care for the world about us. These theologians have also given prophetic insight into the dangers of a literalized patriarchalism which results, not only in a limited theology, but in the disvaluing and, too often, the degradation and suffering of women and sometimes of children and other human groups as well.

She Who Is by Elizabeth A. Johnson (New York: Crossroad, 1992) is a book I have found to be one of the more profound and interesting of these theological studies. I was helped by its rigor and balance and its inclusive Trinitarian awareness.

Professor Johnson knows historical theology. She has, for instance, a very good grasp of what is valuable and of considerably less value in the theology of Thomas Aquinas. While she contends that insights into God's womanly and mother-like attributes need special stress in our time, she well values the biblical and spiritual significance of God as father-like who we may daringly, through Jesus' example, call upon as Abba-Father, the caring parent-like God. She understands this because, while she is aware of the importance of contemplating the many ways God reveals divinity, she knows how essential the personal is to Christian theology. "God is not personal like anyone else we know, but the language of person points in a unique way to the mysterious depths and freedom of action long associated with the divine" (p. 55).

Such theological perspectives may seem new and challenging, but they are lifting up some of the most important traditional theological questions and issues for Christian living, worship and prayer. If your God these days seems to be too small or distant, or too comprehensible or, for that matter, wholly incomprehensible, you may find such theological explorations stimulating and enlivening.

God in Person

I n every respect...made like us...in every respect...tempted as we are, yet without sin." So wrote the author of "The Letter to the Hebrews," and Christians ever since have been wondering and wrestling with this faith.

Once, after I had preached a sermon on the beatitudes, a man came up to me and said, "Those are wonderful ideals that Jesus put forth. But then, we have to remember that he was God." How then, I wanted to ask, was he like us in every respect?

One early church theologian thought he had it figured out. Jesus was a godly being who entered this world in human semblance. He was a kind of super angel who adapted to human ways.

Yet it was finally realized that such a hybrid creature could be neither truly God nor fully human to save and to redeem.

Forms of popular piety have often presented Jesus as a divine being dressed in a human suit. Yet it was a kneeling, suffering humanity which could not accept this seeming simplicity. How then could he be the redeemer of our mortal lives if he had not entered into all that is human—the heartbreak and horror as well as the color and pageantry? If he did not face uncertainty and death as we must face them, how could he be our brother?

Still, if it was not truly God that shared in the life and death—if Jesus was only a great human figure, how are we then saved?

Another theologian gave it a more sophisticated try. Jesus was fully human in his body and mind, his emotions and feelings, but his spirit (that amazing capacity to be aware of and to begin to transcend self) was divine in him.

But again it was the folk on their knees who wouldn't have it. Yes, he had somehow to be God as God is God, but all of what it means for us to be human can be saved only if he was wholly human...in every respect.

The world goes on. Suffering and death go on. It seems too good to be true. We do not understand...truly God and truly human. It is hard to make rational sense of it.

Yet what does make sense? "What God says" writes Frederick Buechner, "is the life you save is the life you lose. In other words, the life you clutch, hoard, guard, and play safe with is in the end a life worth little to anybody, including yourself. Only a life given away for love's sake is a life worth living. And to bring His point home, God shows us one (His son, Jesus Christ) who gave His life away completely for our sake."[1] In human person God does so for us all.

Note

1. Frederick Buechner, *Wishful Thinking: A Theological ABC* (San Francisco: Harper & Row, 1973), 28.

Christian Realism:
Without Illusion or Despair

R einhold Niebuhr was the most influential theologian of this century. While he did not develop a systematic theology, his penetrating insight into basic Christian truths, coupled with his teaching, his involvement in the societal concerns of his times, and his prolific writings profoundly affected more than two generations of clergy and theologians, along with a great variety of politicians, academics and other leaders.

In a fine new intellectual biography *(Niebuhr and His Age: Reinhold Niebuhr's Role in the Twentieth Century,* Trinity Press International: Philadelphia, 1992) Charles C. Brown describes how Niebuhr first came into prominence during his 13-year pastorate at Bethel Church in Detroit. As a pastor and teacher he became concerned with the injustices of society and the need for a prophetic and realistic faith to sustain people in their lives and commitments. His writing brought him a wider audience, and in 1928 he began a teaching career at Union Theological Seminary in New York City which lasted over 30 years.

Little escaped his ethical vision and concern. His international travels and contacts made him an early sentinel of the dangers of Nazism. When the war in Europe broke out, he lost a number of pacifist friends because of his belief that evil had sometimes to be opposed by military means. He saw what was happening to the Jewish people in Europe and became an advocate for a Jewish homeland in Palestine, while also having concern for the Palestinians of that country.

A socialist at least through the 1930s, Niebuhr soon perceived the despotic character of Russian communism. He came by some to be regarded as a Cold War warrior in his warnings regarding the deep flaws in communist politics and practice and the dangers they presented to the world. At the same time he could often be sharp in his critique of the arrogance and self-deceit of American foreign policy, particularly when it tried to disguise or hide from the mixed motivations that are regularly involved in human activities.

At home Niebuhr was involved in the struggle against racism. An active supporter of the union movement (in Detroit he had denounced Henry Ford for his treatment of his workers), he worked with others to try to make society more just and fair. A founding member of Americans for Democratic Action, he would have been regarded by many in his time as a radical liberal. Yet he antagonized some of his more radical colleagues by his willingness to compromise and work for proximate means which fell short of the goals of the liberal agenda.

Niebuhr was certain that we do not live in a perfect world. Perhaps what made him most stand out, particularly in his early years as a theologian, was his insistence on the embeddedness of sin. The events of the times were of course on his side. The optimism of various schools of belief in human progress had been severely undermined by world wars, depression and then the failure and threat of communism.

Niebuhr's 1932 book, *Moral Man and Immoral Society* (New York: Charles Scribner's Sons), spoke powerfully to many Christians and others who felt themselves forced to question the hopes that goodwill and intelligence were sufficient to bring about a more just society. In the book Niebuhr concentrated on the sinful aspects of institutions and societal structures. In later years he came to give additional stress to the significance of individual sinfulness. He quipped that he might better have titled his book *The Not So Moral Man and His Less Moral Communities*.

More and more influenced by his reading of Augustine, Niebuhr described the human condition as one of tension between freedom and finity. Consciousness and self-awareness gave humans a measure of self-transcendence, while yet they were limited by their mortal nature. Sin sometimes manifested itself in pride which wanted only to be free and autonomous—to be one's own god. At other times, sin was to be found in sloth—in the excusing of self from the struggle for fairness and rightness in life by saying "I'm only human" and using human limitations as an apology for inaction. The great challenge of life was to negotiate gracefully the tension of living between human freedom and finitude. The challenge was often heard in the call to work for justice and fairness in society.

Niebuhr regularly spoke against what he regarded as Christian sentimentalism—appeals to love and charitable acts while ignoring systemic and structural injustice in society. Indeed, justice was the way in which a deeply caring love for others—one's distant neighbors and particularly those in need—made itself known. It was the way in which God's concern for the powerless and marginalized (in biblical terms, the widows, orphans, the poor and the stranger in your midst) was made known. At the same time, when such justice was the goal, then acts of love to those whose lives one could directly touch with compassion and mercy, had their vital place. "Love as a substitute for justice is odious, but love as a supplement to justice is an absolute necessity."[1]

Those who argued that Christians should not involve themselves in societal issues, politics or international affairs found little approval from Niebuhr. "There is no such thing as neutrality in human affairs,"[2] he wrote. Those who want Christianity to remain only spiritual and to stay out of worldly issues, he argued, have already taken sides. With his contemporaries Barth and Tillich (who was for some years also a colleague at Union) Niebuhr found himself not infrequently in debate. While he saw much to admire in their theological work, he worried that, in their different ways, they showed too little concern for the role of reason and collective responsibility in human history.

Niebuhr was, however, never naive about what human action alone could accomplish. His emphasis fell on the stubbornness of evil and the complexity of every situation. "There is always an element of moral ambiguity in historic responsibilities. Our survival as a civilization depends upon our ability to do what seems right from day to day without alternative moments of illusion or despair."[3]

Without illusion or despair! How well and prophetically that challenge seems to speak to our lives as Christians today. Twenty years ago a number of commentators predicted that it would be Barth or Tillich, or even Niebuhr's reknowned brother Richard, whose theological views would have the most lasting impact. Reinhold Niebuhr even fell into some disfavor with those who were looking for more systematic theologies or absolutist ethics. Yet it may well be his tough and persistent realism that will continue to serve as a better guide. It may be a better prod to our illusionist tendencies which want an easy grace, love without justice, or certainties rather than more profound and complex truths. It may be a better corrective to our tendencies to despair which can show themselves in ethical sloth, seeking to avoid the ambiguities and complexities of living in and acting through communities of faith, or the current forms of negativity and criticism from the sidelines which pretend to contemporary prophecy.

Neither of these was Niebuhr's way, while he yet recognized that the hardest part was just to keep on going, knowing that our efforts were always partial and incomplete. God's grace and the purpose of God's reign, he believed, yet acted through our efforts, while still their lasting significance was only to be known in the mystery of the resurrection, "grounded in a power and purpose beyond our comprehension, though not irrelevant to all our fragmentary meanings."[4]

Notes

1. "The Gospel in Future America," *Christian Century* 75 (June 18, 1958), 714.

2. "Is Social Conflict Inevitable?" *Scribner's Magazine* 98 (Spring 1935), 167.

3. "The Condition of Our Survival," *Virginia Quarterly Review* 26 (Autumn 1950), 491.

4. *The Self and the Dramas of History* (New York: Charles Scribner's Sons, 1955), 238-39.

Getting What They Deserve
Understanding Justice

It is often noted how generous Americans can be. Sometimes this seems particularly true when we hear on television or read in the newspapers of some individual family or child in great need.

A child born with a rare heart disease requires a delicate and expensive operation. Generous people, many of whom live thousands of miles away, send in donations to help the child and the destitute parents.

Yet, strangely, we as a nation seem reluctant to fund programs to help several hundred children around the country with the same problem. We even seem reluctant to fund programs which would provide pre- and post-natal care for the children of the poor, although it is often pointed out to us that it costs society much more to deal further down the line with the problems created by the lack of such care.

Some of the same short-sighted, tight-fisted attitudes seem to control our willingness to help the mentally retarded and those who are just not mentally very able in our society. One would think that a people with so many generous instincts would want to help take care of them. They are, after all, our own. We do a few things for them, of course, but many of these individuals find themselves in desperate circumstances. They do not even begin to have a decent, moderately enjoyable life. Sometimes the best we can do is to warehouse them in our prisons. Ironically, that probably costs much more than it would to provide decent living circumstances outside prison.

Why? Why are a people who so often can be so generous in individual cases frequently so ungenerous with larger numbers of people?

Some say that we're just not very smart—that we don't see all those people in need, or the consequences of not offering more of our care and help. Yet I think most of us know that there are many people truly hurting in our society. We may want to hide from the reality, but we are not dumb.

Others say that we are, in fact, actually selfish underneath our occasional fits of generosity. We're afraid that there won't be sufficient for us if we tax ourselves enough and otherwise give of ourselves to help the poor and disadvantaged. Yet the truth is, if we rearranged some of our priorities, and sought to distribute what we have more wisely, and were willing to share just another few percentage points of our income, there would be enough to go around.

I think that the basic problem is actually of a moral and spiritual character. I think we are deeply afraid that some people may get something for nothing, something they haven't earned. We are concerned that this would be unfair to those who work hard for a living. We don't want to reward laziness, or allow other people to learn a welfare mentality. This is the hard other side of our work ethic, an ethic which is often thought to be based in religious morality.

I am certainly not against an ethic which supports the value of labor and proper incentives. But there is a lot of evidence that the vast majority of people out of work would very much like to have work. Clearly it would be best if there were jobs for them, but that is apparently not always possible in our economy. It is also true that some of the poorest people in our society work incredibly hard at very low-paying jobs. Then there are the many poor who are too young or too old or too sick or retarded to earn much of anything.

Let us suppose it is true that 10 or 15 percent of the needy in our society are able-bodied and just plain lazy. Should we punish all the rest just to make sure that those others don't get what they don't deserve? Or, as is sometimes said, to make sure they do get what they deserve?

We talk and pray a lot about justice in our churches, but people often have different ideas about what justice is. Some people concentrate primarily on the justice of deserving: getting what is fair for me and mine—what I have earned. Sometimes they also want to make sure that others do not get what they *haven't* earned. That attitude has some merits and a place in social thinking. But it doesn't need to be the dominant and controlling attitude, nor be given full moral and religious sanction.

There is another understanding of fundamental justice, and that is that every human being deserves the basic needs of life just because they are human beings who hurt and are in pain when they are cold or without food, or when they are given a lousy education or little or no medical care. A growing concern for this form of justice would likely do more than anything else to bring about a kinder, gentler America.

Abortion

Humility, Reverence, Faithfulness and Intelligence Should Guide Us All

The recent Supreme Court decision, which again allows individual state legislatures more scope in limiting abortions, will heighten tensions in the increasingly bitter struggle between so-called pro-life and pro-choice groups. The two groups find it diffficult even to talk with one another because they begin from quite different starting points within different value systems. Although they are not regularly brought to expression, different views and attitudes toward human sexuality in general strongly affect the opposing positions.

To one group every abortion is a murder—a killing (with exemptions sometimes given in instances of rape and incest). The other group stresses the rights of a woman to have control over her body and to make her own decision about matters which so profoundly affect her life.

Those opposed to abortion often argue from their understanding of natural law and theology: God is the Creator and Sustainer of all life and from the moment of inception each mating of sperm and ovum is not only potential for human life but is that life already begun. No human agency has a right to terminate what is already a Beethoven, Mother Teresa, Mary Smith or Fred Borsch, moving toward birth. Statistics show that there are now nearly two million abortions a year in our country. If it has not already done so, abortion is rapidly becoming just another method of birth control, a matter of convenience. Roman Catholic and other ethicists worry that such "irreverence for life" will sooner or later have profound tragic effects on the treatment of the elderly, handicapped persons and the value of life in general.

Those on the other side of the debate view the natural law position of anti-abortionists as at best outdated. Hardly anyone today maintains that everything that happens in the physical world is the result of a direct action of God to which human beings should simply submit. Pneumonia and cancer also naturally occur, but we use God-given intelligence and compassion to try to shape a better quality of life for each one and everyone. No one wants an abortion when there are other good altenatives, but sometimes it may be the only moral choice for a woman trying to take into account the quality of life of other children and her own God-given potential.

At least up to a certain point, a mated sperm and ovum are essentially a yet-forming tissue only potential for human life, the rights of which must be deemed less than those of the already living. In the last analysis, it is only the individual woman who is in the moral position to make this judgment. It is wrong for the state to interject itself into this intensely private matter, especially in such a way as to make it relatively easy for women of means to obtain abortions, and to leave poor women with little or no choice—or the choice of illegal and dangerous abortions.

In such a polarized context of debate, where emotions and slogans often seem to dominate, it is not easy to find a helpful way forward. Along with others, however, our Episcopal Church has struggled to set forth some faithful guidelines on the basis of which more profound insights and understandings may grow.

I sometimes think the most important single dimension we can bring to the debate is one of humility and awe. Standing before God, and within the wondrous vastness and intricacy of creation, we can together turn in awe and reverence. Who can claim to know all the answers? Surely we must reverence our creative sexual roles, but just as surely we are called to great responsibility for lives already born and our capacity to make complex and difficult moral choices.

Perhaps one thing we can all agree upon is that we are called to take much better care of the children we already have. It does not make any sense to oppose abortion and then not do all we can to provide vastly improved prenatal care and physical and emotional protection and support for infants and children. At least most of us can also agree that we need to do all we can to help both married and unmarried persons be more wise, responsible and caring about their sexual lives whenever conception is a possibility.

The General Convention and House of Bishops of our Church have held that "abortion is always a tragedy" and that "all human life is sacred from inception." Their statements allow that there may be cases when abortion is the lesser tragedy and, therefore, an acceptable moral choice, but it is not to be used "as a means of birth control, family planning, sex selection or [for] any reason of mere convenience." Within the context of these perceptions it is also understood both that individuals can and must make informed moral choices and that we are responsible to each other to support one another by providing education, counseling, compassion and help for each other in the care and raising of our children.

The Church has gone on to say, "We believe that legislation concerning abortions will not address the root of the problem ... Any proposed legislation regarding abortions must take care to see that individual conscience is respected, and that the responsibility of individuals to reach informed decisions in this matter is acknowledged and honored."

Much more, of course, can and needs to be said. The debate and the anguish will continue. We are called, I believe, to struggle as faithfully as we can with both minds and hearts. Humility, reverence, faithfulness and intelligence should motivate and guide us—and in all things love, which, when from God, will redeem all.

Euthanasia

The Bible can be seen as providing general rather than specific guidance with respect to euthanasia issues. Life is a gift from God. The ending of any life by human means requires, at the very least, extreme justification. On the other hand, mercy and compassion are to be shared in extreme measure.

Although there are blurred and grey areas, a distinction is often made between passive and more active forms of euthanasia.

Passive euthanasia: Many teachers and others in the Episcopal Church, myself included, strongly support individuals' and families' rights, with proper moral and legal standards, to withdraw or refuse to activate extraordinary medical treatment, allowing the individual to die more naturally. This understanding is also given strong support by a resolution from the 1991 General Convention of the Episcopal Church printed below.

More active forms of euthanasia: The same 1991 Convention resolution holds, however, that "it is morally wrong and unacceptable to take a human life in order to relieve the suffering caused by incurable illness." I also do not support acts of euthanasia when a person can be said to retain any reasonable quality of life or is not in great and unrelievable pain. Euthanasia because a person is depressed over or fearful about illness, or wishes not to be a burden to others, is a form of assisted suicide which deprives family, friends, the community and the individual of the opportunity to continue in care and service to others.

When, however, unrelieved pain has become dominant and/or the nearness of death means that no opportunity for meaningful relationships or any participation or enjoyment of life are left, I personally would maintain that the painless assistance to death, with proper legal and moral guards, can be supported by Christian theology and ethical understandings.

While sympathetic with several of the provisions of the proposed California ballot measure (Proposition 161) on terminal illness and assistance in dying, I find it, however, much too broadly drawn and not sufficiently restricted to the latter stages of dying. I am, therefore, opposed to the Proposition.

Resolution of the General Convention

1. Although human life is sacred, death is part of the earthly cycle of life. There is a "time to be born and a time to die" (Eccl. 3:2). The resurrection of Jesus Christ transforms death into a transition to eternal life: "For as by man came death, by a man came also the resurrection of the dead" (I Cor. 15:21).

2. Despite this hope, it is morally wrong and unacceptable to take a human life in order to relieve the suffering caused by incurable illness. This would include the intentional shortening of another person's life by the use of a lethal dose of medication or poison, the use of lethal weapons, homicidal acts, and other forms of active euthanasia.

3. However, there is no moral obligation to prolong the act of dying by extraordinary means and at all costs if such dying person is ill and has no reasonable expectation of recovery.

4. In those cases involving persons who are in a comatose state from which there is no reasonable expectation of recovery, subject to legal restraints, this Church's members are urged to seek the advice and counsel of members of the church community, and where appropriate, its sacramental life, in contemplating the withholding or removing of life-sustaining system, including hydration and nutrition.

5. We acknowledge that the withholding or removing of life-sustaining systems has a tragic dimension. The decision to withhold or withdraw life-sustaining treatment should ultimately rest with the patient, or with the patient's surrogate decision-makers in the case of a mentally incapacitated patient. We therefore express our deep conviction that any proposed legislation on the part of national or state governments regarding the so-called "right to die" issues, (a) must take special care to see that the individual's rights are respected and that the responsibility of individuals to reach informed decisions in this matter is acknowledged and honored, and (b) must also provide expressly for the withholding or withdrawing of life-sustaining systems, where the decision to withhold or withdraw life-sustaining systems has been arrived at with proper safeguards against abuse.

6. We acknowledge that there are circumstances in which health care providers, in good conscience, may decline to act on requests to terminate life-sustaining systems if they object on moral or religious grounds. In such cases we endorse the idea of respecting the patient's right to self-determination by permitting such patients to be transferred to another facility or physician willing to honor the patient's request, provided that the patient can readily, comfortably and safely be transferred. We encourage health care providers who make it a policy to decline involvement in the termina-

tion of life-sustaining systems to communicate their policy to patients or their surrogates at the earliest opportunity, preferably before the patients or their surrogates have engaged the services of such a health care provider.

7. Advance written directives (so-called "living wills," "declarations concerning medical treatment" and "durable powers of attorney setting forth medical declarations") that make a person's wishes concerning the continuation or withholding or removing of life-sustaining systems should be encouraged, and this Church's members are encouraged to execute such advance written directives during good health and competence and that the execution of such advance written directives constitute loving and moral acts.

8. We urge the Council of Seminary Deans, the Christian Education departments of each diocese, and those in charge of programs of continuing education for clergy and all others responsible for education programs in this Church, to consider seriously the inclusion of basic training in issues of prolongation of life and death with dignity in their curricula and programs.

Health Care

Our society is engaged in one of its most important discussions about values and ethics with enormous practical results.

Should we view health care as primarily a private good or a public good?

Is health care a right or a privilege?

Should we place some limits on health care for the majority in order to expand basic health care to all?

The complexity of the issues comes to light in particular stories. The story of one's eighty-five-year-old mother whose best chance for a few more years of quality life lies in a risky and very expensive operation.

The story of a wife faced with the likelihood of spending all her retirement assets before her husband with Alzheimer's disease will be eligible for Medicaid.

The story of a laborer without medical insurance who puts off going to the doctor for his stomach pain until one night he is rushed to the emergency room. The operation and after-care cost $25,000. These costs the hospital and doctors are forced to absorb, and they are then passed on in the form of higher costs to patients with insurance.

Siamese twins, with little chance for life, are separated in an operation costing over $1,000,000, while many pregnant mothers and babies in the same city do not receive basic preventative medicine—eventually costing the society more millions in problems which could have been prevented.

A young family joins a Health Maintenance Organization (HMO) in order to save money. They like the preventative and regular care features, but are concerned that, if one of them develops a rare illness, they might not receive the best and most costly treatment.

Many of the basic facts about health care in the United States are well known. For many people we provide the best health care in the world. But for uninsured persons (37 million and, in fact, 65 million at one time or another in a given year) and many underinsured persons there is not only insecurity but often very inferior care. More than nine million children have no health insurance. We are behind many other countries in basic services like inoculations and infant care.

Our infant mortality rate is the highest among developed nations.

We spend far more on treatment of disease than prevention.

The United States spends twice as much per person on health care than does Germany or Japan.

There are also some things we know as Christians. From the beginning Christianity has been involved in healing ministries of various kinds. In a number of our communities we have hospitals which were founded by Christians in order to extend health care to as many people as possible.

Most, if not all Christians and people of biblical faith would agree that Scripture teaches us that we have a responsibility to speak up on behalf of the less fortunate among us. We would agree that a society can be measured by its care for its weaker members.

Many of us would also agree that health care, while a business, should be more than a business, and that individual needs must be balanced with the common good and a sense of responsible stewardship for our whole society and environment.

These beliefs and values lead most of us to hold that some form of health care coverage for everyone would be our bottom line for any genuine health care reform in our country.

But the tough questions and even dilemmas remain. Universal coverage will bring many benefits and perhaps even savings, but it will also require some trade-offs. These are hard to face up to since they involve our self-interest and a care system which is very important to us personally.

So far as a society we haven't shown a lot of willingness to face up to the harder questions. We leave, for instance, any questions about limits on health care up to those kind of situations like that of the laborer who was afraid of the cost of dealing with his stomach pain.

If as an individual, or as churches, you would like to exercise the responsibility of thinking further about these matters, there is an excellent resource. *A Vision of Wholeness: Responding to America's Health Care Crisis* is available from the Comprehensive Health Care Education Project of the California Council of Churches. Then also consider letting your senators and congressional representatives know what you, as Christian citizens, believe is best.

Who Are We?

When the American Association of Retired Persons recently endorsed health care reform plans which could begin to lead to more universal coverage, it was reported that the organizations switchboard lit up with angry phone calls from some of its members. " I don't want my insurance to change," said one sixty-nine-year-old woman. "Maybe that's selfish but, damn it, I feel I have earned the right to be selfish."

Were we able to hear more of what this woman wanted to say, she might tell us how she had worked hard much of her life to earn her government's benefits. Maybe she had lost her spouse or had experienced a recent illness. She could be feeling vulnerable and frightened, perhaps particularly by advertising she had seen directed against health care changes.

One can also hear at least a whisper of an awareness that she had once been taught a larger understanding of the responsibilities we can have for one another. Whatever her particular upbringing, in every major religion, and in forms of humanism as well, one finds a version of the golden rule: one should seek to do for others what one wants for oneself. There is also its corollary: not to do to others, and, when possible, not to let happen to others, what you wouldn't want to happen to you.

There is renewed talk about the teaching of virtues these days. Traditionally much of what has been understood as central to the virtuous life is a readiness to stand in another's shoes, to feel something of another's pain and vulnerability, and to do something about it.

Such virtue does not come naturally. Cute as little children may be, they are quite self-centered. Every major religion also understands maturity, often as a development involving God's grace, to include a capacity to keep one's own needs and wants from being the center of the universe.

Freedom, then, is not understood as being able to do whatever one pleases. That, in fact, is bondage to a self-centeredness from which one seeks some measure of freedom in order to be free to be of service to others and to the community.

Such an understanding of freedom may seem contrarian in the present climate of political discussion and debate in which self-interest appears not only to be accepted as the basis for participation but rather roundly affirmed. Indeed, one can see heads nodding when the woman says she has *earned* the right to be selfish. From various parts of the political spectrum there us abroad a spirit of libertarianism which exalts economic self-centeredness and the absolutist rights of individuals, families or particular groups. Many of our political representatives evidently have no qualms whatsoever about making such self-interest not only the bases of their votes but the bases of their appeal to voters as well. Some of them at least, and some economists, and evidently some religious folks as well would tell us that this is exactly how politics and the economics of our common life ought to work.

Yet when we speak of our concerns about the mean spiritedness of much that is happening in our times, it is very likely this societal inability to stop being so self-centered that bothers us. We know that we can be generous in other ways, and we at least have a vision of ourselves as a different kind of people.

Another way to say this is that we at least feel there ought to be another bottom line below the monetary line. Economics (as the root meaning of the word implies) should also be about how we live together, and the bottom line needs to take into account larger considerations including some form of the golden rule. If the boomers or the busters or seniors or the beat or X generations are looking for a cause, this is the bottom line that could be there in our debates and in our votes about health care, our responsibility for our environment, control of violence, discipline about guns, providing jobs, and many other common issues.

Some may regard such a perspective in politics as naive, but we shall see. History has a way of reckoning with societies which lose their sense of a shared life—of community.

If I am not for myself, asks the Jewish proverb, who will be? But if I am only for myself, who am I? And, we may ask, if we are each one only for ourselves, who are we?

Taking the Bible Seriously

In recent weeks the Bible has been in the headlines. The Jesus Seminar, which has been debating and voting on the authenticity of the words of the historical Jesus, reported that only a small portion of the words attributed to Jesus in the Gospels were actually spoken by him. Episcopal Bishop John Spong of Newark has written a widely commented upon book, *Rescuing the Bible from Fundamentalism*, in which he debates the problems with fundamentalist or singularly literalist uses of the Bible.

Both the book and the results of the seminar are of considerable value to contemporary Christians.

While in a world of uncertainties one can have pastoral understanding of the fundamentalist desire for an inerrant Bible with immediately accessible answers to help people follow God's will, the Spong book points out the darker side to such a use of religion. Together with the Seminar, the book sparks thought and discussion about the Bible, reminding Christians, among other things, of the distance that stands between people today and any sure historical knowledge of biblical events and figures or direct understanding of their world views.

It is a basic theological insight that, just as the human Jesus was fully incarnate in the limitations of history, so also is the Bible. Scripture is inspired by the same God who accepted the constraints of the incarnation.

This awareness is essential to a wise interpretation of Scripture. It helps contemporary Christians guard against reading the Bible with only their own culture in view. Over the past quarter century a number of studies have pointed out how prone even scholars have been to assume, for instance, that western understandings of self and sexuality were, at least in some measure, shared by biblical authors.

Both the reports from the Seminar and Bishop Spong's book, however, seem themselves curiously dated. The Bishop and participants in the Seminar are clearly cognizant of the fact that we all must live within our time period and that none of us escapes the "circle" from within which we must do our interpreting. Yet in listening to them one feels rather caught in a liberal Protestant perspective which is not profoundly aware of its own presuppositions. One senses a perspective which has not had much to do with other than historical-critical approaches to the Bible. Nor has it heard much of the post-enlightenment critique of the enlightenment's confidence in human knowledge and progress.

Bishop Spong tells us, and it may be true of a number of the participants of the Seminar, that he comes from a fundamentalist background. Perhaps that is one reason why many catholic Christians find it hard to know quite how to react to the rather dramatic tone he and the Seminar participants give to their results and to the ways in which they seem to be arguing within terms set by so-called fundamentalists.

When I began my theological education more than 30 years ago, I was given books to read like R. H. Lightfoot's *History and Interpretation in the Gospels,* written in 1934. Lightfoot concluded his study with these words:

> It seems, then, that the form of the earthly no less than of the heavenly Christ is for the most part hidden from us. For all the inestimable value of the gospels, they yield us little more than a whisper of his voice; we trace in them but the outskirts of his ways. Only when we see him hereafter in his fullness shall we know him also as he was on earth. And perhaps the more we ponder the matter, the more clearly we shall understand the reason for it, and therefore shall not wish it otherwise. For probably we are at present as little prepared for the one as for the other.[1]

Not just my theological education, however, but also my Christian upbringing assumed that there was not very much that we could know for certain about Jesus or the rest of the Bible in historical-critical terms. Historical criticism had great value. There was much that challenged and strengthened faith which could be learned from it. But faith was not dependent upon criticism's often shifting results. Indeed, one had to note the degree to which fundamentalism had locked itself into a struggle with the historical-critical approach in which both sides seemed to agree that questions about whether something happened or was said in the manner described in the Bible pretty much exhausted the important issues.

Oh, yes; we needed to understand that Jesus actually lived, and that who he was historically and the impact he had on his first disciples did not in some profound way contradict the Gospels' presentations of him. And, in fact, there are important, basic things that can probably be known about the Jesus of history. But knowledge about Jesus came not just from history or, indeed, from the Bible. It was found in the life of the community and in Christian experience. It was especially in the liturgy and sacraments that we learned of Jesus. In this setting the biblical stories and teaching became living words which, more than providing us with specific answers to questions, guided us into the presence of God.

While there has always been room in Anglicanism for different emphases in the understanding of the inspiration of Scripture, the final authority for the church was never the Bible alone, but the experience of the mysterious and transcendent God learned of through the Bible in the ongoing worship of the community and in trying to live out the commandments of love and service in the contemporary world. The final authority for Christian living was this presence of the Spirit of God of the living Jesus guided by the biblical witness.

This awareness called for much responsible freedom on the part of disciples, but with its use of stories in response to questions and in other teachings, this seemed to be a responsibility the Bible itself engendered. I was taught these words of Phillips Brooks: "The Bible is like a telescope. If a man looks through his telescope, then he sees worlds beyond; but if he looks at his telescope, then he does not see anything but that. The Bible is a thing to be looked through, to see that which is beyond, but most people look only at it; and so they see only the dead letter."[2]

This larger perspective also helped one to keep in mind the whole of the biblical witness and not just particular verses. One recognized, too, that this witness comes very often in the form of stories which ask for participation and interpretation, stories that shape communities of faith and convey meaning at several levels of knowing. Scripture always had to be entered into and probed for its different kinds of truth. Literary criticism was as valuable as historical criticism in one's hearing of the Bible. Poetry, song and story were useful for the Bible's understanding. As an Anglican, one recognized that Shakespeare, Donne, Herbert, Milton, Carew, Blake, Coleridge, Austen, Keble, Eliot, Auden, Williams, Sayers, Lewis, Paton, Hill, and L'Engle were among the Bible's chief interpreters.

These understandings, too, were part of the catholic heritage, for Scripture had been interpreted differently and often at several levels of meaning throughout the Church's history. John's Gospel, with its use of misunderstandings and words of double meanings, was the most obvious warning against being guided only by appearance and literal readings which, when all is said and done, might be only our attempts at literal reading.

I used to teach my students that listening to John's Gospel was like hearing through a set of stereophones. Through one ear one heard the voice of the historical Jesus. Against those Christians of his time who said it did not matter whether Jesus actually lived, the evangelist insisted on Jesus' physical fleshly life. Yet the Spirit that guided the Church was not a dead figure from the past but the Spirit of the living Lord. This risen Jesus one heard through the other ear.

The historical-critical mind wants to take the earphones off and listen first to the historical Jesus and then to the risen one. But the Gospel will not allow its hearers to do that. The evangelist fears that then hearers will misunderstand. The historical Jesus and the risen Jesus are finally the same Jesus, and the Spirit of Jesus speaks to the Church with one voice. While the other Gospels each present Jesus somewhat differently, in the last analysis they are really doing much the same thing the fourth Gospel is doing: it is both the risen and the historical Jesus that is speaking to his followers.

To the degree that reports from the Jesus Seminar and media comments about Bishop Spong's book have caused anxiety among Christians, one assumes a lack of the larger catholic heritage and perspective. Although I would disagree with the Seminar regarding some of their presuppositions and conclusions, and even with their optimism about what can be known about the historical Jesus, one can be grateful for their bringing the questions to a more public forum. While Bishop Spong's book surprised me with some of the meanings and significance of Scripture it seems to pass by, its willingness to debate within a perspective similar to that of fundamentalists, and with some of the things he believes we might know in critical terms about historical figures from long ago, I am grateful to him for presenting much helpful information about the Bible and for so strongly warning of the dangers of fundamentalist-like approaches to Scripture. Mostly I am made aware again of the values of a more catholic use of the Bible and the need and opportunity to share this perspective in which the Bible is read so fully and deeply and can be so forthrightly offered to others.

Notes

1. R. H. Lightfoot, *History and Interpretation in the Gospels* (New York: Harper and Brothers, 1934), 225.

2. On the Brooks quotations, see my reference in Frederick H. Borsch (ed.) *Anglicanism and the Bible* (Wilton, Conn.: Morehouse Barlow, 1984) 257, n. 32.

The Word of God

The Bible is a collection of books composed over a twelve hundred year period. It is made up of a variety of types of writings. Much of it is in stories, reflections on human circumstances and conditions in which God is frequently seen to be directly or indirectly involved. Often the voices heard in the Bible indicate that they are engaged in interpretation, seeking to understand and make relevant and pertinent for their time the traditions and experiences given to them.

These traditions are often about struggle—between order and chaos, freedom and slavery, justice and injustice, life and death. Amid suffering and evil they tell of hope and the victories of the power of God's righteousness and love, especially in the resurrection of Jesus. Above all, the Bible is about God's love and concern for God's people.

While there have always been different emphases with regard to an understanding of the inspiration of the Scriptures, the catechism of The Book of Common Prayer (p. 853) states the basic Anglican and catholic view. Scriptures are called "the Word of God because God inspired their human authors and because God still speaks to us through the Bible." On the one hand, the Bible is fully a historical book. An analogy can be made with the incarnation. Jesus was fully a human being. "He had to become like his brothers and sisters in every respect..." (Hebrews 2:17). Yet we believe God was mysteriously and wondrously present in this circumscribed life. The Bible, then, is a historical book. Its viewpoint is regularly limited by the understandings and even prejudices of its time. And, we also believe, God speaks through these very circumstances.

The Bible itself, however, is not to be worshipped. We call Scriptures the Word of God because we may hear God's Spirit speaking to us through the Bible, but the Bible functions as a kind of icon, pointing its hearers through its words to the Word of God—to the Divine—revealed particularly as the eternal, incarnate and risen Word of God.

Anglican and catholic theology has always understood the importance and the necessity of interpreting the Scriptures. Although some passages may or may seem to speak more directly than others, there is still the task of setting them within the larger context of the entire biblical drama and revelation. In this sense no one passage or verse can tell the whole story or be interpreted in isolation. What gives the Bible its ultimacy is its over-arching narrative power for shaping our understanding of life and of God's purpose and character—its telling of how God's reign can be already present in a world which often seems inchoate and broken. Each passage of the Bible is a part of that adventure.

The tradition of the Church, together with human reason reflecting on experience, are the means of interpretation. Tradition itself is not an unchanging body of lore and information. In recent years women and others, whose predecessors might at first not seem to have played that great a role in the Bible or tradition, have helped bring a hearing of other voices within the Bible and tradition. They have brought new perspectives and insights.

The Bible may regularly be used to critique tradition and reason, but it never can be heard without them. It is not a matter of whether we will use them to be part of the conversation with the Scriptures. They are always present. The important question is whether we will use them in a conscious, mature and prayerful way.

The biblical writings were formed in communities. While individuals can, of course, read and study the Bible for themselves, it is through the hearing of and reflection upon the Bible in gatherings of disciples that the Bible has its most important role in convicting, guiding and inspiring, the Spirit taking what is of Jesus and "declaring it to you," and, indeed, bringing more truth. (John 16:12-15).

The fullest hearing of the Bible will come in communities that are open to a diversity of voices, women and men, different races and ethnicities, ages, orientations, well-to-do and poor. We are rightly suspicious as to whether we have fully heard our Scriptures when our group is composed of persons who share only the same class and ethnicity. On the other hand, a Bible passage often takes on new power and conviction as hearers open themselves to diverse voices. The story of the disciples eating as they passed through the grainfields on the sabbath day, for example, (see Mark 2:23-28) will be heard differently if there are persons with little food in the community of hearers.

The Scriptures themselves contain many voices and perspectives. It is often pointed out that the four Gospels give us a much richer view of Jesus because of their differences. This diversity is true of all of the Bible. Indeed, it is a mistake to think of the Bible as presenting only one religion. Religious practices and even many beliefs vary and change from the time of a wandering desert tribe to the era of temple worship, through exile and return, with emphases on kingship, prophecy, priesthood and wisdom teaching. Even in the New Testament, written over a much shorter period of time, one finds that the church for whom the Gospel of John was written was quite different from those churches out of which the Gospel of Matthew emerged, and that the church of Corinth was clearly quite different than the one to which the Letter to the Hebrews was written.

What gives the Bible its unity throughout all these changes and variations is its constantly recurring and passionate calling to worship the one and only God, the holy God who is both demanding of justice and righteousness while full of compassion and mercy. This God calls the people of God to "be holy, for I the Lord your God am holy" (Leviticus 19:2). The calling to follow the ways of God and to know God's holiness comes for Christians to its fullness through the life, death and risen life of Jesus.

Jesus and Women Exemplars

J esus' disciples marveled that he was talking with a woman" (John 4:27). Careful readers of the Gospels will say, "they shouldn't have." In his pivotal story about Jesus' speaking with the woman at the well, the Johannine evangelist makes much of the fact that Jesus was not just talking about mundane matters but having a discussion regarding religious concerns with a woman who was also a Samaritan ("For Jews have no dealings with Samaritans," John 4:9). Although our evidence from this period can never be as definitive as we would wish,[1] it is clear that Jesus was effronting well established teachings and mores to have been holding such a conversation, especially in public. One scholar speaks of Jesus' associations with women being "without precedent in contemporary Judaism."[2]

The Synoptic Gospels as well as other material in the Fourth Gospel preserve a lively and memorable tradition that Jesus had a number of significant relationships with women. New Testament scholarship, and particularly the work of women scholars, has allowed this picture to reemerge with clarity. By any reckoning, what is to be marveled at in these first century documents is the frequent and regular role of women, especially in the context of a strongly patriarchal religion and androcentric cultures. Less noted, but of perhaps even more surprise and significance, is the fact that many of the stories and sayings in which women play a role are of great importance for advancing the distinctiveness of the gospel message. Women have no comparable role in rabbinical stories of the period. It is not just that Jesus associated and talked with and about women. In a number of cases they appear to have been deliberately chosen to carry important lessons. In some instances the women seem to have been selected because they were without much status or standing in society and in law. Theirs are stories of Jesus' ministry with and on behalf of the lowly and marginalized.[3] In other cases one can believe that there was a more general concern with the discipleship of women. As it becomes increasingly evident that at the heart of Jesus' ministry was a passionate desire to gather and reform the people of Israel in as inclusive a manner as possible for the coming of God's reign,[4] one recognizes how fully women were to be part of this renewed community. In a number of cases they are presented as witnesses and actors, helping to make the new community happen.

The most significant role given to women in the Gospel's story was not directly within Jesus' control. Yet it is doubtful that women could have found their prominent place in the resurrection narratives unless Jesus had earlier drawn them into close and meaningful association with his ministry as those who "followed (ακολομthein) him and ministered (diakonein) to him in Galilee" (Mark 15:40-41//Matt. 27:55-56//Luke 23:49; and see Luke 8:2-3). The two Greek words have a quasi-technical meaning of discipleship and ministering in the New Testament.[5] The fact that a number of these women are given names, and that there were said to be "many others," indicates both the specificity and strength of this tradition. What is particularly to be remarked upon is not that the women assisted Jesus in various ways (for this was true in case of other rabbis of the time) but that women of various stations in life (Joanna in Luke 8:3 is the wife of Chuza, Herod's steward) traveled with him.[6]

While the four Gospels vary in indicating whether one, two, or three or more women followers of Jesus were the first to learn of Jesus' resurrection, they are all clear that women were first and that Mary Magdalene was one of them or the one. Dispirited and perhaps feeling guilty because they had either deserted or not been of any help to Jesus, the male disciples were led to resurrection faith by the women followers who, as is so often true of women, appear at first just to be attempting to pick up the pieces and help life to go on by visiting the grave to anoint and honor Jesus' body. Having come with Jesus from Galilee, they had been able only to look "on from a distance" while he was crucified. But they were there (Mark 15:40-41// Matt. 27:55-56//Luke 23:49; see John 19:25). They also waited, the narrative informs us, to see "where he was laid" (Mark 15:47; Matt. 27:61; Luke 23:55-56).

The questioning of the women's testimony in Luke 24:11 underscores the inferior status of women in that era as far as being legal witnesses was concerned,[7] but also further serves to emphasize the strength and unanimity of the early tradition in this regard. The women's crucial role was likely an embarrassment to a number of men and to all those concerned to demonstrate the truth of the resurrection by the standards of the time.

Mary of Magdala's foremost place as the prototype witness to the resurrection in all the Gospel traditions [8] (particularly in the moving scene in John 20:11-18), along with her inclusion among those who "ministered to Jesus," has led to more than a little speculation about a special relationship

117

with Jesus. In fact, however, we know very little about her. Luke informs his readers that she had once been possessed by seven demons which now had left her (8:2). One must assume she had been in a bad way whether physically or spiritually or both. Although there is no reason to link her with the immoral woman in the preceding passage (Luke 7:36-50), much less the woman taken in adultery (John 8:3-11), she must have had serious problems and been an important exemplar of Jesus' readiness to associate himself with those in difficult circumstances—the poor, the sick, and the rejected. One can imagine the particularly harsh circumstances of a woman with several or all of these problems.

A number of commentators, discussing the scene between Jesus and the sinful woman in Luke 7:36-50, have suggested that she is not in fact the best illustration of the little parable embedded in the longer passage which instructs that those forgiven much will love much (7:41-43). Jesus only pronounces her forgiveness after she has cared so personally for him.[9] This criticism, however, misses the awareness that Jesus had already shown his acceptance and forgiveness by allowing the woman to minister to him. As so often in Jesus' ministry, actions spoke louder than words and likely brought him into much more trouble. It is one thing to talk about forgiveness and acceptance of those regarded by others as low in life and irreligious. It is another to do it. Strong in the reminiscence of the disciples was the awareness that Jesus did as he said and, in this as in a number of other significant instances, that a woman in difficult circumstances (yet more so if, in fact, she was a prostitute, since then as now almost all prostitutes came from impoverished conditions) was at the center of his controversial action, playing a critical role in his groundbreaking ministry.

Because they also picture a woman ministering lavishly to Jesus and both scenes have a figure named Simon (in Luke a Pharisee; in Matthew and Mark a leper), Mark 14:3-9//Matthew 26:6-13 are often regarded as coming from the same tradition which Luke 7:36-50 may have developed. While Mark's and Matthew's vignette has a different function with respect to foreshadowing Jesus' death and burial, the scene again conveys the strong memory of Jesus' association with women and their use as primary actors. In John's Gospel the story of the woman who anoints Jesus in preparation for burial (12:1-8) has more in common with Luke 7:36-50. (She anoints his feet and wipes them with her hair.) Here the woman is identified as Mary, the sister of Martha and Lazarus.

While the uncertain textual history of the story of the woman taken in adultery (John 8:3-11) means that its direct association with Jesus' activity is problematic, one can still regard it as the kind of story which became linked

118

with Jesus because of his other teaching and actions. The memory of his acts of forgiveness and his concern for the defenseless and women helped make the story part of the tradition. Similarly and correspondingly, the powerful words of Mary's song are meant to anticipate themes of Jesus' ministry:

> God has scattered the proud in the imagination
> > of their hearts;
> God has put down the mighty from their thrones,
> > and exalted those of low degree;
> God has filled the hungry with good things,
> > and the rich God has sent empty away.
> > > (Luke 1:51-53)

Frequently noted is the place that women have in Luke's Gospel.[10] On several occasions he seems deliberately to follow a story about a male actor with one about a woman. Whether all of these stories are to be traced to Jesus' historical ministry, whether they are all or in part the result of Luke's special interest, or whether they stem from some other period of the tradition's development, their place in the Gospel can still be regarded as resulting from Jesus' special concern for and the distinction he gave to women.

Widows, of course, were of particular moral concern in Israel and to Israel's God who is "Father of the fatherless and protector of widows" (Ps. 68:5). Without a husband to help them in a male-dominated society, widows had few rights or protections, and therefore, the Bible urges, special care and fair treatment. That this was not always the case is rather humorously illustrated in Jesus' story of the widow who persistently made a nuisance of herself until a judge, who had no regard for God or human opinion, finally granted her justice as a way of getting her off his back (Luke 18:1-8).[11] The story may imply that the judge was waiting for some kind of a bribe from the widow or her opponent, but the widow, presumably without money or much legal clout, used her insistent nagging to gain her rights. She becomes a hero in a story which Luke uses to underline the importance of perseverance in prayer, though one can guess it might have been used earlier to stress the importance of steadfastedly and single-mindedly seeking God's justice and expecting to receive it. If this uncaring judge would grant that widow her wish because she was such a nuisance, how much more, the parable suggests, will God give the good things of the reign of God to those who persist.

In a story which reaches beyond our modern-day understandings,

Jesus raises to life the only son of a widowed woman from the town of Nain (Luke 7:11-17). The Gospel presents the story in order to portray Jesus' compassion toward the widow and especially to help later disciples realize that the creative healing power of God's reign was ultimately greater than even the awesome power of death. "A great prophet has arisen among us!" the crowd exclaims, and "God has visited God's people" (Luke 7:16).

In Luke 13:10-l7 a bent over woman is healed on the sabbath day and becomes an important example of Jesus' actions and teaching in this regard.[12] Similar to his description of Zacchaeus ("he also is a son of Abraham, " Luke 19:9), she too is "a daughter of Abraham" and is to be fully included in God's restored people.

Women can play significant roles in Luke's Gospel while not fully comprehending Jesus or what is happening to him. The woman who calls out "Blessed is the womb that bore you, and the breasts that you sucked!" is told, "Blessed rather are those who hear the word of God and keep it!" (11:27-28). The women who, bewailing and lamenting, follow Jesus on the way to the crucifixion (23:27-31) can be remembered for their compassion, but they do not really understand what is taking place.

In a parable closely linked with that of the shepherd who leaves the ninety-nine sheep in the wilderness to seek one that is lost, we hear of another woman in Luke's Gospel who, having lost one of ten silver coins, diligently searches for it until she finds it (15:8-10). The evangelist sees the incident as an illustration of how there will be joy before the angels of God over one repentant sinner. In another yoked parable found in both Luke (13:20-21) and Matthew (13:33) a woman puts leaven in three measures of meal, a simile for the apparent insignificance of God's inbreaking reign, which will yet transform all. The result is at least a half bushel of meal, enough for more than a hundred people and a festive occasion. In the Matthean parable of the wise and foolish maidens (25:1-10) some women are illustrations of unpreparedness for the reign of heaven while others will know its joy.[13] The fact that women could be portrayed in less favorable as well as favorable roles in situations both fictitious and real would seem to indicate that Jesus thought of women as persons and not idealized figures. Similarly, in addition to the two men, of whom at the time of judgment one will be taken and the other left, also "there will be two women grinding together; one will be taken and the other left" (Luke 17:34-35//Matt. 24:40-41). Women will share equally in the blessing and judgment of God's reign. They apparently will also share in making judgment. Not only will the men of Nineveh arise at the judgment day to condemn this generation for its lack of repentance and readiness to live in hopefulness, but also "the queen of the

South" (the Queen of Sheba who came to hear Solomon's wisdom: 1 Kings 10:1-13) will arise to offer her condemnation (Matt. 12:41-42//Luke 11:31-32).

Luke (21:1-4) and Mark (12:41-44) use the story of the widow and her donation of two coins to illustrate truly sacrificial giving. Similar stories are known from other cultures, but it is significant that the hero of Jesus' story is again a woman. It should also be noted that some scholars find in this illustration a critique of an attitude which would encourage a widow to donate the whole of her living. [14] (See Mark 12:40//Luke 20:47 on the condemnation of the religious officials who devour widows' houses.)

It is the daughter of Jairus who is raised from death or the point of death (Mark 5:21-24; 35-42//Matt. 9:18-19, 23-26//Luke 8:40-42, 49-56) into which story is interpolated the healing of the woman with an issue of blood (Mark 5:25-34//Matt. 9:20-22//Luke 8:43-48). The significance of the faith of this woman (impoverished by her medical expenses and no doubt without societal protection) for her healing is emphasized. Remarkable also, in this and similar stories where Jesus heals women, is his willingness to be touched or to touch when the women's illnesses would have caused others to regard them as unclean (cf. Lev. 15:25-30). Here he not only allows it to happen but calls attention to the fact. Peter's mother-in-law is another woman whose healing is specifically noted in the Gospels (Mark 1:29-31//Matt. 8:14-15//Luke 4:38-39).

Of still more import for the development of the Gospels' story is the healing of the daughter of the Syrophoenician or Canaanite woman (Mark 7:24-30//Matt. 15:21-28). Although the story was valuable to the early churches as one of the few examples of Jesus' reaching out to gentiles, the seeming coarseness of Jesus' dialogue with the woman and his hesitation in responding to her request may also have given the evangelists pause in using it.[15] It is often thought that Luke has declined to include it in his Gospel for these reasons. But for those same reasons it is possible that aspects of the story reach deep into the tradition to a time when gentile sensitivities were of less importance and Jesus did indeed believe he was "sent only to the lost sheep of the house of Israel" (Matt. 15:24)—on a ministry to restore the people of Israel for the advent of God's reign. As it stands in the Gospels the story now represents a kind of breakthrough on Jesus' part, his finding himself called to reach out beyond his own idea of his mission. In a sense he is being challenged to live up to his sermon which immediately precedes this story (Mark 7:1-23//Matt. 15:1-20), instructing in the importance of what is inside, rather than outside appearances. The individual, whose courage born of desperation and whose bold banter causes Jesus to reach out, is not only a gentile but a woman. His healing of her daughter must, at least at first, have seemed even more surprising to many of the early followers of Jesus than the healing of the gentile centurion's servant (Matt. 8:5-13//Luke 7:10).

While they are now often employed as the Gospels' one great legalism, some commentators suspect that Jesus' sayings on divorce originally were more concerned with the protection of women than insisting on the indissolubility of marriage *per se* (cf. Mark 10:2-12//Matt. 19:3-9; 5:31-32// Luke 16:18). "Moses allowed a man to write a certificate of divorce and to put his wife away." While certain protections were in place, evidently in Judaism at that time a man could obtain a divorce for almost any reason he chose.[16] "For your hardness of heart Moses wrote this commandment," Jesus responds. That is not God's purpose. A man is to "leave his father and mother and be joined to his wife, and the two shall become one. What therefore God has joined together, let not man put asunder." Men are not to divorce their wives, leaving them in many ways helpless, anything like that easily. Whoever does this, Jesus may well have said in the oldest version of these words, commits adultery against his wife when he marries another woman and also makes his wife an adulteress (i.e., he forces her to join herself to another man as the only way she can find protection). [17]

A parallel concern for women seems to be signified in the new teaching that "everyone who looks at a woman lustfully has already committed adultery with her in his heart" (Matt. 5:28). Many of the limitations on women in Jewish society seem to be based on a fear that men could not control their sexual desires. It was best, therefore, to control women socially and in other ways. Standard teaching of the time usually concentrates on the dangers of female seductiveness. This teaching of Jesus, however, seems to expect that his male disciples can learn to control themselves. Perhaps, above all, there is found here a severe condemnation of thinking of women and relating to them only or even primarily in sexual terms.

At several important points in the Gospels Jesus seems among the first to be concerned with what we today would call inclusive language and its implications. When Jesus is told his mother and brothers are asking for him, he uses this as an occasion to teach about a still more important relationship: "Whoever does the will of God is my brother and sister and mother" (Mark 3:35//Matt. 12:50). By taking "it for granted that women, equally with men, can do the will of God, and thereby be his true kindred" Jesus is presenting "a radical redefinition of the Old Testament and Jewish relationship between women and men and God." [18] When Peter rather plaintively says, "Lo, we have left everything and followed you," Jesus responds:

> Truly I say to you, there is no one who has left house or brothers
> or sisters or mother or father or children or lands, for my sake
> and for the gospel, who will not receive a hundredfold now in
> this time, houses, and brothers and sisters and mothers and
> children and lands.
> (Mark 10:29-30//Matt. 19:29//Luke 18:29)

That seems like a great deal of family, and it certainly is remarkably inclusive. It is particularly interesting that leaving sisters, who would usually have been seen at that time as a burden and responsibility, is considered a sacrifice.[19]

While Jesus' mission seems in the Synoptic Gospels to have required him to keep himself at some distance from his family, in the story of the wedding feast at Cana the Fourth Gospel gives his mother an important role. They are portrayed in frank, and on Jesus' part even somewhat strained exchange. Mary appears to sense Jesus' authority and power for this occasion but not fully to realize the importance of timing for his mission. Mary's faithfulness, along with Jesus' concern for her, is demonstrated in the poignant scene at the foot of the cross (John 19:25-27). The later development of Mary's role in the birth narratives of Matthew and Luke is the result of several factors, but gives to her an exalted place in the reverence of the churches.

While it may not be right to call them his second family, Jesus appears to have been especially close to Martha, Mary, and Lazarus. Traditions about Martha and Mary form one of those intriguing links between the Third and Fourth Gospels and are often thought to go back to the churches' early memories.[20] The two sisters play vital roles in the final and greatest of Jesus' miracles in John's Gospel, the raising of Lazarus (11:1-44). Their hesitant coming to faith in Jesus and the power of resurrection, and the ways in which they do so are meant to be models for all disciples.

Martha seems the more outgoing, her faith both trusting and questioning. "Even now I know that whatever you ask from God, God will give you" (John 11:22). When Jesus says, "Your brother will rise again," Martha responds with her belief in the general resurrection: "I know that he will rise again in resurrection at the last day." But Jesus tells her the power for resurrection is here and now, with him. "I am the resurrection and the life; the one who believes in me, though dying, yet shall live; and whoever lives and believes in me shall never die." Then Jesus puts her faith to the test: "Do you believe this?" Martha is able to answer, "Yes, Lord, I believe that you are the Christ, the Son of God, the one who is coming into the world" (11:22-27). She has a personal trust in Jesus. Indeed, her witness is more powerful even than Peter's "confession" at Caesarea Philippi in the Synoptic Gospels and earlier in this Gospel (6:68). Yet she does not fully answer Jesus' question. She knows Lazarus is quite dead, and in a moment she will warn Jesus that the body has already become odoriferous because it is decaying (11:39).

Mary comes to Jesus when she learns from her leading sister Martha that he is calling her. She simply repeats Martha's initial plaintive statement of trust in Jesus' power to heal: "Lord, if you had been here, my brother would not have died" (11:32; see 11:21). Then she can only weep. Her weeping and that of other Jews who are there bring Jesus to tears (11:33-35).

The picture of Martha as active and Mary as more quietly attentive to Jesus is further drawn in John 12:1-8 and yet more clearly in Luke 10:38-42. In John 12:1-8 Martha serves the supper while the woman who anoints Jesus' feet with costly ointment and wipes it with her hair is identified as Mary.

Many commentators focus on Mary in the Lucan story, her sitting and listening to Jesus (who is again teaching a woman, perhaps here either a group of women or a woman in mixed company) and being commended for recognizing that which is most important. It is Martha, however (in whose house this scene takes place), who is actually the more prominent figure in the story. Most people who feel that they take upon themselves more than their share of the world's work can identify with her in her resentment, because Mary seems to be enjoying herself instead of helping. In these terms the story becomes a challenge to all hard-working disciplined followers of Jesus. Can they serve without resentment of others, while recognizing the importance of contemplation along with action, of listening and being as well as doing and accomplishment? As a result of all her activity, Martha, Jesus perceives, is troubled and anxious about many things, along with her resentment. But Jesus stresses what is most needful and, in what appears to be a little word-play at this meal, tells Martha that Mary has chosen the good portion, the main dish that is needed.[21]

In recent years a number of women have voiced their concern with aspects of Luke's presentation of the Mary and Martha story. Whatever is said about the significance of the two women, the story remains male-centered in that Jesus is the main actor, and the narrative clearly is told to preserve his decisive words. The story sets two women against each other and seems to see them only in domestic roles.[22] It is important to remember, however, that Jesus is the central figure throughout the Gospels in which male disciples also play lesser and frequently far from flattering parts. Mary and Martha may be somewhat caricatured in Luke's vignette, but the narrative still recalls the vital place in his ministry of two sisters whose roles as disciples and witnesses may emerge more clearly in John's Gospel.

Finally we return to the story of the Samaritan woman at the well (John 4:7-42)—still a surprising narrative, although by now readers have grown accustomed to stories of Jesus' deliberate efforts to make clear the full inclusion of many different women in the new offer of God's reign. With typical use of irony, misunderstandings based on overly-literal hearings of words, and the use of words of double meanings, the fourth evangelist employs this extended narrative and dialogue to advance several of his important themes. Indeed, one of his messages to hearers may well be, "Don't get stuck with overly literal understandings. Truth often lies deeper."

When Jesus speaks of his gift of "living water," the woman thinks he means water that is moving, running water. She advises him that the well is deep and that he has nothing to draw with. Uncomprehendingly she asks, "Are you greater than our father Jacob?" She soon comes to understand, however, that one greater than the patriarchs of the Samaritans and Jews is here. She learns to ask for water that will cause her never to thirst again. To both the people of Israel and the Samaritans water was another of the symbols for Torah—the water of life. This Jesus himself now gives in his words and person, with perhaps an allusion to the water of baptism as well.

As the dialogue continues, Jesus slowly penetrates the woman's incomprehension, suspicion and defensiveness. She is at first both fearful and surprised by his insights into her. While hearers may be meant to understand that she had five husbands in the literal sense, they are probably also intended to think of the five peoples with whom Samaritans were said to have intermarried and their gods. Never mind! Salvation can now come to Samaritans as well—beginning with this woman. She learns that true worship will no longer be identified with either this sacred mount in Samaria or with Jerusalem. It is not where people worship but how they worship and with what sense of God that matter. The woman learns that the one who is telling her these things is the Messiah.

The disciples return and marvel that Jesus is talking with a woman. But the woman is now a convert and through her witness brings many other Samaritans to faith. She is a prototype evangelist through whom others come to believe that "this is indeed the Savior of the world" (John 4:42).[23] Once again hearers of the Gospels learn of Jesus' intention fully to include women in "the God movement." [24] They hear of his concern to show care for women as persons often disadvantaged in society, and to employ them in their variety and reality as crucial exemplars of the ways in which God through Jesus' ministry was breakng down old barriers and making a new community of God's people.

There is a sense in which stories like that of the Samaritan woman take on even greater significance when they are not regarded as coming from the early Jesus' traditions. Along with the stories of Mary and Martha of Bethany, Mary Magdalene, and others, these narratives may well give a glimpse of a time in the life of the young Christian communities when women had leading parts as evangelists, teachers, and witnesses, [25] in some cases because of their earlier association with Jesus. They played vital roles in carrying on his ministry and his concerns. Even the all male evangelists and the generations of male-dominated churches have not fully eclipsed that record.

Notes

1. The nature of our sources and the problems with dating particular traditions make it difficult to reconstruct the world of early first century Judaism with certainty, but it seems sufficiently clear that women of the time were expected to have a role almost exclusively in the home and were to be passive in almost every public setting. There is some evidence that contact with Hellenism and Roman society may have given some impetus to an improved status for women. See Joachim Jeremias, *Jerusalem in the Time of Jesus: An Investigation into Economic and Social Conditions During the New Testament Period* (Philadelphia: Fortress Press, 1969), 358-76; Ben Witherington III, *Women in the Ministry of Jesus: A Study of Jesus' Attitudes to Women and their Roles as Reflected in His Earthly Life*, SNTSMS 51 (Cambridge: Cambridge Univ. Press, 1984), 1-10; Phyllis Bird, "Images of Women in the Old Testament," in *Religion and Sexism: Images of Women in the Jewish and Christian Tradition*, ed. Rosemary Radford Reuther (New York: Simon & Schuster, 1974), 41-88; Barbara J. MacHaffie, *Her Story: Women in Christian Tradition* (Philadelphia: Fortress Press, 1986), 6-9; Mary J. Evans, *Women in the Bible* (Exeter: Paternoster Press, 1983), 33-43; and L. William Countryman, *Dirt, Greed, and Sex: Sexual Ethics in the New Testament and Their Implications for Today* (Philadelphia: Fortress Press, 1988), 151-67.

2. Werner Förster, *From the Exile to Christ: A Historical Introduction to Palestinian Judaism* (Philadelphia: Fortress Press, 1964), 127. On the danger, however, either of making Jesus look better by painting the patriarchy of the Judaism of his time in the worst colors possible (there is evidence that practice was sometimes better than theory), or of separating him from his own people and culture which would have helped inspire his teaching, see Elisabeth Schüssler Fiorenza, *In Memory of Her: A Feminist Theological Reconstruction of Christian Origins* (New York: Crossroad, 1983), 106-10. Fiorenza then, however, goes on to stress the distinctiveness of Jesus' ministry and message regarding women.

3. See Pheme Perkins, "Women in the Bible and Its World," *Int* 42 (1988): 33-44.

4. See Gerhard Lohfink, *Jesus and Community: The Social Dimensions of Christian*

Faith (Philadelphia: Fortress Press, 1982), 7-73; and E. P. Sanders, *Jesus and Judaism* (Philadelphia: Fortress Press, 1985), 61-119.

5. See Elizabeth M. Tetlow, *Women and Ministry in the New Testament* (New York: Paulist Press, 1980), 97.

6. See B. Witherington, *Women in the Ministry of Jesus*, 116-18.

7. Cf. ibid., 9-10.

8. The earliest of the traditions in 1 Cor. 15:3-8 makes no mention of Mary Magdalene or any of the other women. Whether this was because Paul did not know of or here did not wish to present the empty tomb tradition, or whether it was due to his androcentricity, or some other reason, is not known.

9. On various interpretations of Luke 7:36-50, see B. Witherington, *Women in the Ministry Jesus*, 53-57.

10. See Hans Conzelmann, *The Theology of St. Luke* (New York: Harper & Brothers, 1960), who on pp. 46-47 suggests that Luke may have had a special interest in women because of their importance as witnesses distinct from the male disciples. It is often thought that women may have played important roles in the Lucan community. On the other hand, there are also some indications in the lack of full comprehension by some of the women who call out to or speak with Jesus that Luke may subtly be playing down aspects of women's importance.

11. For more on this story, see Frederick H. Borsch, *Many Things in Parables: Extravagant Stories of New Community* (Philadelphia: Fortress Press, 1988), 111-16.

12. E. Schüssler Fiorenza, *In Memory of Her*, 125, regards this as the oldest of the tradition's stories about sabbath healings.

13. For more on the parable, see F. Borsch, *Parables*, 84-89. This is the only distinctively Matthean story about women, and one notes that he shortens several Marcan stories that portray women. While Matthew regularly shortens narratives, it has been suggested that Matthew is the Gospel least interested in women's roles, and that the evangelist may be deliberately limiting their place lest too much scope be given to women in his conservative community.

14. See A. G. Wright, "The Widow's Mites: Praise or Lament?—A Matter of Context," *CBQ* 44 (1982): 256-65.

15. For more on the story and its place in the Gospels, see Frederick H. Borsch, *Power in Weakness: New Hearing for Gospel Stories of Healing and Discipleship* (Philadelphia: Fortress Press, 1983), 51-66.

16. On the issues generally and these sayings in particular, see B. Witherington, *Women in the Ministry of Jesus*, 2-6, 18-28.

17. Mark 10:12 speaks of the possibility of a woman divorcing her husband. Such a reference would have been unusual in Judaism of the time and may come from a later stage in the development of the tradition, perhaps under the influence of Roman society.

18. Joanna Dewey, "Images of Women," in *The Liberating Word: A Guide to Nonsexist Interpretation of the Bible*, ed. Letty M. Russell (Philadelphia: Westminster Press, 1976), 62-81, 75.

19. See M. Evans, *Women in the Bible*, 46.

20. On the Mary, Martha, and Lazarus traditions, see Raymond E. Brown, *The Gospel According to John 1-XII*, AB 29 (Garden City, NY: Doubleday & Co., 1966), xliv-xlvii, 432-35.

21. On the textual problems with Luke 10:42 and the passage more generally, see B. Witherington, *Women in the Ministry of Jesus*, 100-103.

22. See Elisabeth Schüssler Fiorenza, "A Feminist Critical Interpretation for Liberation: Mary and Martha. Lk. 10:38-42," *Religion and Intellectual Life* 3 (1986): 21-35.

23. Raymond Brown finds that the use of αποσέλλειν in John 4:37 tends to enhance the missionary function of the Samaritan woman, perhaps preserving a memory that women

played an important role in the mission to Samaria. R. E. Brown, "Roles of Women in the Fourth Gospel," *TS* 36 (1975): 688-89, 691-92.

24. Clarence Jordan's translation of "the reign of God." See *The Cotton Patch Version of Luke and Acts: Jesus' Doings and Happenings* (New York: Association Press, 1969).

25. See Sandra M. Schneiders, "Women in the Fourth Gospel and the Role of Women in the Contemporary Church," *BTB* 12 (1982): 35-45.

Ordination of Women
Reviewing the Case

The election of Barbara Harris to be Suffragan Bishop of Massachusetts has raised again the fundamental issues with respect to the ordination of women. This is true not only for individuals and the Episcopal Church, but also for the Anglican Communion and all members of the catholic tradition of Christianity.

As I have listened to and engaged in the discussion and debate over the years it has seemed to me that the basic arguments used in opposition and the responses might be stated succinctly in this manner:

(1) In the incarnation, God was present in the world in a male human being. Ordained persons in various ways are meant to represent Jesus, particularly in the Eucharist which is, in part, a reenactment of the last meal of Jesus with his disciples. It is at least odd to have a female playing a male role.

Response: In the incarnation, God was present in human life for the salvation of every human being. It is a serious category mistake to fasten on the maleness of Jesus as somehow being a necessity for those who would represent him and his message. To do so could lessen the understanding that salvation is for all. Having ordained women celebrate the Eucharist helps in the understanding of the fullness of God, of the inclusiveness of the Church, and that the sacraments are for all. Similarly, the early Church had to learn that the fact that Jesus was a Jew did not mean that all who represented him had to come from a Jewish background.

(2) As Creator, God is initiator and active. These are more properly male roles, which is why God is most often thought of as "male" in the scriptures. Women's vital and distinctive roles tend to the more passive and nurturing. Bishops and priests act for God in their sacramental and authoritative roles and therefore should best be males.

Response: More and more such role descriptions are seen as stereotypes. Many men resent being called less nurturing, less peaceful. Many women do not see themselves with less active and initiatory roles in life. We also have to be careful about projecting our stereotypes onto God. We need to examine the scriptural teaching about God and distinguish that which is essential from that which results from the cultural attitudes of the time. God is a God of all cultures and times.

(3) If Jesus had wanted women disciples in leadership roles, he would have chosen at least one to be among the twelve.

Response: Incarnation means that Jesus was a part of his culture—a culture that would not have recognized women in highly visible leadership roles. What is remarkable is the key roles women do play in association with Jesus' ministry and in the early churches.

(4) The Church catholic has existed for almost two thousand years. One should not change a solid unanimous tradition regarding the male priesthood and episcopate.

Response: The primary orientation of the Church has never been backward but rather forward in hope, in expectation of the fullness of redemption and God's new age. God is a God of our future as well as our past. The future brings change and we can welcome that change when we believe it is of God. In any event, this change may be seen as a further sign that the Church is trying to become a foreshadowing of the community of God's new age where there is radical equality of all God's people before God.

(5) The ordination of women represents a giving in to the women's liberation movement and the ways of the world. It is sociological rather than theological and spiritual.

Response: We should expect the Holy Spirit to speak to the Church in and through the world's cultures as well as in scripture and the Church. The Spirit cannot be limited. It is better to see what is happening in the world as a response to a fundamental truth that has always been present in Christianity, but has taken long to develop. In Jesus Christ, women and men are equal. They are different, of course, but the differences are meant to complement and support one another not to give one gender authority over the other.

(6) The ordination of women—especially of a woman bishop—is going to create grave difficulties for our ecumenical relationships.

Response: Not to ordain women would create grave difficulties for our relations with Lutherans, Methodists and many other churches of the Reformed traditions. Although a number of officials of Roman Catholicism do not accept the ordination of women, many Roman Catholics do welcome it. Others are glad to see us practice women's ordination so that they may discover its benefits. One thing to be remembered about Roman Catholicism is that it can change its mind very speedily. In the meantime, there are still many ways we can cooperate and share with Roman Catholics. Some of the same things could be said about our Orthodox brothers and sisters, though they tend to think more in terms of centuries than generations.

In fairness, one recognizes that others would put these arguments rather differently and want to expand on them and make other points, using particular scriptural texts. The above outline may, however, catch the essence of the debate—a discussion that is becoming repetitious in the hearing of some, and which has led a number of theologians on both sides to say that there are at least no significant theological reasons against the ordination of women.

While I continue to be sympathetic with those who still find the change difficult, I want ours to be a Church that is inclusive in every way possible. I also feel that we are a Church that has tried faithfully, prayerfully and boldly to make a decision in response to the leading of the Spirit. It seems time for us not only to accept the ordination of women, but vigorously to work out its implications throughout the whole life of the Church.

From my perspective I must say how much the ministries of ordained women have meant to me and my hopes for the mission and evangelism of the Church. I believe their ordination is also helping and supporting the ministries of all women as well as men. I feel that the ordination of Barbara Harris will widen and strengthen my episcopal ministry.

All of us must continue to reach out and to listen to others in a time of change and transition, but we also should move forward in hope and faith into God's future.

> Drawn from slavery, oppressions child,
> Still the malign of color's poverty
> And gender's bar to equality,
> Around her hung
> Her own decrying words
> As through a calumny.

She cannot be, will not be allowed,
Is impossible, her gender most,
But surreptitiously her race and
Those angered, cadenced cries
For all others, within and out
This supposed genteel house,
Bring refusals, even to know her,
Especially her.
Yet now she rises, called of God
From among those last made first
One among apostles. Adorned,
Her words now mitred flames
On female brow, in her hand
A staff to protect and set free,
Poverty and womanhood all clothed,
Radiantly, she stands, and turns,
And is, with all hers before and after,
As with her God all things possible,
She is, for us, apostle.

God Not Man: In Prayer and Worship

All men are created equal. A number of people would understand these words from our Declaration of Independence to refer to both men and women. Yet many contemporary women and men do not. They do not hear them as inclusive of both sexes, especially when we remember that at the time they were written women could not even vote. Nor did they have a number of other rights and responsibilities that we believe are important for equality today.

It's not a matter of mere words. It rarely is. Our language comes from the way we think and treat each other. Our language profoundly affects our relationships.

Most people today wish strongly to affirm the understanding that women and men, although, of course, different, should share in a basic social, political, and economic equality. While it does not always work out that way, this certainly should be the goal and intended practice.

Many think that this understanding comes primarily from secular culture, but there were and are powerful forces in this regard at work in the Bible, particularly in the ministry of Jesus. Within a male-dominated culture his interrelationship with women and his use of them as examples in his stories surprised not only his opponents, but often times Jesus' disciples as well. Several times he seems pointedly to have used a form of inclusive language; for instance, when he says, "Whoever does the will of God is my brother and sister and mother" (Mark 3:35; Matthew 12:50). One scholar writes that by taking it "for granted that women, equally with men, can do the will of God and be his true kindred" Jesus is presenting a "radical redefinition of the relationship between women and men and God."

And then, to Peter's rather plaintive words, "Lo, we have left everything and followed you," Jesus responds: "Truly I tell you, there is no one who has left house or brothers or sisters or mother or father or children or fields, for my sake and for the sake of the good news, who will not receive a hundredfold now in this age—houses, brothers and sisters, mothers and children, and fields..." (Mark 10:29-30; Matthew 19:29; Luke 18:29). That may seem like a great deal of family, and it is remarkably inclusive. It is particularly interesting that leaving sisters, who would at that time usually have been seen as a burden and a responsibility, here is considered a sacrifice.

Given Jesus' attitude and concerns, it is not surprising that Paul, despite the pressures he clearly felt in a male dominated society, envisioned the new community of Christians with these words: "There is no longer Jew or Greek, there is no longer slave or free, there is no longer male and female; for all of you are one in Christ Jesus" (Galatians 3:28). Obviously Paul does not mean that there are not differences, but in the community of the followers of Jesus, ethnicity, economic privilege and gender are not meant to bring either privilege or inferiority. A startling new equality is to guide all relationships.

Christianity has not always followed this new understanding by any means, but it has been an exciting leaven—an opportunity which contemporary disciples can now seize upon.

We can listen again to some of the words of our prayers. Many of us, when we hear a phrase like "to give thanks for all men," will feel, at the least, quite uncomfortable. The phrase does not seem to catch the wonderfully inclusive spirit of Jesus who, throughout his ministry, was eager to extend the invitation to God's reign to a rich tax collector like Zacchaeus and to a woman like Mary Magdalene, and to all kinds of people, rich and poor, lame and lepers, women and men.

Similarly, although one recognizes the historical context of certain biblical phrases, it seems truer to their original intent, especially when they are used in liturgical settings for the whole community at worship, to translate them as inclusively as possible.

Thus the peacemakers who are blessed in Jesus' Beatitudes are not meant to be just the sons of God but all God's sons and daughters.

And then the familiar words: "Peace on earth among men with whom God is pleased." I don't imagine that any of us would think that the angel who announced this message was trying to exclude women from God's favor. Wouldn't it be better, then, to translate the real intent of the words into contemporary English: "Peace on earth among those with whom God is pleased"?

Such translations and usage are among the most basic features of what we call inclusive language. Most of us see great opportunities for being clear about the nature of Christian community and following our Lord's will for the Church today in easily adapting to such usage.

I know for myself that language which is not inclusive sounds exclusive to me, and I believe it is oppressive to women. With a little practice, inclusive language comes to sound both right and normal, while the use of the words men or man or mankind, where we mean women and men, begins to sound strange.

Then there is still another vital area of liturgical and theological language where the concerns go even deeper and raise more profound questions and opportunities.

The cultures of the biblical period were what we call patriarchal in character: that is to say, they took it for granted that only men would play leading public roles in work, in social and political life, and in religion. Naturally, their understanding of God was strongly influenced by this cultural context. Deities in the ancient world were often thought of in human-like terms and described as male or female, the chief god usually being male. The one God of the people of Israel was, understandably, most frequently described, though with some important exceptions, as though masculine.

It is of primary theological importance to recognize that, while it is necessary to use human ideas and language to speak of God, these words must be regarded as very limited when applied to God.

On the one hand, it may seem that the Bible recognizes and affirms the human need to imagine God *anthropomorphically*; that is, in human-like terms. Indeed, for Christians astoundingly and wonderfully God is most decisively and uniquely revealed in human life. We look to Jesus for our chief understanding of the divine character.

Yet a central purpose of the incarnation is to help us realize something of the character and purpose of God who transcends all human life. In Jesus, disciples by faith glimpse divinity, but the human Jesus is always pointing beyond self to God. The Bible is also full of warnings against assuming that anthropomorphisms, our human ways of talking, are anything like sufficient. "God is not man (that is, God is not human) that God should lie..." (Numbers 23:19; see also 1 Samuel 15:29). "The Lord sees not as a human sees," Samuel is told (1 Samuel 15:29). "God is greater than human life," Elihu reminds Job (Job 33:12) "...for I am God and not human, the Holy One in your midst," God proclaims to Hosea (Hosea 11:9).

I often think in this regard of the title of the popular book by J. B. Phillips, *Your God Is Too Small*. It would be such a mistake for theology and for faithful living to understand God as reduced to the human categories which can only hint at the source of the life and being of this vast and incredible universe.

There are some theologians who maintain, however, that the predominantly masculine oriented ways of speaking of God in the Bible are of theological importance. While God is not, of course, masculine in human terms, God may be realized to have certain masculine rather than feminine attributes. The masculine is, in the creativity of sexuality, generally the initiator, the active one. The feminine has been characterized as more passive and receptive. Historically, men have been seen as rulers and makers; women have been more the nurturers, protectors and preservers.

Yet many people today would find such descriptions to be misleading stereotypes. Women can and often do initiate at least as much as men. They can be just as aggressive and fierce in protective and other roles. As a man, husband and father, I do not hold to the idea that nurturing is only a feminine role or characteristic. In several places in the Jewish scriptures and in a number of Jesus' stories and phrases, some theologians say they hear the feminine, nurturing and protective side of God. I prefer to say that they are hearing of the depths of God's love.

This is not to maintain that there are not differences between the human genders, but the categorizing of divine attributes as predominantly related to one human gender is problematic at best. Many contemporary theologians and students of the Bible do not regard the use of masculine pronouns and titles (king, etc.) to be essential to worship and to approaching an understanding of God. Neither God nor our understanding of God is bound to particular cultures. Clearly, in the New Testament we see Christianity reaching beyond cultural limitations.

But did not Jesus himself frequently use the word Father in speaking of God? Did he not use the Aramaic word "Abba," which some have seen as reflecting an intimacy that might better be translated as "Dad" or "Papa"?

Jesus most significantly did, and I am among those who think it would be a great mistake to diminish the importance of the word in our vocabulary for God. It is right to point out that the analogy does not work well for everyone. Some people have had painful experiences of human fathers. For some the word primarily suggests a domineering or punishing presence. Jesus' use of the word, however, suggests both a strength and an intimacy of care and affection, a loving, personal relationship that can be lost in other expressions.

At the same time, it is critical to remember that "Father" used of God is an analogous way of speaking. Father is an analogy for what God is like; it is very near to metaphorical language.

We can see Jesus using a lot of figurative language to try to tell of God's ways of being present in the world. It is a kingdom—the kingdom of God.

But, of course, it is at the same time not like a human kingdom. So, it is also like a time of sowing and of reaping. It is like a dinner party or a marriage feast. It is a time of judgment. It is as when a tiny mustard seed is planted and grows suddenly—when a woman puts leaven into a meal, a father with two sons, a master who pays all-day and one-hour workers the same wage, a woman who finds a lost coin. Many analogies, parables and metaphorical ways of speaking are needed to help in the understanding of how God's ways of justice and mercy are in the world.

Father has a very special place in the Bible and in Christian prayer and worship, but it, too, is a figurative way of speaking. The word can greatly help in our approach to God, but, if one imagined it too literally, it would limit understanding of God and begin to get in the way rather than pointing to God. Other forms of language and imagery are needed.

Sometimes, very interestingly, the Bible uses impersonal images. Impersonal images can warn against too much anthropomorphizing. In the Psalms, God is addressed as "Rock" or "Our Shield." Rock can help us understand something of God's steadfast, unchanging character, though we would never make the mistake of thinking that God *is* a rock. Similarly we should never make the mistake of imagining God *is* a father, even while this word has a very special role for us in revelation and in worship.

Other language is needed both to help us avoid being too literal in the use of "Father" and to help us understand that God is always more than any of our words or ideas about God. Here our belief in the Trinity of God may particularly come to our help. God is also Spirit—the *ruach,* the wind, breath and spirit of the Jewish Scriptures. God's Wisdom in Jewish revelation has been interpreted as an earlier revelation of the second person of God. Both *ruach* and Wisdom are often said to have more "feminine" attributes in the Bible.

It is a fascinating aspect of Christian history that a number of the mystics and other men and women of deep prayer were often the most daring and inclusive in their approaches to God. Sometimes the intimacy of their language can almost take our breath away. The divine Christ can be described as like a mother offering breasts to suckle. Their language seems to be breaking through normal phraseology in order to point to the God who is beyond all our words, yet mysteriously at the heart of life.

Some of the newer inclusive language liturgies are meant to offer us similar opportunities. Perhaps a part of us fears that the traditional and familiar is being taken away. But the point is not to take away, but to add to our ways of thinking of and worshipping God. We may need to see that some of what is familiar can have become limiting, and then we are able to hear in new ways that can help us reach outside of ourselves in prayer and thanksgiving—making use of the new and new use of the old.

We are still learning how best to use these opportunities, and no human liturgical language is perfect. But I believe we are living in a time full of opportunities for more revelation—for our ideas of God's presence among us to deepen and grow.

"Love Bade Me Welcome"

George Herbert was born in 1593 into an established Welsh family, known for its service to the crown and its readiness to take up arms for country and for honor. Herbert's father died, however, when the boy was quite young and he was brought up by a remarkable and cultured mother. This upbringing together with his unsteady health turned him at an early age toward a different manner of life. Through his years as a student at Westminster School and Trinity College Cambridge, with their training in Latin rhetoric and rigorous Anglican piety, Herbert was drawn toward a career as a clergyman with various scholarly interests. He felt a strong desire to dedicate his life wholly to God.

There remained with him, however, a measure of worldliness, perhaps particularly evident in his love of fine clothes. When, after several years of teaching at Trinity and the private study of theology, Herbert became public orator of the university at the age of twenty-seven, he found a new way to use his skill with words by writing letters of supplication and congratulation on behalf of the university. During this time Herbert also developed his musical abilities and his talent for composing elegant Greek and Latin poetry in the rather stylized fashion of the period. These talents, his position at Cambridge and his family background all began to draw him closer to the political life of the times and to service in the Court of King James. In 1624 he was elected to Parliament, and, had King James lived, might well have continued to rise in government service.

Herbert wanted to see his political activity as a way of serving God. In later years people would express surprise that George Herbert and men like the saintly Bishop of Winchester, Lancelot Andrewes, could so loyally serve the rather pompous King James with his exalted ideas about his limited abilities. But in an age when rulers could be all too free with the lives of their countrymen in pursuit of wars—at a time when much of England wanted to crusade against Catholic Spain, James stood tenaciously for peace, and Herbert and Andrewes felt called by God to support him in that dedication. Several of Herbert's poems take up the theme that all things can be consecrated and made known as God's if people will offer them to God.

Teach me, my God and King,
In all things thee to see;
And what I do in anything
To do it as for thee.

All may of thee partake;
Nothing can be so mean,
Which with this tincture "For thy sake,"
Will not grow bright and clean.

"Nothing," he wrote, "is little in God's service."

Nevertheless it also becomes clear from Herbert's poetry that he often experienced uncertainty and anguished doubt as to whether he was truly serving God. Underneath his piety much of his life seemed to him useless and drifting. He thought he knew where he wanted to go, but how to get there?

To have my aim, and yet to be
Further from it than when I bent my bow...

And slowly, now that there was a new king and Herbert had lost his patrons in court, and as his own search for God and God's service deepened, Herbert felt himself coming back to his earlier calling. Strongly influenced by the sanctity and dedication of Nicholas Ferrar, Herbert moved over the next several years to ordination and acceptance of the vocation to be a country parson in the Wiltshire parishes of Fugglestone and Bemerton. He married happily and devoted himself to be the most serviceable of country clergy—a position that was, however, held in little repute by most of his former friends and acquaintances. As a guide for his own life he wrote the manual, *A Priest to the Temple or a Country Parson*, which served as well as a practical and devotional guide and inspiration for many later generations of clergy. He also rewrote a number of his earlier religious poems and composed new ones which he fitted into a loose structure relating to the various parts and furnishings of a church building and also of the seasons of worship and inner life of the Christian.

Though many of his friends thought he had lost his way, Herbert wanted to believe that he had begun to find it. His poetry reveals that faith, but also his ongoing uncertainties. How could he see himself as worthy to serve God as a priest? He continued to rebel against the confinement of his natural instincts and freedom which his priestly life seemed to require of him.

I struck the board, and cry'd, "No more!"
....
Recover all thy sigh-blown age
On double pleasures: leave thy cold dispute
Of what is fit, and not. Forsake thy cage,
Thy rope of sands,
Which pettie thoughts have made, and made to thee
Good cable, to enforce and draw
And be thy law,...

And where was this difficult and demanding God anyway—so often absent from his prayers?

As good go any where, they say,
As to benumme
Both knees and heart, in crying night and day,
Come, come, my God, O come,
But no hearing.

So much of life seemed without purpose or plan—disordered and enigmatic. Music and poetry were ways of arranging and composing life's disorder—of giving it a shape and then probing it for significance. At Bemerton Herbert taught and prayed for his people, set some of his poetry to music and continued to write and rewrite his poems. Into the poetry he now poured all he was and had been——rhetorician, musician, courtier, statesman, scholar, lover, pastor. Poems which may once have been but poetic observation and skillful rhyming now became at once more clearly passionate and mysterious. He learned how to report a mood until it no longer was a report but a work of art and prayer.

Herbert had less than four years to serve in Bemerton. Before he was yet forty—in the winter of 1633—he knew himself dying. He had not published any of his English poems during his lifetime. In an age of reticence he probably considered them too personal—perhaps their language too colloquial to be valued by others. As he lay dying he sent them—structured into a book called *The Temple*—to his friend Nicholas Ferrar with the instruction to publish them if Ferrar thought they might be of any help to others in similar struggles, but otherwise to have them burnt. He described his poems as "a picture of the many spiritual conflicts that have passed between God and my soul, before I could subject mine to the will of Jesus, my master, in whose service I have now found perfect freedom." The last of the poems in the major section of the manuscript was "Love Bade Me Welcome..."

Love bade me welcome: yet my soul drew back
Guiltie of dust and sinne.
But quick-ey'd Love, observing me grow slack
From my first entrance in,
Drew nearer to me, sweetly questioning,
If I lack'd any thing.

A guest, I answer'd, worthy to be here.
Love said, You shall be he.
I the unkinde, ungratefull? Ah, my deare,
I cannot look on thee.
Love took my hand, and smiling, did reply,
Who made the eyes but I?

Truth, Lord, but I have marr'd them: let my shame
Go where it doth deserve.
And know you not, sayes Love, who bore the blame?
My deare, then I will serve.
You must sit downe, sayes Love, and taste my meat.
So I did sit and eat.

In a country now moving toward civil war Herbert's poetry spoke to people of different camps—Puritan and high church, Cavaliers and Roundheads. This was in part due to their remarkable conversational quality—the manner in which Herbert had caught cadences of everyday speech yet held in extraordinary metrical control. The poetry also made use of concrete imagery drawn from daily life and coupled this with an intensity of passion that often makes one think of the Psalms. Many of Herbert's motifs and images were taken from the Bible, the church year and liturgy, and the architecture of the church building—all so familiar to his country-men. But what may well have held the most appeal was the central theme of *The Temple*: the love of God.

More than we perhaps realize today the people of England during this period had been pervasively influenced by a Calvinist doctrine of God. This would have been especially true of anyone who went to Cambridge. God's grace and election were seen as coming from a stern and rather distant patriarch. This view of God Herbert seems to have accepted intellectually but not in the deepest levels of his spiritual need and prayers. Here Herbert was met by a far more intimate lover of souls. Yet to this meeting the pastor-poet also brought a deep sense of his own unworthiness and the magnitude and corrupting power of human sinfulness.

The occasion of much of Herbert's poetry is the contrast between the human perception of self as unworthy and unlovable and the gentle yet persistent love of God seeking to make human beings lovable by loving them. The individual soul, flawed by sin and unable to direct the unruly and confused will toward God, is lured and courted and finally overcome by God's infinite love. A number of the poems are a dialectic of this spiritual duet, moving through a sometimes heated struggling with God to a calmer resolution of acceptance of submission. Thus the poem "The Collar," which begins with the poet-priest railing against the discipline and sacrifices of his profession, builds to intensity and then concludes in this way:

> But as I rav'd and grew more fierce and wilde
> At every word
> Me thoughts I heard one calling, *Child!*
> And reply'd, *My Lord.*

The poem "Deniall" begins with the musician-poet feeling out of tune with his craft, his life and God.

> When my devotions could not pierce
> Thy silent eares;
> Then was my heart broken, as was my verse:
> My breast was full of fears
> And disorder:

The poem ends with Herbert—his soul still "untun'd, unstrung"— pleading with God, but the final *m* sounds and the added rhyme of the last line bring him to a note of composure and hope, even reaching toward tunefulness

> O cheer and tune my heartlesse breast,
> Deferre no time;
> That so thy favours granting my request,
> They and my minde may chime,
> And mend my ryme.

The sometimes deceptively simple but at other times intricate inventiveness of Herbert's metrical patterns and rhyme schemes are the music to which he sets his themes and metaphors—often layered on one another, being sung, as it were, at different levels of meaning. He frequently employs a kind of verbal shorthand of interthreaded motifs and stories not fully told by which he alludes to possible meanings while allowing the hearer's imagination to guess and explore more fully. Between the lines one hears of life's mystery and the possibility of God offering value and purpose. Metaphors and words with double and even triple references help weave all together into a madrigal both engaging and profound.

"Love Bade Me Welcome..." has been called one of the finest poems in the English language. It is also one of the most attractive pictures from Herbert's spiritual biography, and a number of Christians have carried it in their hearts as a reminder of the character of God's grace. It can be especially helpful in preparation for holy communion.

One strand of the poem begins as a kind of parable verging on allegory. We are not told how the dust-covered traveler arrived or entered into this feast, but now he feels unworthy while the host gradually but persistently presses him to join in the meal. The reluctant guest finally consents on the condition that he serve at table rather than sitting and being served. His host, however, gently turns aside this condition and, vanquished by courtesy, the guest sits and eats.

Mingled with the outline of this story is its spiritual interpretation of the soul come to its Lord. The place might be heaven and the messianic banquet, but it is also the eucharist clearly and even coarsely referred to as "my meat." This is the Lord who gives himself to be the food of salvation.

The soul, covered with sin's dust, draws back from Love's invitation. But the host-Lord comes nearer and asks what is lacking. The guilty guest fends the Lord off with his unworthiness. Who can be worthy to share in the Lord's feast? "You shall be he," says Love, astounding the soul much as Jesus must have surprised Zacchaeus in the gospel story. Throughout the poem one hears allusions not only to Zacchaeus' story, but to parables like that of the Great Banquet, to the Last Supper, and Jesus' description of himself as the one who came not to be served but to serve.

The words of endearment, otherwise seemingly incongruous in the poem—*Love, sweetly, my deare*, the taking of the hand and smiling, now suggest a further dimension: It is the lover inviting the beloved, a poem of mystic love which is almost a ritual—a dance of the wedding banquet. The questions, refusals and answers, gestures, touching and moments of silence all heighten the tension and lead us on.

It is, too, a form of gentle debate—not without humor and gentle irony. Once more human evasion tries to use guilt as a kind of defense against the gift it can never earn. Hanging its head, the soul refuses even to look upon its Lord. Yet, "Who made the eyes but I?" and we are reminded that this Lord is all life's creator.

The soul tries again. It is true that the Lord has created, but the soul has misused and marred even the gift of sight. Love responds, "Know you not ...who bore the blame?" The creator is also the redeemer. The one who made the eyes redeems—gives new value to their purpose.

The soul makes one last try. If, overcome by Love's courtesy, it cannot leave the banquet, then the soul will be the servant, waiting at the table— still trying to earn what it has so much difficulty accepting. Yet Love firmly persists and the poem, full of intricate emotion, now comes to its resolution in monosyllables—more passionate for their simplicity. It is as though to say that human words can say no more, and the poem—and in a sense Herbert's poetry and life—concludes by pointing to the one of whom our words can but hint.

Giving in Thanksgiving

In days of old, it is reported, when a king converted to Christianity and ordered his knights to be baptized, many of them held their right arms out of the water. As they were submerged in the baptismal water they kept their weapons arms dry so that they could continue to use them in the ways of killing and war.

I sometimes have a picture of modern-day Christians undergoing our baptisms while trying to hold our wallets and checkbooks out of those converting waters. "I'll give you my all, Lord, but..."

I have another, sometimes scary, vision that when I get to that checkpoint between heaven and the place downstairs, St. Peter is going to ask to see my checkbook. "No, St. Peter," I'll say, "Wouldn't you like to see my letters of reference and my résumé? I have a list here of good things I have done."

"The checkbook will do just fine," Peter will say. "More than anything else it will tell me about how you spent much of your time and energy and the things you were most concerned with in life. You remember our Lord's words: 'Where your treasure is, there will your heart be also.'"

It isn't as though you and I haven't been told about the basics expected of us. Plain and simple, we are to tithe—we are to give at least 10 percent of all that we earn and receive in life for the purposes of God—the mission of the Church and the care of those in need. That doesn't necessarily take care of all the giving and sharing we are to do in our lives. We are, of course, to give of our time and talent, too; but the tithe is a basic building block of our Christian discipleship.

People say to me, "But right now we have a big mortgage (or maybe a rent hike). We have to take care of our children's education." I am very sympathetic. I've had or have those bills, too. But tithing isn't supposed to wait until we have some extra money. In fact, the most important thing about tithing is how it is meant to set our priorities straight. It's only when we tithe that we can begin to control the materialism that otherwise tends to dominate our lives.

The only exception I can think of to tithing is for those without enough to eat or to house or clothe themselves. These are, of course, people the rest of us should be trying to help.

There are questions we can discuss. Should I tithe on what I earn and receive before or after taxes? That is an individual decision. How much of my tithe should I give through the Church and how much to other charitable causes? That, too, is an individual decision, but I would say that something is pretty odd in a disciple's life if at least half of that person's giving isn't going to the work of the Church.

I've had relatively well-do-do people say to me, "Oh, if I gave a tithe to the Church it would unbalance their budget." Or, "The Church wouldn't know what to do with big sums of money. I give to my college or opera or museum."

On the contrary, I say to them, if your congregation doesn't know what to do with more than it is spending, perhaps it has a small vision of mission, mainly just taking care of its own. There is so much the Church is doing, often on short budgets, and so much more its Lord is calling it to do for others, not only at the parish level but beyond. Let me tell you about all the opportunities your diocese has in youth work, in Christian education, in helping the homeless, the hungry, the prisoners, those suffering with AIDS and other diseases including alcoholism, the elderly, those who need tutoring. Do you know about the institutions that work with seafarers, take in abused children, assist the elderly, provide chaplaincies for hospitals and colleges?

I can promise you something. Tithing will make a profound change in your life. I have seen it happen time and again. So much else begins to fall into place.

Maybe you feel you just can't make 10 percent yet. Okay, but if you are serious, sit down and figure out what it will be. Eight percent? Five? Two?

You know what the toughest thing is? The toughest thing is to get people to be honest enough about what they are giving to actually sit down and figure out what 10 percent or five percent or three percent of their annual earnings and other income is. They'll talk about giving X number of dollars, but hard-headed business people, who know all sorts of things about dollars and cents, deliberately won't figure out what a tithe would be. They are going to keep that wallet and checkbook out of the baptismal water!

But tithing—or even just beginning to get serious about giving—can dramatically change lives. That's the wonderful part of it. Finally we are giving not because we feel guilty about money or because we feel we should or because the bishop told us to, but out of thanksgiving. We give because we realize we have been given so much. In our gratitude we want to help others. It is that giving in thanksgiving that changes us.

Comprehension

D o you think the Episcopal church compromises too much?" a bishop
once was asked. He thought for a few moments and then responded,
"Well, yes and no."

From the earliest years of its separation from the Roman Catholic
Church in the 16th century the Church of England has been seen as the
product of compromise—an effort by Elizabeth and her secular and church
advisors to keep Catholic and Protestant Christians united in one church
and with loyalty to one monarch.

From the beginning, however, there was also much more involved.
Despite often sharp disagreements among differing groups, many Christians
appreciated the insights that divergent perspectives and expressions could
bring to the church when people remained in communion with one another.
Instead of leaving to form their own denomination with a more homogeneous view of Christian truth, disciples could continue to influence one
another and provoke one another to take into account understandings and
experiences different from their own. People from different classes and
educational and economic backgrounds—people with different personalities and spiritualities—kept on talking and praying together and sometimes
learning from each other's experiences of God calling.

Richard Hooker was the great theologian of what came to be known as
the Elizabethan Settlement. A catholic Christian with deep sympathies with
the reforming movements, especially on the continent, his wisdom and spirit
are summed up in words from the prayer for the day of thanksgiving for his
life and witness:

> O God of truth and peace, you raised up your servant Richard
> Hooker in a day of bitter controversy to defend with sound
> reasoning and great charity the catholic and reformed religion:
> Grant that we may maintain that middle way, not as a compro-
> mise for the sake of peace, but as a comprehension for the sake
> of truth.

In fact, there is also much to be said for a just peace that will enable people of differing views to work and share together, but that peace will best come about when people recognize that God's truth is hard for any one group to hold in its fullness. There is often much to learn from others.

St. Augustine once said that orthodoxy—Christian truth—rather than being seen as a straight line should be viewed as a fence around the truth. In other words, truth may be seen as a large space. Yes there are limits, but there is also considerable room for exploration and different experience.

As representatives of the Episcopal Church return from General Convention, having fashioned various compromise resolutions, it is understandable that some would regard these statements as mere attempts to keep the peace. Those who wished for more in one direction or another may feel that God's will has not been fully upheld or set out with enough prophetic vigor.

Yet there may again be wisdom in trying to make room for differing understandings. In an article concerning the debate about sexual issues at the convention, Peter Steinfels of the *New York Times (July 20, 1991)* found reason to appreciate "true dialogue...(with its) willingness to search out common ground, to engage someone else's viewpoint and to reexamine one's own."

Speaking specifically of the presentations made by Bishop William Frey and myself, Steinfels wrote, "Some people might find the mixtures of convictions held by Bishop Frey and Bishop Borsch surprising or incongruous. But it is probably only by such surprises and incongruities that many religious bodies can escape the stalemate they have reached in debating their teachings on homosexuality and human sexuality generally."

On other matters, too—on international political issues, on questions involving both individual and community rights, with regard to more inclusive language in speaking of God, on the need for free enterprise but also governmental action and control—efforts were made at the convention to take more than one perspective into account.

I understand that some people may not always like this way of going about things. People have said to me that the Episcopal Church's struggles to find the middle way forward often seem messy to them. They would like clearer answers for many of life's issues and problems, and perhaps more often to be told what to think than to be told to think. I imagine in the back of their heads there is that fearful quote from the Book of Revelation, "So because you are lukewarm, and neither cold nor hot, I will spew you out of my mouth."

But Hooker's way of seeking to comprehend the truth may in fact be the most demanding way when it is practiced with integrity, compassion and commitment. It is a major reason why many of us are Episcopalians and Anglicans. In the midst of the messiness, the incongruities and surprises and the ongoing dialogue and exploration, there can be some of the greatest opportunities for the Holy Spirit to enter into our lives and for us to draw nearer to the God who creates and redeems a world so vast and intricate and so full of mystery and grace.

Other Faiths and Ours

Chaim Potok tells the story of a young rabbi visiting a Buddhist shrine in Japan with a friend. Seeing an old man with a prayer book in hand slowly swaying back and forth, the rabbi asked his companion, "Do you think God is listening to him?"

"I don't know," his friend responded. "I never thought of it."

"Neither did I until now," mused the rabbi. "If he's not listening, why not? If he is listening, then, well what are we all about?"

A generation or two ago most people lived in cultures where their religion was pretty much the only religion. They might also say, "I never thought of it."

Today, however, other religions are on television and studied in college. Increasingly for many people throughout the world, and certainly here in Los Angeles, one daily meets people of other faiths. They are at school, at work; they are our neighbors. In times of earthquake or civil upheaval we find ourselves responding alongside Muslims and Jews, Buddhists and Hindus, with people of other faiths, cultures and philosophies and of mixed marriages.

Such experiences bring with them the challenge of relativism, such as the young rabbi felt, and the challenge and opportunity for dialogue and learning. Hans Küng is among the theologians and other commentators who emphasize the importance of this learning for the future of the world community. Along with all the good religion brings into many peoples' lives, religion also can be a source of misunderstanding, distrust and even hatred. It can be a cause of strife and war within religions and between religions. Religion is very easily mixed with the goals of cultural and political supremacy, and this, together with the challenge of relativism, has also brought a response of religious fundamentalism and even fanaticism in a number of countries.

On the other hand, better religious understanding and cooperation may be the most important factor in helping to make for peace among nations and cultures. Religious communities, with their traditional sense of the common good, could also, acting together, provide the necessary spiritual response to the world's environmental crisis.

Genuine dialogue calls for listening and learning as well as talking. It means allowing others to explain their beliefs and practices on their own terms. When I was a university chaplain, I was privileged to gather together an interfaith council of students. In addition to the fascinating and enjoyable experience of cooking for one another, we talked about our scriptures and worship, holy days, and our differing understandings of the sacredness of certain times and places. We reflected on various views about authority, God, gender and sex. We experienced the difficulties and pleasure of praying together. When one of our members died in an accident, we spoke of suffering, death and theodicy (how we might reconcile God's goodness with all the evil and suffering in the world).

Ross Reat and Edmund Perry have noted the paradox that, while particular religions often claim to offer a supreme understanding of God or reality, they also in their scriptures and at the heart of their theology emphasize the elusiveness of God and the inability of human words or comprehension to know God or God's ways in any sense fully. There is an attractive modesty at the heart of many faiths which can be coupled with other commonalities such as the awareness that all the major religions espouse versions of the Golden Rule in its positive and negative forms. They share in common a trust that, in the face of tragedy, suffering and death, God and/or the ultimate reality is good.

Thus, while many important differences in religion remain (perhaps chief among them whether there is a God to be understood as "personal" or "impersonal" or in ways which transcend these categories), a number of people have adopted some version of a pluralistic view toward religion. There are, on this understanding, many lamps but one light. Many roads go up the mountain, but they all lead to the same height. Building upon Aquinas' teaching that "Things known are in the knower according to the mode of the knower," one may say that the same divine reality is being viewed through different lenses.

Such pluralism offers particular challenges to traditionally evangelistic religions which hold out salvation for all people. How are Christians, we especially ask, to understand Jesus' role as the Savior of all the world? How are we to interpret "I am in the Father and the Father is in me" (John 14:11); "I am the way, and the truth, and the life; no one comes to the Father except through me" (John 14:6); "in him the fullness of God was pleased to dwell" (Colossians 1:19); and "there is salvation in no one else, for there is no other name under heaven given among mortals by which we must be saved" (Acts 4:12)?

The response among a number of theologians recommending a full pluralism is to find ways to "lower" Christology (that is, understanding of Jesus). They acknowledge that sayings like those from John's Gospel above are unlikely to have come from the historical Jesus. They are statements of faith by later Christians, while, in fact, the churches from earliest days had a number of ways of viewing and exalting Jesus. He can be seen, for instance, as a great teacher, exemplar and prophet with whom God had a very special relationship. This would not preclude God having equally important special relationships with people of other faiths in other ways. Thus Christians in dialogue with people of other faiths need not have an overt or covert agenda of converting others to their faith in Jesus as God's *only* special self-revelation.

While recognizing the value of dialogue and cooperation with those of other faiths, there are, however, many Christians who have difficulty squaring such a view of Jesus with their tradition and experience. Thus, another form of response has been to seek a way to understand Jesus as an incarnation of God while recognizing that there will be many people who, because of time, geography, culture or other reasons, cannot know and value this incarnation. They can, however, in their own ways, be people of faith and goodness who, in this sense, follow in the way of Christ. In Karl Rahner's phrase they are "hidden Christians," a perspective which was interestingly set forth by Justin Martyr more than eighteen hundred years ago:

> It is our belief that those who strive to do the good which is enjoined on us have a share in God; according to the traditional belief they will by God's grace share his dwelling. And it is our conviction that this holds good in principle for all people. Christ is the divine Word in whom the whole human race share, and those who live according to the light of their knowledge are Christians, even if they are considered as being godless. (I Apology 46:1-4)

There are, however, obvious difficulties with this stance when it comes to full and open dialogue with those of other faiths. It more than implies a superiority of religious understanding and leaves a strong sense of "if you knew what I knew" along with a covert desire to convert others.

The value of Justin's approach, on the other hand, is that it makes place for a much higher Christology. Just as many of us would not want those of other faiths to lower their own commitment and depth of faith in order to have dialogue with us, so we cannot change our faith for the purposes of dialogue. Our understanding of God's grace, of God's way of dealing with sin, and our call to right and just living are not based in a low Christology, or a mythological understanding of resurrection, much less of crucifixion and God's presence in that.

This last point is of great importance and is not given sufficient place in a number of recent theologies of interfaith dialogue. If life is "cruciform"; that is, if suffering is necessary for there to be life (with the higher the form the greater the sense of this suffering), then God's intimate presence in that suffering can be seen as an essential rather than an option of Christian theology.

The suffering of God in Christ, and then the ultimate victory of God's love can, however, be believed in and shared with others in Christian humility which still allows a genuine pluralism. God's presence and disclosure of Godself in Jesus, while essential for Christianity and paradigmatic of God's character and purpose for all people, does not exhaust all that God is or can be for and with others. God's presence in Jesus is a presence in a human life. However decisive Christians believe the fullness of that presence to be, there is obviously more to God and even the "second person" of God than this one life reveals. In other ways the compassionate God can be present to others from whom we can learn and with whom we can share.

For Further Reading

Borsch, Frederick H. *God's Parable.* (Philadelphia: Westminster Press, 1975). *Jesus: The Human Life of God* (Cincinnati: Forward Movement Press, 1987). Cobb, John C., Jr. *Christ in a Pluralistic Age.* (Philadelphia: Westminster Press, 1975). Eck, Diana L. *Encountering Fod: A Spiritual Journey from Bozeman to Banaras.* (Boston: Beacon Press, 1993). *An Interpretation of Religion: Human Responses to the Transcendent.* (New Haven: Yale University Press, 1989). Küng, Hans, Joseph van Ess, Heinrich van Stietencorn, and Heinz Bechert. *Theology for the Third Millennium: An Ecumenical View.* (New York: Doubleday, 1988). Reat, N. Ross, and Perry, Edmund F. *A World Theology: The Central Spiritual Reality of Humankind.* (Cambridge: Cambridge University Press, 1991). Smart, Ninian, and Konstantine, Steven. *Christian Systematic Theology in a World Context.* (Minneapolis: Fortress Press, 1991).

The Blind See: Our Common Vision

A kind of riddling goes on through many New Testament passages. How do the first become last and the last first? How does one lose one's life and find it? How can a person have ears and not hear, or eyes and not see? How are the deaf able to hear and the blind see? Often these challenges come in story form. Such is the character of the story which the evangelist Mark presents when he tells of Bartimaeus, the blind beggar (Mark 10:46-52). The story takes place at the pivot point of the Gospel and has been artfully anticipated. It has been described as a coda about the meaning of discipleship, following as it does a long section in the middle of the Gospel which also begins with the healing of a blind man (Mark 8:22-26). Between these two healings we hear of the struggles of the disciples to perceive the meaning of their faith and relationship with Jesus.

Previous to this section, we have been introduced to religious leaders whom one would normally regard as having very good sight. Their eyes were trained in the reading and interpretation of the Scriptures. Their prayer and religious devotion would have put most of us to shame. Many of them would have felt that they had gained special insight into God's purposes. Yet, they could not see Jesus as much other than a threat to their understanding of how God related to the world.

For a time, Jesus' disciples begin to perceive how God is acting in the ministry and person of Jesus. Peter glimpses this for a moment and confesses Jesus to be the Christ, the Expected One from God, but then he cannot understand how God would be acting in Jesus as the Son of Man who will suffer and be killed. Together with James and John on the Mount of the Transfiguration, Peter catches sight of Jesus as the one through whose humanity God is disclosing the divine character. Again, however, the mystery becomes opaque, and before long the disciples grow fearful and resort to arguing among themselves as to which of them is the greatest.

Still later on in the narrative, James and John ask Jesus whether one of them can sit on his left hand in glory. By seeking to interpret their association with Jesus as a matter of privilege and special merit on their part, they, too, have become blind. They also have eyes, but they do not see at all well.

It is at this point that the evangelist brings Jesus and his little band of uncertain followers to the town of Jericho. Immediately ahead awaits an obscure but already ominous encounter in Jerusalem. An excited crowd wants to catch sight of Jesus, to look him over and perhaps hear him. The disciples are tired, fearful, wishing they had never left Galilee. It is a blind beggar who, out of his need and hope, calls out. He uses a title for Jesus which may not have been regarded as the most propitious and was likely even dangerous considering the circumstances, but one which was perhaps the best he could imagine: "Jesus, Son of David, have mercy on me!"

The crowd tries to silence him. Jesus must have more important concerns. Yet, Bartimaeus' desperate hope is shouted even more loudly: "Son of David, have mercy on me!" Jesus stops in the midst of his own profound journey and says: "Call him." Those nearest Bartimaeus turn to him, saying: "Take heart; rise, he is calling you." The blind man gropes his way from arm to arm in the direction of Jesus' voice. And then: "What do you want me to do for you?" "Master, let me see again." "Your faith has made you well," Jesus responds. Immediately, we are told, Bartimaeus received his sight and followed Jesus "on the way."

Clearly, the evangelist means this to be a master story about how one comes to true discipleship. In contrast to the religious officials and the ambitious disciples, Bartimaeus brings to Jesus, in John Calvin's phrase, "nothing but the begging." Persistently beseeching Jesus out of his great need and hope, Bartimaeus has pure faith in the Lord's healing as a gift of love, a sign that the Messiah has come and that the new age has begun. The gift brings Bartimaeus the vision he needs to follow Jesus "on the way" to Jerusalem, to Calvary, and to the new life of resurrection.

It is a story told over and over again throughout the history of Christian discipleship. It is also St. Paul's story, the story of a man who thought he perceived and owned God's will, until the day he was made blind and then was given the vision of who Jesus was for him and for the world. Well might he then have joined with Bartimaeus in singing: "Amazing grace, how sweet the sound that saved a wretch like me. I once was lost, but now am found, was blind, but now I see."

In times of ecumenical meeting and discussion, when Christians are acting together in response to our Lord's prayer "that they may be one" (John 17:21), it can be especially important to remember again this master story of coming to faith and discipleship. It is when we become most possessive of our vision—our way of seeing, our interpretation of Scripture, our sacraments and liturgical rites, our formulations of faith, our traditions and customs, our ethical practices, our forms of church government, our ways of worshipping and serving—that we are most in danger of blinding ourselves as individuals and as communities. When we once again recognize that our faith is before all else an act of God's grace and that our eyes are not meant to be focused on our liturgies, or our creeds, or our polities, but rather on Jesus who heals and gives us sight, then it is that we may begin to have a greater common vision.

Our Heart's Desire

What do you want? What do you want most in life? What is your heart most yearning for?

Perhaps in this season of buying and exchanging presents we might fasten on some particular gift—clothing, something for the house or perhaps the money to purchase these things. Or we may look to our careers, or, particularly at this time of year, to family and friends.

Other words and phrases may come to mind: life, liberty and the pursuit of happiness. Life: health, soundness, strength and attractiveness of body. Liberty: freedom of speech, to make one's own friends, to come and go as one pleases.

Many of these freedoms we take for granted in our society, and we find that we want more. We want the freedom to control many choices in life—to control our time, to live where we want in the style we desire. Whether we recognize it or not, those opportunities for choice usually depend on power, the power that comes with position, with influence and money, sometimes with sexual attractiveness. And, while power has its pleasures, we also learn that it can corrupt and hurt those who use it as well as those over whom it is exercised or from whom it is taken.

Then there is the pursuit of happiness—toward enjoyment, fulfillment. But is happiness really to be found in the pursuit of it? Or is happiness to be pursued but never attained, as with Keats' figures on the Grecian urn forever frozen in their pursuit of pleasures? Or is happiness only fleetingly attained—like cotton candy which, almost as soon as you bite into it, is gone?

Even though we have experienced a number of life's pleasures and attainments, there still seems to be a yearning, like when you are thirsty and keep on drinking until your stomach is full—even bloated, but still you thirst, not sure even for what.

We may find the experience confusing, disturbing even to the point that we don't want to ask the question any more, or we try to overwhelm it with distractions. Maybe we do this because what we suspect we really want seems impossible—so unattainable.

159

George Herbert once wrote a poem in which he suggested that God, in creating us, had a pitcher full of blessings to pour out onto humanity:

> So strength first made a way;
> Then beautie flow'd, then wisdome, honour, pleasure:
> When almost all was out, God made a stay,
> Perceiving that alone of all his treasure
> Rest in the bottome lay.

God refused to pour out the last gift of rest, fearing that men and women would then focus all their attention on the gifts and not the Giver, that they would not then search for life's ultimate goals and purposes.

Similarly Augustine wrote, "You have made us for yourself, O Lord, and our hearts are restless until they find their rest (*ad te*) toward you." Dante expressed it this way, "In God's will is our peace."

The prophets and teachers tried to find words to tell what that peace would be like:

> If you pour yourself out for the hungry and satisfy the desire of the afflicted, then shall your light rise in the darkness and your gloom be as the noonday. You shall be like a watered garden, like a spring of water whose waters fail not. ...to do justice, and to love kindness ...love your neighbor as yourself. Keep justice and do righteousness and soon my salvation will come...for the earth shall be full of the knowledge of the Lord as the waters cover the sea.

Deep in our being—at the heart of our thirst—the prophet's poetry suggests that what we most long for is a world of God's wisdom and justice, of fairness and reconciliation, trust and true peace. The vision offers the hope that we might be part of such a world, and what we now most want is to be able to move toward that hope—to anticipate it now by beginning to work toward God's purposes for humanity.

Our desire is to participate in the new age by seeking, through the knowledge of the Lord, those things which restore human dignity to others and which make for community and peace—even though we fear the measures of giving and giving up, of sacrifice and willingness to suffer that such a life will call for.

There is the rub: to have what we most want, we must share what we have. It is in giving that we most are growing, in loving that we most are lovely, in letting go that we are most living.

A vital clue to how this might be once lay in a manger on a cold and dark night—a baby, whispering to us about how God is starting to accomplish this vision for human life, beginning in humility that we may discover that it is often in surprisingly small and humble ways that we will realize how God's fairness and justice and peace and joy can begin their reign in our lives.

Christmas is a special season for hoping and for strengthening us as disciples of the one who came among us as a child. For most of us there will soon be presents—clothes and games and electronic thises and thats, music, phone calls, much food and family fun. But beneath all the tinsel and wrapping paper and good times, there will still be our piercing hope for the meaning of Christmas in the little child who will lead us.

Some will say that is only a seasonal dream. Yet it is this vision which enables many of us to deal with life's hard realities. It is that hope which equips us to go on caring when others have abandoned hope to keep on in the faith that evil and wrong and that hurt and oppression can be transformed by grace into community and healing and justice and kindness.

That is what most we long and yearn for. That is what most we are restless for. That is what most we want. There is our peace and our Christmas joy.

The Giver and the Gift

The young teenager was hoping for a B-B gun for Christmas. Instead he received a new dictionary and desk lamp.

Dad had asked for a VCR. Instead he got new garden tools.

A young wife had hinted broadly that she would be glad to have some inexpensive, practical kitchen dishes. But her husband suprised her with a very expensive gold necklace and a fancy nightie.

Everybody in the family was expecting the usual $50 check from grandfather. What they received were notes saying that this year their present would go to help a needy family in a drought-stricken area of Africa.

The staff was expecting a little Christmas bonus. Instead they received individual carvings from the boss working at her new hobby of soap sculpture.

You can tell a lot about givers by the gifts they give. As the gift is unwrapped one learns about their motivations, their likes and dislikes, their tastes and values.

We tell a lot about ourselves by the gift we give. Suppose, for instance, we had a arranged one of those "Secret Santa" Christmas swaps among a group of us. Each of us draws a name to bring a present for, while the gift is given anonymously.

Yet, even though you would not know from whom you had received the gift, I imagine you could make some good surmises about the giver depending on whether the gift was a box of UNICEF cards or some homemade jam or a book or a box of candy, or a gift certificate for Saks or McDonalds or Radio Shack, or a picture or flower seeds.

It all makes me think about our relationship with God at Christmas. I mean, God can kind of seem anonymous. By worship and faith and prayer, by caring and service, by loving and being loved we may find that we are aware of certain things about God. Yet, though at times close to our lives, God may often also seem—well, transcendent, "other" than our world and lives.

We may feel we know something about the Creator through creation—through the vastness, beauty and complexity of the universe, although this isn't at all easy to comprehend.

And then we are given this gift!

What were we hoping for? One who would answer all the world's problems? Who would overcome world hunger? End wars? Compel religious belief through mighty acts and wonders?

That is what a lot of people were expecting and perhaps some people still are, before they will put their trust in God.

Instead we are given a baby—one who we know will grow up to be mighty, but with a might very different from the world's standards. It is to be a might that is vulnerable and crucifiable—self-giving and forgiving.

What—on earth—is the message? What on earth can we tell about the giver from this gift? Is it something very simple? Or very profound? Or perhaps very simple and profound at once?

A baby is a sign of new life and new hope, but it is also weak and vulnerable. A baby does not have much to offer us, but instead calls us to give—to protect and nurture and try to make our world a better place for this infant. We are invited to be braver, more caring, more faithful, more generous. The baby cries for what is best in us to be reborn and gain new strength. It helps us to understand how God is part of our world.

One hears those later words of Jesus: "I was hungry and you gave me food; I was thirsty and you gave me something to drink; I was a stranger and you welcomed me; I was naked and you gave me clothing; I was sick and you took care of me; I was in prison and you visited me."

Perhaps by the time you read this it may seem a little late to do very much about Christmas presents. But it's not too late at all. In a way it's all beginning again—you and I unwrapping and discovering again in and among ourselves all our possibilities for tenderness and care, courage and new hope.

And then we have all the days of Christmas and all the days ahead to share this gift with others. No wonder the angels are singing.

The Golden Rule—Is It Enough?

Many philosophers and teachers have held the Golden Rule to be that basic moral teaching about which the wisest may agree. In the Sermon on the Mount, it seems to have this aura: "In everything do to others as you would have them do to you; for this is the law and the prophets" (Matthew 7:12).

Yet, there is much in the surrounding Gospel context which might seem to undermine the idea that the Golden Rule could be the basis for a fully Christian way of life. This issue becomes yet more acute in Luke's Gospel where Jesus may appear to be attacking such an understanding:

"But I say to you that listen, Love your enemies, do good to those who hate you, bless those who curse you, pray for those who abuse you. If anyone strikes you on the cheek, offer the other also; and from anyone who takes away your coat do not withhold even your shirt. Give to everyone who begs from you; and if anyone takes away your goods, do not ask for them again. Do to others as you would have them do to you.

"If you love those who love you, what credit is that to you? For even sinners love those who love them....If you lend to those from whom you hope to receive, what credit is that to you? For even sinners lend to sinners to receive as much again. But love your enemies, do good, and lend, expecting nothing in return. Your reward will be great, and you will be the sons and daughters of the Most High; for God is kind to the ungrateful and the wicked. Be merciful, just as your Father is merciful" (Luke 6:27-36).

It would be easy to question the morality of the Golden Rule as merely serving self-interest: a sort of "I'll do this, if you'll do the same in return. I'll act fairly if you'll act fairly," although, as such, it still might serve better than much else as a guideline for society's interaction.

In fact, however, the Rule appears to go beyond any such basic attitude of equivalence by setting forth a willingness to anticipate the response of the other. But, in a recent article, the distinguished philosopher and interpreter Paul Ricoeur points out that in most contexts there still seems to be an aura of equivalence—the expectation that one's own ethical behavior will find reciprocation.[1] "I will live fairly in order that you will live fairly too."

There remains the question: What if others do not act fairly? Does this release one from the Rule?

Jesus' teaching can best be seen not as undermining the foundational Golden Rule but as its reinterpretation. The Rule is artfully set in a new ethical perspective that leads beyond the logic of human reckoning and may oftentimes even appear beyond reach. Its basis is in God's holiness. "Be merciful, just as your Father is merciful." Or, in Matthew's version, "Be perfect as your heavenly Father is perfect" (5:48).

The measure of love for Christians is not what will bring a gentler, fairer world for us to live in, but the love and mercy of God. The Golden Rule remains in place as a valuable guide for justice and morality, but Christians, realizing in their lives the abundance of the mercy and compassion of God, are called to a way of living in which doing good to others is to be beyond calculation. Every system of justice and every interpretation of law will be profoundly affected by this abundance.

Note

1. Paul Ricoeur, "The Golden Rule: Exegetical and Theological Perplexities," *New Testament Studies* 36, no. 3 (1990): 392-97.

"Jack"

"Jack" was how he was known to his friends. Many of us first came to know C.S. Lewis through his tellingly insightful *Screwtape Letters*, correspondence between the devil and one of his minions, which is full of pointed warning about the pitfalls of the spiritual and ethical life of a Christian. Or perhaps it was his book *Miracles* which first caught our attention, or *Mere Christianity* or *The Problem of Pain*. These books were written to try to reach a generation that had come through two terrible wars and to offer them the continuing hope and challenge of Christian faith.

For others it may have been *The Lion, The Witch and The Wardrobe* and those other tales from *The Chronicles of Narnia* which first entertained and then caught their imagination and longing. Or possibly it was one of the books from his curious and heavily allegorical space trilogy that provided an introduction to this fertile mind. For another group, students of literature, it was the *Allegory of Love* or his monumental *English Literature in the Sixteenth Century* and his strongly formed and widely read approach to literature that made us want to read more. Although I never knew Lewis personally (he was teaching at Cambridge when I was a student in Oxford) his reputation and influence ran deep in much of the Christian community in Oxford and for those who studied English literature there.

At the time I thought there were things I did not like about Lewis. His approach to some of the profundities of Christianity seemed to me a little high-handed, even arrogant. There were times when his insights sounded almost too barbed, his temperament a little sour.

In later years some of my feelings for him changed, and it would seem he did, too. Many people have now seen the made-for-television drama or the play *Shadowlands* (or then the movie with Anthony Hopkins), which tells of Lewis' love for his wife, Joy, her agonizing death from cancer and his struggle to keep her faith, and then its deepening.

Last summer I picked up A. N. Wilson's *C.S. Lewis: A Biography* (London: William Colins, 1990) with great anticipation. After a few pages, however, I almost put it down. At first Wilson seemed antipathetic to Lewis' faith. Clearly he was going to show him to be a man emotionally crippled by his mother's early death. He would help us see the psychological complexities of Lewis' conversion and the ways in which he could be an intellectual bully. Wilson obviously meant to take delight in the manner in which some Christians wanted to have Lewis be defender of their conservative approach to faith, while seemingly ignoring Lewis' own struggles and the fact that he was a heavy smoker and drinker—far from the conventional saintly portrait sometimes drawn of him.

But I could not put the book down. Wilson was helping me to see Lewis in all his humanity. His realistic biography is at the same time deeply compassionate and quietly admiring, reminding us again how God's grace and presence are known in earthen vessels—through what Yeats called "the rag and bone shop of the heart."

These words from *An Experiment in Criticism* (Cambridge: Cambridge University Press, 1961. p. 141) call to mind Lewis' powers of insight and expression and his deep humanity:

> Literary experience heals the wound, without undermining the privilege of individuality. There are mass emotions which heal the wound; but they destroy the privilege. In them our separate selves are pooled and we sink back into sub-individuality. But in reading great literature I become a thousand men and yet remain myself. Like a night sky in the Greek poem, I see with myriad eyes, but it is still I who see. Here, as in worship, in love, in moral action, and in knowing, I transcend myself; and am never more myself than when I do.

The Death and Resurrection
of the Beloved Son

There are basic plot themes which the Bible tells over and again. Repetition is a way of teaching. It is a way of telling that something is important. Through variation and different settings it is a way of giving depth and richness of significance to a theme. Such a vital and central theme is the death and resurrection of the beloved son.

Abraham takes his only son, Isaac, whom he loves, to the land of Moriah where he is prepared to sacrifice him. But just as Isaac is about to die, an angel of the Lord stays Abraham's hand and a ram is substituted for his life.

Earlier Abraham's son by the slave woman Hagar was saved by divine intervention at nearly the last moment.

Jacob loses Joseph. He was virtually buried and thought to be dead before being taken down to Egypt, where he was unknown for many years. Then it is Benjamin, the only remaining son from Joseph's favored wife, who must go down to Egypt, before both he and Joseph are restored to their father. Through their sacrifices the people gain new life.

Sometimes the death actually occurs and new life comes, as it were, through a substitute. Adam and Eve lose both Cain and Abel (the rivalry between two brothers for the role of favored son being a repeated subplot), and then Seth is born through whom comes the life of the whole human race. David loses his firstborn by Bathsheba, who is then replaced by Solomon through whom the life of the Davidic line continues.

The theme clearly has its roots in ancient child sacrifice wherein the death of the firstborn (not always a boy) brings safety and is life giving for the parents and the community. In his penetrating study *The Death and Resurrection of the Beloved Son: The Transformation of Child Sacrifice in Judaism and Christianity* Jon D. Levenson argues that the practice was not eradicated but transformed in ancient Israel and that this transformation has had profound effects on both the lore and belief of Judaism and Christianity.

There is, if you will, a kind of dark side to those words, "You are my beloved son"—for the one chosen (not always the literal first born), who seems especially to belong to God, must be chastened, humiliated and tested to see if he is worthy. These chosen ones must become servants and undergo some form of death before they can rule. Levenson touches upon but does not develop the connections of this theme with royal ideology and practice in which the son must suffer before he can inherit the father's throne.

In many ways, of course, it is God's son, the people Israel, in whose experience throughout the Hebrew Scriptures the story of chosenness, exile, death and new life is repeated.

The Gospels' parable of the wicked husband-men may well have the essential plot theme in the background, as could the parable of the prodigal son (this your brother was dead, and is alive) which latter narrative Levenson surprisingly does not discuss. But for Christians the richness of the story, with all its nuances and significance, comes to its culmination in the life-giving sacrifice of Jesus, he who on our behalf took the form of a servant... humbled himself and became obedient unto death. "Therefore God has highly exalted him and bestowed on him the name which is above every name."

In the last pages of his study Levenson reflects on the significance of how, both in rivalry and together, Judaism and Christianity share this ancient, protean, and strongly resilient story of the death and resurrection of the beloved son. For teachers and preachers this provocative book and the vital story itself, with all its consequence and generative power, are well worth our study and continued reflection.

Being Saved by Faith

Bthut whose faith? There is an interesting debate going on in New Testament scholarship over the best way to interpret the phrase *dia* (or *ek*) *pisteos Christou Iesou,* rendered in all modern translations as "by" or "through faith in Christ Jesus" and regularly understood as the faith of the believer. (See Romans 3:22, 26; Galatians 2:16 [24]; 3:22; Philippians 3:9.) Thus Galatians 2:16a (in the Revised Standard Version) reads ". . .we know that one is not reckoned righteous by works of the law but through faith in Jesus Christ." Most of us have heard this understanding emphasized from the pulpit or in seminary: it is not our works that save us, but our faith.

Perhaps, however, you have always been a little bothered by this stress. Do I have enough faith to be saved? Does not "faith" now become the one great good work on my part?

A number of New Testament scholars argue that it is more appropriate (grammatically and exegetically) to translate the phrase as a subjective rather than an objective genitive; i.e., "through Jesus Christ's faith" or "through Jesus Christ's faithfulness." What saves is not our faith, but Jesus' faith in God, his faithfulness.

Various objections are raised to this translation. The phrase regularly occurs in verses where we hear that Christians have believed (put their faith) in Christ. (It is countered that this is strange logic. Is it not rather redundant to speak of those who have put their faith in Christ Jesus by their faith in Christ Jesus?) Others are concerned for Christological reasons. Did Jesus need to have faith? (This criticism seems to suggest that faith is somehow a lesser quality than knowledge, and that the earthly Jesus was not meant to be so fully human that he had a need for faith. But Paul more than once indicates that it is this faith which overcomes human faithlessness. Jesus is the faithful one who overcame Adam's sin.)

The translation "through Christ Jesus' faith" may seem a radical reinterpretation to some, but it actually makes good biblical and theological sense and is well worth pondering. It does not do away with the need for human response, but it helps in the understanding that human acceptance of, and participation in what God has done in Christ Jesus is enabled by

Jesus' faith in God and his faithfulness.

There is, also, a third group of scholars who maintain that the phrase has a certain deliberate ambiguous and mystical quality, suggestive of the mutuality of Christ's faithfulness and our response—the reciprocity of faith-faithfulness, if you will. It has been suggested that we might then translate the phrase "Christ-Faith." But, the emphasis would still fall on what Christ has done that helps us to respond and to follow in his faithful way to God.

Such a debate may seem distant from the everyday life of Christians, but it clearly has vital implications for one's spirituality and ethics.[1] Even when our faith is weak we are still the beneficiaries of Christ's faithfulness. The issues also have relevance to past and present contentions that unless Christians believe correctly about this matter or that (ranging from women's ordination to baptismal regeneration) they may not be of the true Church and may not be saved. It is a healthy reminder to all to realize that it is Christ's faithfulness which is saving us and not our own.

Note

1. Those who want to pursue these arguments more closely can do so in Morna D. Hooker's "Pistis Christou," *New Testament Studies* 35 (1989): 321-42; and Sam K. Williams' "Again Pistis Christou," *Catholic Biblical Quarterly* 49 (1987): 431-37.

PART 3

Adelante!

Ministries Today

Adelante!

ADELANTE! That is a rousing word. Come in! Go Ahead! Forward! That is the way we face and the direction we are going.

There is much in religion about the past. The very word "religion" has roots that mean to "tie back." This is part of Christianity's great power. We are strongly linked to our heritage, our tradition and founding events of revelation and faith. But the way Christians face is forward.

We are not like much of society that forgets the past—which says the past is past and does not count. We bear with us the courage and witness and suffering of all those who have come before us. In many ways they are still with us as we expect the redemption of their lives and ours. With them we face forward.

Our faith is not in progress. Yes, we want to enhance human life, but we do not think of the past as just disposable prologue. Nor are we ourselves but chapters in some future generation's technologically perfect age. We believe the past and present can and will be saved by God. So our face is to the future—forward.

This is the way the early Christians faced—forward in hope and faith. The resurrection of Jesus filled them with expectation. The resurrection was not so much an event to look back on as it was a guide to the future. It offered the clue to human destiny in God. "When he appears we shall be like him" (1 John 3:2). The stories of faith that came to be known as Scripture were not teachings which locked people into a particular worldview or way of thinking. They became a guide book in the adventure forward.

Just off in God's future—already beginning to change lives: This is where the reign of God's righteousness and justice comes—enabling Christians already to live by its ways. This is how we are to go forward in mission—in witness and service to others.

A church that is not facing forward becomes caught up in games over turf and privilege—this committee against that committee—concerned about what people wear in church, becoming preoccupied with sexual matters, this form of worship or that, suspicion, anger and lack of trust. People become dispirited. But that is not how we are to face. Our way is forward.

175

It is not that there is just one path. What we share together is a direction forward—a vision. It is a vision of opportunities to witness, to grow, to heal, to give and to serve—of building communities of hope and welcome and courage. It does not worry about what we do not have—but rejoices in all we have. It is motivated by thanksgiving. It is filled with spirit by the Spirit. It is a can-do way forward.

Adelante!

Were Those Really the Good Old Days?

I have friends who, like myself, are lifelong Episcopalians or long-time members of the Church. They sometimes speak nostalgically of the Church of the '40s, '50s and early '60s. I certainly have many wonderful memories and much to be thankful for as well, but when they begin to talk about how clarion clear the Church then was on certain moral issues and how uncertain and ambiguous the Church is now, I must admit to being nonplussed. Are we talking about the same Church?

Yes, I suppose we then had a more rigorous attitude toward divorce. Homosexuality wasn't even spoken of, and some might have said that men were men and women were women—whatever that was supposed to mean. There still, of course, was a lot of divorce, infidelity, secret abortions, spouse abuse and alcoholism. Many of us know that a number of our clergy and some of our most active and generous parishioners were gay. More than this, we know most of our churches were *de facto* segregated racially and that there were many, many people in our society without educational opportunities and life's basic necessities. Some of us at least must have been conscious of male privilege and the inequality and unfairness that suffused many a woman's life. Our country was swept by spasms of hysteria about communists, and innocent people lost their jobs and their reputations.

Again I do not want to just talk down those "golden years." There were splendid acts of prophetic courage and sacrifice in those times. Many people led lives of quiet devotion and generosity. In some ways, too, I suppose, life was easier. The communities in which Episcopal churches were sited were more homogeneous. The pace of life was less hurried. There were fewer choices that had to be made.

But what I remember all too well about life in our churches then was that we did not talk much about the tough, demanding issues of our culture and society. Not everywhere, and not all the time, but mostly, church—and especially the local congregation—was a haven from all that.

I guess I can understand why some people are nostalgic for that and for a time in the life of the Church when issues and answers at least seemed more straightforward—when we had more of a moral consensus. But I must

177

say I am much more proud of the Episcopal Church as it exists today. Heaven knows (I'm sure!) that we are not exactly all captains of courage when it comes to the difficult issues, but there seems much more readiness at least to talk about them, pray about them, and see what things we can do.

Some people say that is why others have now left the Episcopal Church. I find that sad, if true, while I also know of still others who have come to our Church just because they find it one of the few places in society where people from different backgrounds can come and talk and try to accomplish things together in hope and faith.

I have heard people say that all this means the Church has become more liberal. My highly articulate response is usually something along the lines of "Balderdash. What a sloppy use of labels." By just about any sociological reference of which I am aware, the Episcopal Church would overall be considered a strong conserving force in society—working to hold onto critical values and moral perspectives. But you cannot conserve your most basic values by sitting still. Things change, and if you do not make some changes, your values are left behind.

It is not, in fact, that the Episcopal Church has a lot of definitive things to say about the great personal and social issues. Some people from both the so-called left and right probably do not like that. But what our Church has been more insistent on is the ministry of raising the issues. That is a prophetic task (like that of the prophets of the Bible)—asking, and in some cases insisting, that people see and become reflective about matters they might rather not see: gross economic injustice at home and abroad, racism, sexism, threats to the environment, the dangers of dependence only on weapons for security, the results of our foreign policy in certain countries, millions of refugees in the world today, people lacking basic medical care and homes in our country, the problems in our prisons, convalescent homes and schools.

People may, of course, interpret these problems differently and have different ways of trying to respond to them. But that is not the point—or rather; it *is* the point! Let us disagree. Let us call ourselves liberals or conservatives, Republicans or Democrats, if that makes us feel better, but let us be a Church and churches where we have open eyes and ears and hearts—open to each other to listen and to learn, and open to God's challenge and God's way of peace.

It is not a question of superficial tolerance and a pluralism of indifference. These are serious matters on which some directions must be set, but let us be a Church where we will worship together and draw strength from God's love and be a place where we can talk and try to do something about the tough and important issues of life. Let us be a people who know we are held together by concerns that go deeper than our economic views or status or political stripes.

We did not manufacture these tough issues and problems. In an important sense we can say God has given them to us because it is quite clear that the God of the Bible cares about them. Some may argue that God also gives us a whole set of answers to them. I do not see that nearly so much as I find that the Bible tells us that because God cares, we are to care and wrestle and strive to be compassionate and thoughtful about vital and critical concerns in our time of life. I am proud to be a member of a Church that responds like that.

Ministry as Artistry

The early death of Terry Holmes was a loss to the earthly church. He wrote several thoughtful books dealing with the ministries of all disciples arising out of Christian community. In what I found to be his most provocative book, *Ministry and Imagination*, he reflected on the importance of imagination for modern life and the mystery of the transcendent God's universal presence. The world, he held, could rightly be perceived as "enchanted," and he saw the priest as having a calling to help others realize and relate to this mystery of divine presence.

He suggested several intriguing images for the priest in relation to this calling. The priest is the mana-person, the imaginer and shaman, in touch with the holy. The priest is the clown, showing up false religion and the poverty of much of what is often regarded as important in order to allude to that which is of greater significance. The priest is storyteller, helping old lore to come alive and new stories to be told. And the priest is the wagon master, encouraging and enabling a kind of organized pilgrimage.

All such images have their limitations, and a collection of them are needed to suggest the varied roles and aspects of the ordained ministry. I know people who prefer the image of scout or coach or orchestra director. You may well have several favorites of your own.

One of my favorite images or models for ministries of leadership is that of the artist. Like good artists good ministers are attentive. They have eyes which see and ears that hear. They are contemplative. They pause and listen; they look and gain insight; they sometimes behold and on occasion find themselves beheld.

They help others to see. Like the prophets of old they sometimes cause others to recognize what they otherwise might want to overlook—the sad, the horrible, what is unjust, what needs giving and healing. At the same time they look below the surface and see beauty or the potential for what is lovely where others might not. Living in the connective Spirit they sense as liminal persons; they gesture toward mystery. They are sacramentalists, leaders in liturgy, poets of praise.

Participation in creativity depends on a willingness to trust, on commitment and then love—even surrender, for artists are conservers and arrangers more than users. Assisting in the fashioning of relationships, comings together and community, they share in the work of redeeming— alluding to significance, helping bring to life the possibility of meaning.

Much artistry is, then, as the word implies, a ministry of subservience. Ministers as artists make do with the given. Rather than lamenting what they do not have or wishing for what might be there, they see the possibilities of what is here—the circumstances, the people, the stories, the challenges, the opportunities of the time. There is such artistry in ministry.

Minister Afire

When I was a curate, one of my ministries was to bring the sacrament to individuals in nursing and convalescent homes. With me I brought the consecrated bread and wine in a case which also contained a small cross and candles and a cotta. The short cotta was open at the back and could be put on over a shirt or jacket and then fastened at the top with a button.

The altar guild would faithfully prepare the kit for me and the cotta was carefully folded inside. I'm not sure but that they didn't wash and iron it after each use. In any event it had become thin and a little yellowed and dried out over the years.

One morning I was calling on a quite elderly woman, as I remember for the first time. I recall that she was pleasant and seemed to appreciate our conversation and having the sacrament brought to her. I could tell that she had been a faithful disciple and churchgoer for many years, but she wasn't doing very well now. She was bedridden and probably hadn't too long to live.

For some reason the Rector and others at church persisted in calling these ministrations "sick communions"—a term I thoroughly disliked. Better, I thought, to call them "well communions," helping to bring strength and consolation.

After the woman and I had talked for a while, I unpacked the kit and set up the little cross and lit the candles. There was even a miniature chalice. They reminded me of toys, and it always seemed a bit like playing church.

I read the Gospel and offered the prayers. As I then reached for the bread to bring it to the woman, I accidentally dragged a corner of the cotta through a candle flame. In a flash practically the whole dry cotta caught fire. I yanked it off me and threw it in the corner and stomped on it until it was finally out. There leapt from memory, even at that moment, the line from the Letter to the Hebrews quoting Psalm 104: "He makes his angels winds, and his ministers a flaming fire."

The room was sharp with the smell of singe. My pulse was doing a little jig, and I was confused by emotions of both embarrassment and relief that I hadn't burned myself up and the place down. I turned to offer my apologies or at least to try to say something. What?

She, however, propped up in her hospital bed, still had her hands extended for the sacrament, her eyes closed and a serene look on her face. Relieved, I brought the sacrament to her, quickly finished the service, and picked up and deposited what remained of the cotta in the waste basket. With the fire and the crumbling of the dry rest of it, there wasn't much left.

At the time I think I told myself that the dear woman was sufficiently out of it that she hadn't even noticed. Reflecting later in the car, I wasn't so sure. There had been quite a burst of flame and stomping about. Even if her sight and hearing were poor, there was also that odor of singe. Perhaps she had put it all down to some new liturgical revision or Diocese of Chicago high church hi-jinx. More likely yet, with that humbling tolerance and patience many lay people can have with sometimes bumbling clergy, she may just have decided to let it ride. God bless her now.

I don't recall the altar guild being quite so forgiving. I'm not sure they fully believed me either. Perhaps I'd just forgotten it or otherwise disposed of the relic. In any case, I thought to myself, it was time to get a new one.

"Ministers become a flaming fire." It was just a routine visit with the sacrament to a convalescent home. Nothing very exciting about that. And then suddenly flame and fire! I remembered a burning bush, fire from heaven, hailstones and coals of fire, and the one who will baptize with the Holy Spirit and fire.

One never knows. Maybe sometimes. Maybe more regularly than we imagine, for I often still think of the flaming cotta when I offer the body and blood of Christ.

The Storm of the Century

I t was shortly before noon at an Episcopal Conference Center called Kanuga. It is a lovely wooded site by a lake in the mountains of western North Carolina. Having led and attended a number of conferences at Kanuga, and having hiked its hills and swum its lake, it was a place which I had come to care for and enjoy.

Earlier in the week the weather had been mild for early March. On Tuesday and Wednesday I had been able to play tennis in the late afternoons with other bishop friends, gathered for a meeting of the House of Bishops. But by Thursday it was considerably colder, and the wind was up—strong enough to whistle lowly through the pines and to shudder the leafless trees.

By Friday morning heavy, grey clouds were slipping rapidly over the mountains with an urgency that seemed to confirm the ominous weather reports. Record low pressures were predicted as a moisture laden storm, driven by a cold jet stream which had dipped down toward the Caribbean, now headed north to intensify as it clashed with a still colder front moving southward.

The meeting had concluded on Friday morning and almost all the bishops had left. I was trying to keep together seven of us from the Theology Committee so that we would not need another meeting later in the Spring. My flight was not scheduled until afternoon on Saturday which would still get me back to Los Angeles in time for Sunday visitations to St. Martin's in Canoga Park and St. Michael's in Riverside.

It became increasingly difficult, however, to hold our attention on the assigned topics. My colleagues kept glancing out the windows and at their watches. Phone calls were made to check with airlines. Dutifully we continued talking over lunch, but I had to recognize the meeting was ending.

Two of the bishops quickly left. Three others had a car and were readying to leave for Charlotte, two and a half hours away, in the hopes of catching planes there. A phone call to my airline revealed, however, that all flights were far overbooked. I knew, too, that the Atlantic Coast Conference basketball tournament was taking place in Charlotte that weekend, and it would, at the least, be difficult to find a motel room.

In the meantime, members of the Kanuga Directors' Board were arriving for a meeting. My friend Bishop Charles Duval, also a member of the Theology Committee, was staying to chair that meeting. Parishioners, including families with small children, drove in from a church in South Carolina for a weekend conference.

I had to make a decision. It seemed wiser to stay in familiar surroundings among friends. Probably the storm warnings were exaggerated. Surely it would clear up by Saturday afternoon.

But it was to be called the storm of the century. First there were a few soft flakes. It began snowing heavily just after nightfall. A wind now roaring awoke me several times during the night. In the morning all the air was blowing snow. Everywhere there was drifting and piling—more than eighteen inches of snow in the end. Several times—with air pressure so low —it thundered.

No chance to leave now. The roads couldn't be opened until at least Sunday; perhaps not until Monday or later. There would be no visitations to St. Martin's or St. Michael's. I began to think about meetings I might need to cancel on Monday.

It grew colder. I could see the lake beginning to freeze at the edges. Several times the lights dimmed. Then they were gone. At first it was only part of the system, but suddenly all of it went. No lights and then, I realized, no heat.

We were so isolated it was hard to get information even on a portable radio. But the telephones still worked. I called Barbara in what I knew was sunny Los Angeles. The fierce winds, she told me, had blown over a tree in our son and daughter-in-law's backyard in Tampa. She reported to me from the Weather Channel. The huge seven hundred mile wide storm was moving north slowly. The whole of the east coast was shutting down. All the airports were closed.

We had candles. We had a roaring fire in the fireplace of the main lodge. Blessedly, the gas system still functioned. There were stoves to cook on as long as it was light. There was hot water. One could take a hot shower. I took several. I had never been cleaner in all my life.

By Saturday night the temperature was near zero and my bedroom was without heat. Bedtime was very early. There was a candle to read by, but it was too cold to turn the pages. I took another shower and put on my sweatshirt over my pajamas, falling asleep in fetal position. When I stuck out a foot, I woke up.

During the day on Sunday the sun shone wondrously. The children

185

were playing in the snow. Without the right clothes I bundled up as best I could, and, reminding myself that I am a native of Chicago, I went for a long walk.

Before the great fireplace—almost as fire worshippers—we offered our Eucharist that morning. "Glorify the Lord, O chill and cold, drops of dew and flakes of snow. Frost and cold, ice and sleet, glorify the Lord, praise him and highly exalt him forever."

After lunch I sat for awhile by the sliding glass door in my room. The sun streaming in warmed me so well that I no longer needed the blanket on my lap. When I travel, I invariably carry more books with me than I can possibly read. But this time it paid off.

I dozed too, and I gave thanks to God for the sunshine and the enforced time to sit, and to make new friends and to play with the children. I gave thanks for the courage and stamina of the Conference Center staff. I gave thanks for the sun. "Glorify the Lord, O nights and dark, O shining light and enfolding dark."

I thought of our ancestors, also going to bed as the sun went down and rising with its rising, who would probably consider me comfortable with my glass window, prepared food and hot showers. They could not have imagined a pay telephone on which to call Barbara again and to talk with my children living in the East. I thought of my friends in Canoga Park and Riverside and knew they were worshipping now, or preparing to do so, and praying also for me.

Monday we dug out. It took a long time. There was a further wait for news that a lane had been cleared down to the main road and that the highway itself was open. New friends drove me to Charlotte. There were still further delays with my airline, but I was fortunate to get out on standby nonstop to Los Angeles.

I sat back. I was tired, but I was also rested. And I had survived the great storm and lived to tell about it.

But would any southern Californian believe me?

Adventure in Yucaipa

On the road in Southern California. My chaplain, Mark, and I were headed east on the 91. We had just finished a good visit with the disciples at St. Peter's in San Pedro. It was a bit after 1 p.m. The next occasion was the dedication of the new St. Alban's Church in Yucaipa. Much excitement and expectation surround the dedication of a new church. We were to give thanks to God for all the skill and sacrifice that went into the building program.

The liturgy was scheduled for 3 p.m. We had told them we might be a little late, but we thought we could make it.

On up through the Santa Ana Canyon and Corona. In the back seat I was finishing some mail and going over my sermon. Time flew by and so did the miles. Riverside, Redlands a little before 2:45. Still tight, but we were looking good.

We were on Yucaipa Boulevard only about a mile and a half from the church when Mark suddenly grumbled and said the engine had quit. He pulled over.

We were both surprised. The two-year-old Buick had behaved almost flawlessly. Mark checked the gauges. One of them indicated we were out of oil. Neither of us is a mechanic. It was about 2:50.

We laughed a little nervously about the fact that they couldn't very well begin the liturgy without me. We reminded ourselves that they knew we might be late. Still the picture came to mind of all those people crowded into the new church. The temperature was in the 90s.

We tried to stay cool. I dialed the church number on the car phone, but there was no answer. I learned later that the phone was ringing vainly in the tiny old church. The phones in the new building were installed but not connected.

On another day I might have called Lou Hemmers in Redlands or Victoria Hatch in Banning and asked them to come to the rescue. But they were by now all vested and waiting at the church.

Mark suggested a taxi. I called information. "Could you give me the number of a taxi company?"

"Which taxi company, sir?"

I quickly explained our situation and said I didn't know the name of a local taxi service. I can't give you a number without a name, sir.

Doesn't information have a copy of the yellow pages?

"Could I speak to your supervisor?

Same response. "I'm sorry, sir. I'll need the name of the taxi company."

It was 2:55. I asked Mark to stand outside the car in case someone came by on the way to the service.

I hiked back a block and a half to a barbecue restaurant Mark had noticed. The air conditioning in the car had lulled me. It was hot.

Morbitzer's Bar-BQ. Chicken, pork, beef. No public phone. But they were kind and offered the use of their phone and yellow pages.

Two good-sized young men overheard me describe the predicament. "We'll give you a ride to the church, Father. Do you mind riding in a pick-up?"

Who's to choose? Gratefully, I climbed into the middle of the cab of Tom's and Jim's truck. I felt a flare of exhilaration. What nice people lived in Yucaipa!

I thought I would see mostly relief on Mark's face, but instead he was obviously having trouble hiding his amusement at seeing his bishop in the middle of the truck cab, a bit dwarfed by the two young men.

There were more friendly Yucaipa people, for in the meanwhile a couple had pulled over in a Buick identical to ours. Mark had put my vestments and crozier in the back of Anita's and Richard's car. Richard is a mechanic. He had the hood up on my Buick and soon announced he had fixed some loose wiring. The oil was fine.

Meanwhile, Anita and Jim discovered they knew each other. Conversation ensued. I interrupted. It was 3:05. Could they just get me to the church?

I thanked Jim and Tom profusely. Off the two Buicks went. A couple of minutes later I spotted Kim Saville's spare frame pacing back and forth in front of the new St. Alban's. In his 70s and one of the fine priests of our diocese, Kim, together with his wife, Nellie, had come out of semi-retirement to help this congregation in the building of its church.

As we pulled up, I tried to get Anita and Richard to come into the service. It is, after all, the decade of evangelism! And, how much fun it would be to thank them with the whole congregation present.

They were shy. They didn't feel properly dressed. I wanted to convince them otherwise, but there were all those people waiting. At least I had a good story to tell.

As I vested and quickly went over details of the liturgy with Kim, I remembered another occasion when generous people had helped me. I had tried to thank them, too, but the best thanks, they said, would be to pass it on.

"Pass it on," I whispered.

"What?" Kim asked.

Let's just pass it on.

Backseat Writing

Previous to moving to Los Angeles and becoming a bishop, I always lived where I worked. I lived across the street from the church, or I lived on a seminary or university campus. I walked or rode my bike to work.

Is life getting even with me! Westside to downtown LA, up to San Fernando, and back home. To Compton, San Gabriel and Lincoln Heights. To Good Samaritan or County Hospital, to City Hall, out to Redlands, up to Santa Barbara, down to Huntington Beach.

Try Barstow, Needles, Lompoc, Santa Maria and San Clemente. An emergency pastoral call in Long Beach.

No, I don't do this every day. But the miles and the hours do mount up...too often locked in traffic jams. And one sees some terrific accidents—which is more than a little unnerving.

I used to fret. What kind of life or ministry is this? Where now is my study in Princeton?

Then one day, I think it was the Holy Spirit said to me, "Hey, it ain't all that bad. (The Spirit sometimes talks like that.) You're sitting in the back of the car. Your Chaplain's doing the hard work of driving."

Which is true. Usually I have a comfortable seat in the back with a phone and books and a lap board. I can prepare for meetings, plan ahead, prepare talks and sermons, read, write articles like this one, answer mail, say my prayers, daydream or fall asleep.

I write lots of notes to people—hundreds, no doubt, thousands of notes by now. Maybe you have received one.

One day I got to wondering what people thought of my penmanship—full of bumps and squiggles as the bishopmobile jogged on up the avenue or down the freeway. Sitting there I wrote this poem:

Some palsy must have seized him,
Hand or head now and then shaking,
Wobbling words this way and that.
Bumps over here and there lurching.

Backseat Writing

How else? I imagine them thinking,
Given even the scramble of hurry,
Could account for a pen so awry,
And fully explain their worry?

Sometimes the light is not good,
But mostly it's the lanes we are changing,
The slowing and pace picking up,
And suddenly braking!

As I try not only for sense,
Words rightly meant with some wit,
But also formed and just shaped,
So that on the page they will fit.

The whole task with its many diversions,
Stops, shifting, the to-ing and fro-ing,
Is a challenge to bend yet be steady,
Enough to be read and keep going.

The Non-Anxious Ministry

We've heard it. We've read about it. We've thought about it. We know there is much to be gained from being that less reactive, non-anxious presence for others.

Yet it's not that easy. There is a lot of anger out there in our society—sometimes bounding about in congregations. There are individuals with many of their own agendas and problems who can act them out in church groups. And in any case, building a caring community in our so individualistic and often blaming society is in no way easy.

So how does one keep from getting hooked? One can pretend not to be reacting and repeatedly count to ten, but we know the anger can then manifest in different ways.

But it does help to practice. It can be like practicing a role in which one takes on more and more of the characteristics of the part. And in that role one can come to see the powerful and often healing effects of not reacting to others' anger or blaming.

This is not passivity—not just walking away. It is not weakness but strength and health. It can be a means of developing leadership in oneself and others. It often involves active listening and careful efforts to understand what the issues really are. In that listening one regularly discovers that issues are not nearly as personal as they may have been made to seem. They often are more systemic and ask for more systemic analyses and responses.

It helps not to grow too dependent on other people's favor. This doesn't mean not becoming involved with people and their lives, but for clergy it does mean not being a dependent personality—one trying make up for lack of affection earlier in life or now by drawing that from the congregation. That kind of affection and support should come from elsewhere. If one doesn't get hooked on a congregation's approval of affection, it is much easier to deal with disapproval.

In all this there is a deeply spiritual dimension. It is the psalmist and Paul and the prophets who remind us that our trust is finally in God, whose grace "has made us competent to be ministers of a new covenant." Mind you, none of them found this ministry all that easy (and Paul isn't always our best role model in this regard, is he?), and we also all need human friendship and affection, but we are reminded of the direction in which we are to face to know who is our lasting help and our joy.

And, if we yet find we cannot help sometimes being overly reactive, let us now promise (on that stack of Bibles) never, never, never to do it in sermons or at announcement time, no matter how subtle or loving we think we are being—particularly never in personal terms. If there are things to be talked over, we may do that in forums or other venues where there can be response and listening and conversation.

The Good Episcopalian

How Can You Tell When You Meet One?

"Fred, I'd like you to meet —— ——; he's a Good Episcopalian."
I, of course, had met the Good Episcopalian before. There are quite a few of them in the East, and I was interested to find that there are evidently a number of them here in Los Angeles.

Once or twice I screwed up my courage and said, "I'm very glad to meet you, Mister or Madam Good Episcopalian," but I never have been able to go the further step and ask the individual what it means to be a Good Episcopalian. What are the criteria that can be used to make this judgment?

Sometimes one can sharpen a definition by comparison with its opposite, though I have never been introduced to a bad Episcopalian as such. One can imagine, however, that the day might come. " Fred, I'd like you to meet —— ——. He's a lousy Episcopalian."

"Yes, Bishop. I only go to Church on occasion, usually during one of the holiday seasons when I'm feeling a bit sentimental. I break commandments three, eight and nine with some regularity (although I suppose we shouldn't expect Mr. or Ms. Bad Episcopalian to know the commandments by number). I don't get much involved in anything beyond seeking security and pleasures for myself and my family, and I regard my financial affairs as strictly personal in which God, if there really is a God, doesn't have any say."

I've actually met some people who I think were trying to tell me something like that—whether by way of confession or assertion, I'm not sure. I guess I might commend them for their honesty, while the temptation would be strong to preach to them sermon No. 4 about living in a disenchanted world without an awareness of being part of the creation's excitement, and without a strong sense of purpose and of belonging to an adventure greater than oneself.

Presumably the Good Episcopalian would be the opposite of these things, although I fear that isn't always what is meant. I find out later that some of the Good Episcopalians I am introduced to lead rather disenchanted and unenthusiastic lives. They are usually kind and often generous, nice people to be with, but their faith sometimes turns out to be on the periphery rather than at the center of their lives. The excitement of exploring discipleship and living with a sacrificial concern for the needs of others is not always theirs. At times it seems almost to be a matter of culture. The individual is Episcopalian rather than Baptist or Jewish, helps out some good causes, and tries not to be mean.

One shouldn't, of course, knock these last two accomplishments. The culture we live in is very secular; life can be hard, and it is always good to meet nice people. Moreover, who among us would dare to call oneself a Good Episcopalian?

It has been said that being a Good Episcopalian is harder than measuring up in other denominations because we set so few strict standards and instead ask for a mature self-discipline and decision-making on the part of the individual disciple. This estimate of the challenge to being a solid Episcopalian Christian is in many ways true, although one can also certainly look at the baptismal covenant on pages 302-305 and at pages 845-62 (especially 847-48, 885-86) of the *Book of Common Prayer* to get some helpful overall guidance.

I really won't mind if the next time you introduce someone to me as "a Good Episcopalian" you do not have a set of clear definitions in mind. But I won't be able to help wondering and hoping. Here, pray God, is a man or woman who puts being a member of and supporting the community of faith at the heart of his or her life. They know they are only beginners in this great venture, but they have a passion for knowing the love and justice of God and for showing this loving justice in the care of those in need. May the good Lord help us all to try to be good Christians and good Episcopalians.

Not Challenging Enough?

What It Means to Become an Adult Child of God

One of the favorite criticisms of so-called mainline religious denominations is that they are not demanding enough. It has become a kind of stock in trade with certain commentators to maintain that so-called liberal faith does not offer the rigorous standards of more "conservative" churches and that this is why the latter are thought to be growing.

I sometimes worry that the standards which some people want to insist upon seem more directed at others than themselves, but mostly I am puzzled. I am puzzled by the analysis when, as a lifelong Episcopalian, I think about the challenges and expectations with which my church has always confronted me.

Let's start with sex, since overtly or otherwise, that seems to be mostly on the minds of many of these commentators when they talk about standards. My church challenges me, if I am to express my sexuality physically, to become part of a committed, lifelong relationship in which I can find joy and physical and emotional pleasure, but in which I also will experience vulnerability and a vocation that will call for sacrifice—for caring and self-giving in sickness and in health, tough times as well as good ones. To this relationship I am to make every effort to remain committed.

If children become part of this relationship, I am to care for them—to give of myself for their emotional and physical well-being. Parenting, too, is to become a vocation, requiring considerable sacrifice of time, energy and money on my part. I am to teach them the Christian faith and work hard to see that they are brought up in that faith.

I am also to support the committed relationships of other families of various kinds, perhaps especially those with only one parent.

And I myself am to be part of a community of faith. None of this individual salvation stuff or I can be a Christian by myself. Sometimes I might think I'd prefer that, but that is not the biblical faith. Being part of a community of faith means I cannot always have what I want. In order to worship and serve together, I need to make accommodations with those whose tastes or moods or style maybe different from mine.

This worship I am to do regularly, week in and week out—not based on my moods or schedule but that of the community. Loving God, I am to pray regularly and to learn more about prayer and meditation.

I am also to learn more about my faith. I am not to be educated about many things in the world, but a novice when it comes to interpreting the Bible as a spiritual and historical book. The great stories and central concerns of the Bible are to provide interpretive structure and guidance for my life. I am to know about the spiritual heritage of the church and what my church has to say about important ethical issues.

I am to tithe. This means giving a minimum of 10 percent of all my income to my church and church-related work. I am to do this in thanksgiving, without pride or grumbling. This is over and above what I give to my university and public television—good causes to be sure, but ones from which I also benefit and may be honored.

Nor is my giving to stop with my death. The mission of the church should be in my will.

I am eager to share my faith with others. This is not to be done manipulatively. Nor should I be unwilling to tell of some of the uncertainties and sacrifices of Christian living for this, too, is part of evangelism. But I am to be glad to share what I have been given.

I am to speak the truth in love—to strive to be an honest, truth-telling, fair-minded and loving person in all my relationships. I am never to act in revenge. But knowing myself a person of mixed emotions, I am continuously to try to offer my motivations to God—for cleansing, purifying and redirecting.

Then there are still greater challenges. I am to seek to love my neighbor as myself—to try to show sympathy and compassion for my near-neighbors and to seek love's justice and care for all others, respecting the dignity of every human being. I am to work to change mores and systems which are unfair or oppressive. I am to find ministries for myself and with others through which I can do these things.

I know there are some philosophers and psychologists who say that human beings are not capable of such love—especially when it becomes costly—but this is not what my faith teaches me as the way of Jesus I am to follow.

And, to top all this off, with the support of my faith community, I am to make these challenges my own. I am not part of a church where I am dependent on a hierarchy or charismatic leaders or some other form of infallibility. My challenge is the biblical challenge to grow up into the full stature of the maturity of Christ as a responsible, adult Christian.

Nor is any of this challenge hidden from me. It is there in the Bible and all through the pages of my Prayer Book—in the eucharistic prayers, the baptismal covenant, the catechism and elsewhere.

I realize there may be some people who feel that one ought to be kicked out or at least sharply disciplined if he or she doesn't live up to what they regard as the most important of these standards. I would agree that we Episcopalians could do considerably better when it comes to mutual accountability in the body of Christ, but I also find that it is part of being an adult child of God to learn what is expected of me, to confess and repent my failures, and to know that the community of other faithful, struggling Christians is there to uphold me.

When I feel I have finally gotten somewhere with all of these expectations and challenges, maybe I'll be ready to look for a more demanding form of the Christian faith.

Grand Canyon
Reflections After Rafting

This summer Barbara and I had the opportunity to go down the Colorado River through the Grand Canyon. We did this, with some old and new friends, on small rubber rafts.

Shooting down rapids, we bounced and splashed between the hot canyon air and the cold river water. We took side trips to view more of nature's wonders and to see some of the signs of earlier Native American settlements.

Six days later, unable to make the whole trip because of other commitments, we hiked up the Bright Angel Trail (seven-and-a-half miles long and one mile up). That was quite a trek, and we fell into bed exhausted.

But the next day we were able to look across the vast canyon and down to the thin blue ribbon on which we had paddled the days before.

The Canyon is in so many ways overwhelming: in its size, its beauty, its vivid display of geological time. No words could be right for it, but to remember our summer adventure, I tried a little poetry.

Storied sand, mud and life
Five thousand years by inches,
Pressed, uplifted, billionaire,
More lost than saved in
Temples sculpted without myth
And vastly vaulted awe.

Here a mute shard, saga
Fallen down the layered eras,
Smoothed by this muddy geologian
From a thousand peaks away,
Rushing unhurriedly to draft new tales
Of ancient marine.

Outrage and Hope

Still warm from but one sun,
I behold with infant eyes,
Now drawn the walled aisle,
Past half of earth, in slice of stars,
Some this night shining
Before a canyon day.

A grain of time and space,
Yet now to see and guess,
Not only thinking
But to think of thinking
On all which seems beyond
Our reverence and thanksgiving.

The Ministry and
Authority of Bishops in
a Changing World and Church

The awareness that change is the one constant in life is a frequent subject of philosophical reflection. However much we may want to wade in familiar waters, an appreciation of Heraclitus' dictum that one cannot step into the same river twice is essential to maturity.

Yet this truth is not the whole story. There is, after all, much in human experience that lasts for at least a long time. Many aspects of the river are constantly reoccurring, and, in this sense, the river does continue to be the same for many years. Even more lasting is the experience of running water which I share in common with men and women of long ago and of different places and cultures today.

Contemporary science also teaches us that the astonishing variety, complexity and constant change in the natural world are the result of the interaction of deep organizing principles—basic patterning factors which make the existence of the changing phenomena possible. Change, instability, randomness and the chaotic are fundamental to existence, but so are intrinsic tendencies toward pattern, form and organization. Some scientists —and just ordinary folk as well—may emphasize the place of change or of order more in life. They may even feel that they prefer one to the other, but both are essential to all life.

Afloat on this stream are what may seem at least as astonishing as existence itself—creatures aware of life passing and changing. Human beings are capable not only of thought but of reflection on their thought, and so they realize and create past and future, story, language and responsibility. In some cases and in some measures they can themselves effect change or seek to slow or ameliorate or just understand it.

Other generations have had to deal with some astounding changes in life, but the past fifty or sixty years, particularly in the so-called industrial and informational societies, have brought a cascade of changes in technology, quantities of information, ethics and social relations which have profoundly affected, not only how people live, but how they perceive and understand themselves. Even a catalogue of such changes could easily fill several pages, but one thinks right away of radio, television, computers, automobiles and airplanes, contraception, medicine, now microbiology and soon virtual reality. More basically there has been the development, even among the less educated, toward more scientific ways of thought - the looking for causes and effects in a closed universal system. It is, after all, less than two centuries ago that some church members argued vehemently against placing lightning rods ("heretics' rods") on churches. Only a few people would even think to make this argument today.

To the list of what may seem largely positive gains, with all their complications, one must now, however, also add the intensifying threat to the environment, the dangers of overpopulation, of wars and weapons of massive destruction, and the loss or weakening, in many cases, of the extended family. While, on the one hand, a sense of mass culture grows, many are struggling to find their place in community. And beneath and as a part of all this change there has developed an increasing sense of relativism and even the deconstruction of any assuredness with regard to various forms of truth. Gone, too, for many, is the confidence in human progress which the enlightenment period once seemed to offer. So much relativism has, in turn, understandably produced various types of fundamentalist response, particularly in religion, but in other fields as well.

Every form of community and institution has been challenged by so much innovation and change. Traditional religion, due to its continuity with past events and revelation, and because of the hope it offers in truths or a reality which in some way transcends mortal vicissitudes, has experienced the challenge acutely. The Latin root of the word *religion* means to "tie" or "fasten back," and through recorded time many people have looked to religion for assurance that there are some things which do not (and, one may add, must not) change.

Yet neither is this the whole story for, along with a general conservatism, many religious groups have also shown themselves to be remarkably adaptable over the generations. Indeed, the comprehensiveness of most religions—their involvement with all aspects of life —requires this adaptability if they are to continue to speak to succeeding generations. The history of Israel throughout the biblical period is but one of the best known examples. The constancy is found in the call to worship only the God of both demanding righteousness and great mercy, but, from exodus through exile and return, with and without judges, prophets, wisdom teachers, kings and temple, the outward forms and even many of the main teachings regarding faith in God were changing and adapting.[1]

In retrospect in the study of religions one recognizes that it is often those urging and claiming continuity in life and faith who, wittingly or unwittingly, bring about many aspects of change in form but also in substance. Often, reformers do this while calling for a return to the ways of the earlier faith. But here again Heraclitus' truth cannot be escaped. Later generations will recognize that the "old ways" have, in fact, been remarkably, even ingeniously adapted to very different circumstances and understandings.[2] The several developments of the Reformation are among the best known examples of this adaptation. Much of televangelism is another striking illustration, even while it purports to present the old time religion.

Over recent decades many Christian denominations have employed a variety of strategies and approaches to change with different levels of awareness as to what they were doing. Changes have been accepted knowingly or unawares, gladly or grudgingly. Change has been vigorously opposed, while yet even the more conservative churches have found in their traditions reasons for helping to bring about changes. Some change has been seen of the devil. Some of the same changes have been seen by others to be guided by the Holy Spirit.

The governance and organization of churches obviously makes for important differences in the ways in which change is responded to. The Roman Catholic Church could respond with alacrity to the desire of many to have the Mass in their own language. The Roman Church has recently, on the other hand, been able to make clear for the foreseeable future its opposition to the ordination of women. To this one may contrast the surprising speed, by historical standards, with which women's ordination has been accepted by the majority in several branches of the Anglican Communion and, on the other hand, the many years of trial, testing and debate of revised forms of prayer books throughout the Communion. (It is interesting to note that the revisers again appealed to older forms of prayer and worship, some dating back to the second century of the Christian era, in making their changes.) Other denominations would show an even greater degree of diversity and "local option" in responding to change, regularly conditioned by response to their own cultural settings as well as traditions.

Because of its place in the complicated and interesting story of societal and religious change in recent decades, and, because of my own experience and role, I wish to reflect on aspects of change in the recent history of the Episcopal Church in the United States and more particularly on the responsibilities, challenges and opportunities of bishops within this Church. Still more specifically, I want to look at several of the ways in which the office of bishop is itself changing and at the role of bishops as agents of change as well as of continuity in faith and practice.

It is both paradoxical and ironic that the denomination long characterized as "God's frozen people" and "the Republican party on its knees" finds itself engaged with so much change and resultant controversy. Clearly it is no longer so Republican, and sometimes it even debates whether it should kneel at certain times of worship.

A story is told of a young priest, given responsibility for her first congregation, who was driven to distraction by arguments within the congregation about whether it was in the best tradition to stand or kneel for the final prayer of thanksgiving. She tried everything, including letting individuals do what they wanted, which didn't please those who thought there should be uniformity one way or the other. Finally she went to an old mentor from seminary days. "Which way," she asked plaintively, "has the most to be said in its favor? Is standing or kneeling the more traditional?"

"Both," her mentor replied, "have something to be said for them. Both have a long history behind them."

"But which," she pleaded, "is the tradition? I have to know. Otherwise they'll just go on arguing."

"That," her friend responded, "that, I'm afraid, is the tradition."

There is no doubt that controversy over change has caused some people to leave the Episcopal Church. Interestingly, however, actual Sunday attendance has increased over the past twenty years, and there is evidence that a number of churchgoers and potential churchgoers appreciate congregations where significant issues can be discussed in ways that will bring insight and understanding. At least many people want to hear and talk about fairness, intimacy, love, forgiveness, justice, duty, community and responsibility, although Wade Clark Roof notes the irony that these discussions are more often found in church basements on week nights and weekends (in twelve step groups and various classes, support, sharing and peace and justice groups) than they are upstairs on a Sunday morning - thus creating a "kind of ecclesiastical upstairs and downstairs."[3] What people are clearly much less interested in are squabbles over standing or kneeling, turf battles and name calling. What they evidently will respond to are communities of sufficient trust and care, where, although voices may be raised out of deep concern and conviction, they will not find themselves or their own efforts to be faithful belittled.

Many Christians are evidently more understanding than they may be given credit for of the very real tension between a desire for an unchanging, objective morality and the awareness that codes of ethics are regularly shaped and should be shaped by circumstances. They recognize, for example, that practices which may be good and of benefit to an agricultural community may not have the same purpose or value in a crowded metropolis. They can also see that controversy is hardly new to the church—that it is, in fact, of the warp and woof of the Bible: Should we go back to Egypt? Should Israel have a king, a temple, welcome strangers, use military means? Should taxes be paid? Can one be wealthy and be a Christian? What should be done with a sinful member of the community? On what terms could gentiles become Christians? How is Scripture to be interpreted? And so on and on. A number of contemporary disciples may also rightly at least suspect that it has been in times of great change and controversy that the church has often grown.

"I am not afraid of the words 'crisis' and 'tension,'" maintained Martin Luther King, Jr. "I deeply oppose violence, but constructive crisis and tension are necessary for growth. Innate in all life, and all growth, is tension."[4] Peace at any price may have its seeming attractions, but it is finally not the biblical shalom of the richness of community, trust and growth. "We do not speak of politics or religion here," was said to be the password at certain upper-crust clubs. At least a large number of people recognize that such would not be the hallmark of a church reflecting the concerns and attitudes of the Bible, and that vigorous thought and discussion are signs of health, not trouble.

All this being recognized, it is, however, also true that most churches are, even at their best, only approximations of communities of such trust and care, and that we live in a now highly individualized society in which building and sustaining any community is never easy. The task is compounded by a suspicion of institutions and of forms of authority which make it difficult for people, however much they long for a sense of belonging, to make commitments to and with others. The so-called left and right of United States politics (often reflected in more than guided by contemporary church values) are strongly motivated by a libertarianism of either personal or economic rights which makes it difficult to espouse the rights and needs of all members of the society together. This is particularly evident in basic and critical issues such as health care and environmental sustainability. The Christian understanding of freedom as freedom, not to do what everyone pleases, but to be freed from the self-absorption of sin in order to serve God and others freely, is harder than ever to teach in the churches. Meanwhile, the pace of change seems relentless and often further disintegrating of a sense of common life.

All this, of course, presents great opportunities as well as challenges for faith communities and denominations. While it is somewhat less difficult and often best to respond to these challenges through individual congregations, responses only at this level could also lead to a further fragmentation of church and society. Yet, given the times and challenges, how does one offer leadership for the broader church in ways of worship, mission, teaching about common values and virtues, and in service to others?

Bishops, while far from the only leaders in the churches, have been given vital roles in the church catholic and apostolic and in the Church which calls itself Episcopal (from the Greek word for bishop, the older meaning of which is often translated "overseer"). The monepiscopate or office of a single bishop as the leading liturgical, teaching and administrative figure in a local area did not develop uniformly in the early church, but by the third century it had begun to be the pattern almost everywhere Christianity was known.[5] As the chief presider at the Eucharist, as foremost preacher and teacher, with pastoral and organizational responsibilities, and in the key role of ordainer of others, bishops have continued to be central to the catholic church's life and work.

Particularly in times of stress, but in ordinary times as well, the bishop has been seen as a personal sign of unity and continuity in the life of the church. This unity is, first of all, with Christ and in the Body of Christ in that unity with God which Jesus offers and to which he calls all disciples in John 17. One knows that one is in communion with others in the particular community of faith and with those in the wider body by being in communion with the bishop. This role has given and gives to the bishop a special servant responsibility to reach out and be in communion with all those who can be joined in communion, whatever their situation and however their views may differ. It is part of a bishop's pastoral calling to let other voices be heard, especially the voices of those who are in any way marginalized in the church or society, by himself or herself listening to them and sometimes speaking for them.

The sense of a bishop and of bishops together as expressive of the unity of the church past and future and as bearers and continuers of the apostolic faith has always had more to do with the continuity of community and teaching than any mechanical sense of the passing on of this apostolicity through the laying on of hands.[6] But the connection of hands came after time to be an outward sign of this continuity.

The importance of the personal character of the office should not be underemphasized. However much the church may need to be an institution for its unity and continuity, it is first a community of persons seeking to love and serve its Lord Jesus. Although there is a strain of teaching which views authority in the church as passing along a kind of hierarchical chain from God to Christ to the first apostles and then their successors as bishops, and through them in given times to priests, deacons and (if any authority be left over) to the laity, the older and more biblical model is that of the body of Christ. Among and through the body of Christ's followers the Holy Spirit of Jesus inspires community service and raises up certain functions and offices for the life and direction of the organic whole. Because of its importance for the unity and continuity of the body, and in service to the whole, the office of bishops is given the distinction of visible historical continuation.

These traditional understandings of the office of bishop have not meant, however, that roles and actual ways of functioning have not varied considerably over the years. The scope, authority and duties of the ministry have adapted to internal changes in the church and the culture, the relationship with the secular authority and with the models of that authority as emulated by the church. They have sometimes been expressed through the externals of the office and at other times depended more on the personal authority of the particular individual holding the office. The size of the diocese in relation with other dioceses and with other episcopal authorities was and is another important influence. In recent years advances in means of transportation and communication as well as many of the complexities of modern life, including legal, fiduciary and insurance responsibilities, have had their effect on the exercise of the office.

Particularly of interest for our purposes is the understanding of the role and authority of bishops in Anglicanism. While one finds a considerable variety of emphasis, the churches of the Anglican Communion see the authority of bishops as being exercised with the whole community of faith in their diocese. Thus Anglicanism speaks of the "bishop in synod" or the "bishop in convention," signaling that the bishop is to act on important issues always in conjunction with a group representing all the people of God in a given area.[7] When working effectively together, this collaboration should enable the bishop to act and speak authoritatively for the body, and, of equal importance, strengthen the bishop's ability to guarantee and support the authority and ministries of all disciples. The fact that in the Episcopal Church bishops (this is true of suffragan bishops as well)[8] are elected by majority votes of the clergy and a wide representation of the laity acting in concert should, at least in theory, add to the authority of the bishops to speak and act for the community.

One says "in theory" because there are today, of course, a number of factors mitigating this authority and its actualization in the power of bishops. Chief among them may be the tendency in present society to at least modulate any voice seeking to speak on behalf of the larger community's interests, particularly if it seems to conflict with the perceived rights of individuals. To this is added the general suspicion of any "authority" in our society. Many of the present generation of lay and clergy leaders were, after all, raised and, in many cases, went to college when "Question Authority" was the most popular bumper sticker.[9] And then bishops are also, of course, imperfect and, along with other church leaders, have given enough poor examples of integrity and leadership to fuel the desire to ask "Who do you think you are?" or "Why should I?"

Limitation on the authority of bishops is in no small measure supported by the interpretation of the power of the office of bishop in the Canons or church law. On this point a historical perspective on the Episcopal Church in the United States is of value, recalling that it was not until after the Revolutionary War that this Church had resident bishops. Up until that time bishops had been important for little else than their authority to ordain clergy in England for the Church in the United States. Vestries, meanwhile, had learned to exercise considerable independent authority and power which they were later reluctant to limit.

After the war against England, there was also the memory of certain eighteenth century English "prelate" bishops, figures of considerable secular power, not always with matching pastoral care and faith. One result of this suspicion of bishops was substantial debate as to whether bishops were necessary for the life of the church. Even if they were, it was felt that there was good reason to be sure they never got out of hand. Then, too, many of the lay leaders of the church had just finished helping to draft the Constitution of the United States. They were believers in checks and balances.

The effects of these attitudes and beliefs, encoded in canon law, are still today to give to local congregations, acting through their vestries, considerable autonomy in the effective operation of the congregation, other than directly in matters liturgical, reserved for the rector. This arrangement has many positive benefits. It offers considerable flexibility and scope for local knowledge, initiative and ministry. As with any system, it also has its potential downsides. Even though elected, the vestry may become an inner group out of touch with the larger congregation. Although rectors are given tenure with election, they may find themselves in ambiguous positions if their relationships with their vestries are not good. Then they might wish that their bishop had more power in relation to vestries and congregations.

In other cases vestries will cede much of their responsibility and authority to rectors who may then feel little responsibility to either bishop or vestry, but only to their congregation and ministry more generally as they interpret it.

At its best this sharing of authority and responsibility can lead to productive collaboration between bishops (representing the larger church), vestries and clergy. This is congregationalism doing well for the mission of the church. When not operating effectively it can, however, lead to a narrower congregationalism, unnecessary competition over resources, and clergy with little commitment to acting with and on behalf of their bishop as he or she tries to speak and act for the larger body.[10]

This division or sharing of authority and responsibility is sometimes spoken of in Anglicanism and the Episcopal Church as "dispersed authority." With its virtues in its call for mutual responsibility and accountability, and in its comprehension of various voices and different experiences, this "untidiness" yet sometimes leaves those looking for clearer lines of authority in the life of the church a bit mystified. Since it has its counterpart in the national church (the House of Bishops being required in most matters to act in concert, meeting every three years, with the House of Deputies of clergy and lay representatives) there is a natural bias which makes it difficult to act with rapidity or singleness of voice when responding to change and new opportunities. It has led to such jocular commentary as the response to the individual who claims not to have much interest in organized religion. "Well," the response goes, "have you tried the Episcopal Church?"

And there is still another important area of "dispersed authority." While many branches of Christianity emphasize the interactive roles of Scripture, tradition and reason along with experience as the bases for their authority to teach and act, some are able to speak more univocally than others. It may be the Bible (which they hold not to be interpreting or to need interpretation), or tradition (in the Roman Catholic Church interpreted into ecclesiology in the magisterium of the Church) or reason (as, for example, in the Unitarian Church) which helps give them this authority. Traditional Anglicanism, however, while giving a central place and precedence to Scripture, has insisted on the importance of a complex and ongoing interrelationship with tradition and with reason understood to include contemporary experience.[11] The situation is made more complex and profound by the recognition of both the necessity and importance of interpreting Scripture and of the limitations of human reason. Add to this the modern awareness that tradition is not an unchanging body of lore and information. Just as we now read American history rather differently than was done in decades past, so in recent years women and others whose predecessors might at first not seem to have played that great a role in the Bible or tradition have helped bring a hearing of other voices within tradition. It is also in this context that room is made both for the teaching and values of the community and the rights of the informed, individual conscience.[12]

"Dispersed authority," rapid change and the anti-communitarianism of contemporary society offer challenges to a bishop's authority to act and be a responsible agent for the church in dealing with the change in the culture and the church. Yet, at the same time, I believe it is also true that bishops have a remarkable degree of power which they should responsibly recognize and exercise along with potential for considerable capability to effect and affect change.

Beware of those in authority who say they feel powerless! Bishops, in fact, have a frightening degree of what might be seen as "negative power" in the church. Rather easily they can keep things from happening. Such power can, of course, be helpful if something wrong would otherwise take place, but it can also lead to much inaction and many opportunities missed. In many cases all a bishop has to do to exercise this "negative power" is to look the other way, be preoccupied or tired. The polity of a diocese is such that the office of bishop can easily form a kind of bottleneck. What cannot get through, at least in many cases, will not happen.

There is no single way to deal with what in many cases may be unintended obstructiveness. Perhaps first and of most importance, a bishop should recognize and be candid about this kind of institutional power. A second response, however, should not be to try to redouble one's efforts. Most bishops are busy enough, and more time at work would be counter-productive. Standing back and analyzing priorities can be helpful in order to try to give more time to significant tasks. Likely of more value is finding more ways to share authority and responsibility for initiatives and for the development of the human and material resources to deal with them, sometimes in collaboration with people of other denominations, faiths and of good will. There is enormous talent among laity and clergy for which bishops may provide forms of leadership, or, at other times, work alongside of, or stand aside of in order to let this talent develop new approaches.

With other clergy (and similar to leaders in other professions) bishops, for the most part, are no longer listened to or followed simply by virtue of office and degrees held. They will be expected to show an integrity of life (of word and action) that goes with the profession of their office and to demonstrate the effectiveness of their learning.[13] No human being can do this other than imperfectly, but when performed with courage and humility as part of a servant ministry, the authentic authorization of a bishop to speak and act from and with the body of Christ and its tradition can be very helpful for many within and beyond the church.

It can be particularly helpful in dealing with change. There is tension in the expectation that one will be both a defender of a historical faith and an innovator, but, because a bishop is a personal symbol of continuity, a bishop can be expected to try to see some new idea, opportunity or problem in the light of the ongoing tradition. And, as we have seen, because the bishop is called to be a personal symbol of unity, the bishop should frequently reach out to hear many voices in a time of change, particularly of those who otherwise might feel shut out or passed by.

The exercise of such comprehensive roles could be seen leading to a kind of paralysis, but there is, in fact, scope for considerable creativity in bringing together old wisdom and new learning, revelation and insight, and listening to a variety of perspectives. The novel is neither accepted uncritically nor rejected outright as being apart from God's truth. A contemporary natural law, for example, teaches that things which are different, or even seemingly odd and "unnatural" often have an essential place along with the normative in ongoing life and creativity. Courage is called for in making space for this, and in accepting and making use of change that must come, and in seeking out change which will benefit the church and society.

I shall always remember the ancient city of Oxford in England when I first visited there in 1955. The city streets were choked and its buildings being ruined by the exhaust from cars and heavy vehicles. The city "fathers," unwilling to make any changes to Oxford or its environs were, in fact, allowing the city to be radically and sadly transformed. Only when the ring road was finally built was Oxford able to continue a more traditional process of growth and development.

A strong teacher and prophet is called to help a city or a church see what is happening to it. A prophet often helps us to see what we otherwise might not wish to see—what is happening, for instance, to a church which is so "adult" in many of its practices and use of resources that it too often gives little more than lip service to ministries with children and teenagers. A prophet enables us to see what is happening to a city where more than a quarter of its youth are growing up in poverty. A prophet helps us to define what is most significant, to shape the important questions, and calls us to change what must be changed by those who hunger and thirst for more fairness in this life.

In this teaching and prophetic role the bishop, as one regularly engaged in prayer and prayer's discernment with others, is also a steward and pastor of hope and ultimate trust in the God of the resurrection. In his poem "Ash Wednesday" T.S. Eliot offers one of the shortest and most heartfelt of prayers: "Teach us to care and not to care." It is not, the poet asks, that we are sometimes to care and at other times not. Rather, in the face of the world's wrong and suffering, one continues to trust God's ultimate goodness. Thus, when others might be forced to despair or apathy, Christian carelessness enables one to keep on praying and caring.

Reinhold Niebuhr shared a similar hard-headed faith when he wrote, "Nothing that is worth doing can be achieved in our lifetime; therefore we must be saved by hope. Nothing which is true or beautiful or good makes complete sense in any immediate context of history; therefore we must be saved by faith. Nothing we do, however virtuous, can be accomplished alone; therefore we must be saved by love. No virtuous act is quite as virtuous from the standpoint of our friend or foe as it is from our standpoint. Therefore we must be saved by the final form of love which is forgiveness."[14] In the face of all life's frustrations and challenges the bishop responds by asking the people how they, by God's grace, can live better together and what they are capable of doing for others. While this vision of a fairer, more truthful and compassionate society will never be fully realized in this life, it is of the essence of faith to hope and to seek opportunity and blessing with God for others as well as ourselves.

Complicated as it is by the modern pace of change, the prophetic, teaching task of a bishop can still be seen as seeking to set forth the essentials of the hope and faith which are believed to be always true of God's relationship with us in ways which will reach out to a changing world. Such a well considered theology allows for diversity and even ferment along with creativity and fertility in theological understanding and the life of the church.[15] This teaching mission will regularly have its complexities and not be without controversy. It calls for understanding and care for those who are finding change difficult. Nor is it ever easy fully to agree on what the essentials are and what must accompany them from the past for their correct interpretation. Nor is it easy to agree on the forms and ways which may legitimately be used in the present life of faith.

This is in large measure what the debates over issues involving sexuality are about. Beginning in 1930 and again in 1958 the Anglican Communion rather boldly held that contraception was not only legitimate but could become a way of helping to fulfill God's purposes. Not all Anglicans or members of other churches have agreed with that teaching. Now also many other aspects of the "sexual revolution," good and bad, can be seen, but the decision was a prayerful effort to seek to live faithfully and responsibly before God.

This collective way of reflecting theologically and of teaching in a time of change is another essential aspect of episcopal ministry, but it is one hard to enact in the complex life of the Episcopal Church, and all but impossible to perform for the worldwide body of Christians. Nonetheless, it remains true that a bishop never teaches alone. Even if bishops think they are doing this, they are always affected by and affecting the collegium - the larger body. They speak for the church as well as to the church. In this sense there is one episcopate and each bishop is not just part of that whole, but in one way or another, an expression of it.[16]

This awareness of collegial responsibility could also be understood and applied so as to lead to inertia and a lack of boldness and courage in theology and in our dealings with change and opportunity in our time. It need not, however, mean that bishops must always speak with but one voice. Such full consensus may rarely be possible. Bishops should, nonetheless, not only be looking for common understanding, but for all the ways they can do theological reflection together and in touch with one another. This can still enable them, as explorers of the breadth of God's reality, and especially as those seeking to know and follow the ways of justice and mercy, to take on together any number of issues.

I believe that the House of Bishops of the Episcopal Church had made some progress in this regard. It is true that things got a mite out-of-hand at the 1991 General Convention in Phoenix. It was nothing like the British House of Commons, but voices were raised and a few names called. The issue at the time was homosexuality, as it seems to be with some regularity in recent years. Some bishops did not want it to be discussed at all. Some bishops seemed to be fearful, perhaps for good reason; many people are concerned and restive. Threats regarding the withdrawal of money are part of the fear.

So several bishops were called "unscriptural" and others were "homophobic." There were grumblings about "liberals" who were following the spirit of the age. Probably even "un-Christian" was muttered a few times. As in any group there are some, shall we say, strong personalities who seemed to be making allusions to older battles and grudges. Still it was nothing like the remarks that were shouted at one another, often we are told by groups of bishops in chorus, at the Councils of Ephesus during the fifth century Christological controversies. Talk about dysfunctional!

I believe we have now made some progress in the Diocese of Los Angeles and in other dioceses and congregations with regard to issues of sexuality. We have done this through people meeting people, with prayer, with education and discussion, trying better to clarify what the real issues are and to shine gospel light on them. We strive together to understand how we are to be faithful and responsible, and how we are to educate and guide our children to be intelligent, disciplined, compassionate and respectful of others. I'm proud of the way many disciples have handled themselves, even while sometimes continuing to disagree. We have had to realize that the issues are not always easy to talk about, and that they often involve deep feelings more than intellectual positions as such—concerns with families, fairness and justice, the character of biblical authority, and the future of the church and society.

We have had to recognize that the issues are genuinely complex and that, whatever resolutions or canons are passed in the future, the concerns will likely be with us for our lifetime. We had best, then, find ways to live with them with as much understanding as we can muster. As one woman recently said to me, "If we can learn to talk honestly with each other about this, then that means we can talk about anything." We reckon that this in itself could be quite a witness to the rest of society and that God may often care more about how we deal with one another than with specific stances we take. Not a few passages in the Bible seem to indicate that fairly strongly. And, as someone astutely observed, most of us are more right in life about what we affirm than what we deny.

There is also a deep concern and desire to remember that there are other gospel imperatives to which we should also be giving our best time and creativity. We do not want to be stuck on one issue.

A frustration with being stuck was, no doubt, bothering the bishops in Phoenix. Also it was hot in the desert in July. Still it now seems a mistake for the bishops to have withdrawn into executive session. Hindsight, of course, is easy, but even at the time there seemed something a bit comic about it. The press was naturally irked and soon we had archdeacons, acting like FBI agents, crawling around looking for tape recorders hidden in brief cases.

The House of Deputies was even more irked, and rightly so. We are, after all, both public bodies at General Convention, and the Deputies could claim no such executive privilege, even if they had wanted to do so. The Deputies, moreover, perhaps helped by their greater size and the need for more regulation, had shown themselves more capable of discussing issues heatedly without losing their cool.

What Presiding Bishop Browning was particularly astute about, and what the bishops did do right, was to agree to meet in special sessions over the next three years at Camp Kanuga. It quickly became apparent that the frustration level, especially among a number of the newer bishops, was high. The House of Bishops is sometimes compared to the U.S. Senate, but senators live and work in the same town through much of the year. Many of the bishops, up at least to their pectoral crosses in alligators in their own dioceses, hardly know the other bishops. There at Kanuga, with time to worship together, pass the potatoes to a colleague one had just argued with, with time to talk more freely and intimately in small table groups, a number of stereotypes began to fall away. There were nice opportunities just to swap ideas about the hard work of bishoping.

Some of the fruits of this kind of meeting were borne out at the regular meeting in Baltimore in September of 1992. There, using papers written from differing perspectives, the bishops devoted three days to discussing the authority and interpretation of the Bible—a matter that had been contentious, particularly in relation to passages dealing with homosexuality. Despite differences of emphases, the bishops found themselves in a good deal of agreement with respect to central matters of biblical theology.[17] The Pastoral Letter on Racism and the Study on Sexuality, despite the continuing contention around some of the issues, recently put forth at the 1994 Indianapolis Convention are additional useful examples of this process.[18]

Many of us have come away from these several sessions with a sense of the strength that is in the House of Bishops. My own obvious modesty aside, it is a remarkable group, led by a wise and courageous Presiding Bishop. As with any group, there are , of course, individual problems from time to time, and we grow more diverse too slowly, but the experience, the wisdom, the time spent at prayer and the individual courage of these men and women are a regular encouragement to me. Despite all the tough problems of church and society today, I recognize how much good is being done in their dioceses, congregations and institutions.

There are ways, however, in which this awareness only adds to the frustration. Although to some degree restricted by the care the House of Bishops must take to move in legislative areas only when meeting together with the House of Deputies, the bishops ought to be offering more informed leadership on the great issues and concerns of our time: health care, our severely distressed environment, overpopulation, our wretched penal system, refugees and immigrants, gross economic imbalances and injustice, racism at home and ethnic wars abroad, violence in our society—particularly against women and children, sexism, the need for stronger educational programs for adults and children in our churches (what more we might do with so many astute disciples if they had a more profound grasp of biblical theology, of prayer, and their spiritual heritage!), all our work with youth, the education of parents and the support of families, stronger and more thoughtful forms of renewal and evangelism, better support for laity in their ministries beyond the congregation, our relationship with other world religions, the privatization of religion and the problems created by exaggerated individualism and the dualism of the material and the spiritual in this age, and the great theological issues of this and every time—suffering and evil and how we may better understand the ways God is present to our lives. The House of Bishops needs to look at better structures, a different allocation of resources, and be making better use of our Church's theologians for these purposes.

Yet at least we have begun a number of these tasks and, when one looks at previous Pastoral letters and study documents of the House of Bishops and many resolutions from the General Conventions, one recognizes how many issues have been taken on, at least in preliminary ways. What is then also needed are ways of bringing more of this reflection and discussion to the congregations.

When Rembert Weakland, the remarkable Archbishop of Milwaukee, visited the Convention in Phoenix, he noted that he had in the past viewed Episcopalians as a sort of bridge church between Protestants and Catholics. He was kind enough to compliment us for our efforts toward comprehensiveness. But then he went on to say that he was surprised at the vigor with which we had taken up tough and controversial issues, especially involving inclusion, in a way his church had not. He said he now thought of us as a group of ecclesiastical green berets. I was reminded of how often Archbishop William Temple told Anglicans that they were not the whole of the Church, but that they had distinctive contributions to make to the universal Church.

Probably no one wants, however, to be green berets all the time. Yet I think Archbishop Weakland was telling us that we have a lot more going for us than we sometimes give ourselves credit for. We are, after all, living through decades of enormous change. Tremendous sociological, economic and environmental pressures have led many of us again to the awareness that quality of life must be measured in more than material ways. Communities of faith have great opportunities to be a conserving and creative force in society, but only if they will faithfully and honestly participate in its challenges and changes.

There are at least a number of people who want a faith which recognizes the complexity and the ambiguities as well as tragedies of life. They are expectant of a faith which is less concerned with definitive answers to life's questions, particularly answers which could preclude the moral probing and testing of their readiness to love and to care—and more concerned with what they believe to be important for a living faith. The biblical faith for which they long is concerned with relationship with God and with a sense of belonging in this world and opportunities for purposiveness and ministry. It is a faith which will bring assurance and a passion for faithful living, but which also knows mystery and a modesty in knowledge about God as it worships in poetry, song and sacrament. Too much religious certainty, this faith realizes, can be a human way of shutting God out of life. "To recognize our own uncertainties," T.S. Eliot wrote, "can be a mark of realism and humility, and can make us in the end more willing to acknowledge the great but mysterious certainties of God."[19] This is a faith of memory and preserving, but it is even more directed to the future in hope. It is this orientation which challenges and calls its leaders and all disciples to look for God's spirit and ultimate purpose also acting in the many changes of life.

Notes

1. On this call to worship only the God of justice and mercy through all the changes of religion in the Bible, see Paul Hanson, *The People Called: The Growth of Community in the Bible* (San Francisco: Harper & Row, 1986).

2. Max Weber was one of the earlier sociologists of religion who particularly emphasized the historical role of religion as a source of change as well as conservatism. See his *The Sociology of Religion* (1922; reprinted Boston: Beacon Press, 1963).

3. In Wade Clerk Roof, *A Generation of Seekers: The Spiritual Journey of the Baby Boom Generation* (San Francisco: Harper & Row, 1993), 210-11.

4. In *A Testament of Hope: The Essential Writings of Martin Luther King, Jr.* ed., James M. Washington (San Francisco: Harper & Row, 1986), 350.

5. See the discussion by J. Robert Wright, "Origins of the Episcopate and Episcopal Ministry in the Early Church," pp. 10-32, and Mark Dyer, "Theological Reflections on the Patristic Development of Episcopal Ministry," pp. 33-43, in *On Being a Bishop: Papers on Episcopacy from the Moscow Consultation 1992*, ed. J. Robert Wright (New York: Church Hymnal Corporation, 1993). See also *Episcopal Ministry: The Report of the Archbishops' Group on the Episcopate 1990* (London: Church House Publishing, 1990), pp. 13-38.

6. On continuity through the episcopate, see Richard A. Norris, "Bishops, Succession and the Apostolicity of the Church," in *On Being a Bishop* (ed. Wright), pp. 52-62. See also his essay "Episcopacy," in *The Study of Anglicanism*, ed. Stephen W. Sykes and John Booty (Minneapolis: Fortress Press, 1988), 296-309.

7. Cf. K. S. Chittleborough, "Towards a Theology and Practice of Bishops in Synod," in *Authority in the Anglican Communion: Essays Presented to Bishop John Howe*, ed. Stephen W. Sykes (Toronto: Anglican Book Centre, 1987), 144-62; and the brief discussion in *Belonging Together: A Study Document of the Inter-Anglican Theological and Doctrinal Consultation 1992* (London: The Anglican Communion Secretariat), 24-25.

8. A number of aspects of the office and ministry of episcopacy discussed in this essay

apply to the ministries of suffragan and assistant bishops as well as extensions of the diocesan episcopal office, but I have concentrated on the ministry of diocesan bishop.

9. Stressed by Roof at several points in *Generation of Seekers.*

10. Richard F. Grein notes the tension which can result when "responsibility and expectations placed on the office are not matched by a resultant canonical authority" (p. 65) in "Introducing 'The Ministry of Bishops: A Study Document Authorized by the House of Bishops of the Episcopal Church,'" in *On Being a Bishop* (ed. Wright), pp. 63-77.

11. See my discussion in "All Things Necessary to Salvation," in *Anglicanism and the Bible,* ed. Frederick H. Borsch (Wilton, Conn: Morehouse Barlow, 1984), 203-27.

12. See the discussion by H. R. McAdoo, "Authority in the Church: Spiritual Freedom and the Corporate Nature of Faith," in *Authority in the Anglican Communion* (ed. Sykes), 69-93.

13. The differences between the authority of office and degree, on the one hand, and of an authentic piety and demonstrated ability to teach are discussed by Jackson Carroll in *As One with Authority* (Louisville: Westminster /John Knox), 57-58.

14. Reinhold Niebuhr, *The Irony of American History* (New York: Charles Scribners' Sons, 1952), 63.

15. Cf. the discussion by Ian G. Barbour on pp. 60-62, 66 and at other points in his *Religion in an Age of Science,* (The Gifford Lectures 1989-91, Vol.1-San Francisco: Harper & Row, 1990).

16. See J. Robert Wright, quoting Cyprian, in *On Being a Bishop* (ed. Wright), p. 29.

17. The papers, with an introduction describing the process and a study guide, are available as *The Bible's Authority in Today's Church,* ed. Frederick H. Borsch (Philadelphia: Trinity Press International, 1993).

18. Further on sexuality issues, see Frederick H. Borsch, *Christian Discipleship and Sexuality* (Cincinnati: Forward Movement, 1993).

19. T.S. Eliot, *The Dynamic of Tradition* (London: Faber & Faber), 58.

Centennial

A centennial can make us a little giddy as we are asked to look backward and then turn forward, followed by further references to the past and then future hopes. We give thanks and seek to draw strength from the faith and accomplishments of those who have come before us so that they may help us look forward with renewed commitment and vision.

As a people enmeshed in our time we cannot really escape this turning about and the limits of these horizons, but for a moment, with eyes of faith, rise up with me. What do you see?

I believe we can see the communion of saints. We "believe in the communion of saints," we often say. We believe not only that this community in which we remain in communion with one another exists but we believe in—that is, we put our trust in it. In the life of God we do not forget and are not forgotten. In the life of God and in the body of Christ we carry with us all the good as well as the evil endured and the pain and suffering and faithfulness and compassion of those who have come before us. And they carry us with them. So we believe—we lead our lives of faith—in the communion of saints.

In this communion in this centennial time we have many stories to tell. Some are better known than others. Some are remembered in the wider community—others in their churches. Some are more clearly heroic. Others tell of those who lived their faith and made their contributions in quieter ways.

In these stories we see and we can hear vestries meeting, churches being built, readers reading and musicians singing. God, wild and wondrous, is thanked and praised. The sick and the elderly are visited, children and older disciples educated. Sins are forgiven. The troubled are counseled and new friends given hope and faith because of Jesus. Schools are founded and a hospital. Here there are programs for neighborhood youth and their families, there a home for abused children. So much of this founding and building and caring is done by lay persons—especially lay women and deaconesses. Outreach and ministry to seamen is established, and a place for those recovering from addictions, and homes for the elderly. There is a medical clinic for children and their mothers, food pantries and thrift shops, after school programs and learning centers. Camps are created. Generous hearts give regularly and faithfully in thanksgiving for the church's ministries. New missions are begun and more churches are built along with low cost housing and homes for persons with AIDS and a Cathedral for worship and service and hospitality, where young people who have had problems can finish high school and where more families are counseled and supported. People from all over the world come to Los Angeles and our churches. Missionaries are sent abroad to share the gospel and teach and establish a program for handicapped children. The homeless are sheltered and abused women harbored. New priests and deacons are educated. Chaplaincies to colleges, hospitals and prisons are developed along with a new comprehensive venture for the area youth and a credit union which can make loans in low-wealth communities.

And all along, amid wars, depression, civil upheaval and earthquakes, there are secretaries and salespersons, and doctors and nurses and teachers and business leaders, fire fighters, police, carpenters, mothers and fathers, brothers and sisters, godparents and grandparents, aunts and uncles who, strengthened in their communities of faith, go about their daily work and ministries seeking to be honest and caring and faithful and to love their neighbors as themselves.

It is, of course, far from a perfect church. Too many stories—and even some of the best stories—are scarred by racism and its results, by sexism and toleration of gross economic disparity and disadvantage. But then, again, prophetic voices are raised and action taken for greater understanding, fairness and compassion. One cannot hear these many stories without learning of saints—people of dedication and devotion called together by God to holiness.

Even from this perspective, it is hard, however, to see one hundred years forward. Yet I think I can catch a glimpse of a great gathering of disciples in similar celebration. I hear them rehearsing your stories, giving thanks for you and asking for your encouragement in the communion of saints.

It is easier to look forward another five or so years, and on into the beginning of the next millennium, and to see ourselves called—in our new and challenging circumstances—to many like tasks of sharing hope and building communities of faith and service. This, we can be sure, is the vision God wants us to have for ourselves as God's people. Our times may seem to us, as they are often described, to be a more mean-spirited age, dominated by consumerism and with less sense of community responsibility and caring.

But in every generation the churches of the Lord Jesus have had to confront apathy and meanness from within as well as without. It is now our challenge and opportunity, drawing strength from holy women and men past and present, to go forward as reconciling and healing communities. Guided by our three priorities of ministries for and with all our youth, an evangelical and welcoming multiculturalism, and education in the faith, we are to be the adelante, welcoming and going-forward people.

Knowing ourselves forgiven and accepted, we, in the power of God's sanctifying Spirit, are to be the builders and prophets, the pure in heart, the merciful and the compassionate in the years to come in the communion of saints.

Many Ways of Eucharist

Many things happen during the Eucharist. The people gather. This is not what is done individually but as a community. It is *common* prayer. Nor is this *common-unity* a coming together we fashion by ourselves. It is because we recognize ourselves to be equally accepted, forgiven and loved by God that we can come together equally in unity. In God's love we are also linked with those who have come before us and those who will follow in the body of Christ.

Re-presenting Christ to us and representing all of us before God, the celebrant of the Eucharist does certain representative acts. But this is not a performance. We are all together ministers of this sacrament. And so we pray together for purity of heart and mind. We praise God and collect our lives and prayers together in the collect of the day.

We then listen to the stories and teachings of our faith. These are the stories common to us all which help to shape us into a people reflecting the holiness of the God of justice and mercy. Moving through the liturgical year - from advent expectation, Christmas presence, the epiphany stories of our Lord's ministry, lenten fasting and discipline, through Easter joy to the outpouring of the Spirit, saints' days and regular time - these are stories of Adam and Eve, of Cain and Abel, Noah, Abraham and Sarah, Isaac and Jacob, Joseph and his brothers, Moses, Miriam, Ruth and Esther, Sarah, David, Bathsheba, Solomon, Amos, Micah, Isaiah, Jeremiah and Ezekiel, of prophets, kings and judges, of exodus, exile and return, of wisdom and temple worship, of a child's humble birth, meals shared, of lost sheep, dinner parties, times of sowing and reaping, the good Samaritan and the prodigal son, of healings and controversy, of betrayal, passion and death, and of new life on the roads to Emmaus and Damascus.

The stories are often about struggle—between order and chaos, freedom and slavery, justice and injustice, chance and providence, life and death. Amid suffering and evil they tell of hope and victories of the power of God's righteousness and love.

And we respond with psalm and canticle. We respond in the words of the preacher and in our thoughts and reflections. We think of our own lives, challenges and hopes. We reflect on stories of our own forgiveness and healing and how we are called to serve God within the complexities and opportunities of our time.

We respond, too, by praying for ourselves and others—for a more just and peaceful world, for the church, its missions and all its ministers, including each of us. We pray for our country, for our community and all leaders and representatives of our government, for the healing and sustainability of the land, water and air, for the aged and the sick, for all who suffer or who are in any trouble, for the unemployed, prisoners and refugees, for those who are lonely and without hope. We pray for those who care for others, who speak and act in care and for fairness, and we ask to share in these ministries. We pray for those who have died. We ask for the forgiveness of our sins, and we know again the power of our belonging with God and one another.

So we share with one another the peace of the Lord. This is God's peace which is far more than tranquility or the absence of difficulties. It is the peace of trust and forgiveness and belonging, the fullness of compassion and service and ministry.

In the context of the Eucharist we from time to time baptize and renew our own baptismal covenant. We confirm disciples in their faith and in various forms of ministry and service. We celebrate new ministries and ordain. We consecrate churches and bless homes. We marry, anoint the sick and at our end have our lives offered to God's undying love in thanksgiving and hope.

After we share the peace, we bring before God bread and wine as Jesus first offered them with his disciples. We give thanks for food and drink and all that sustains life - for those who grow and prepare and market them. We offer our gifts of money, and perhaps of food and other things, to carry forward the mission of the Church and to assist others. We give sacrificially and gladly in thanksgiving for all we have been given.

Here and again we may sing in thanksgiving and praise. We lift up our hearts and join with angels and archangels and all the company of heaven in the ancient hymn: "Holy, holy, holy...heaven and earth are full of your glory." In the churches of the west we sense the company of heaven coming to gather with us around our altar. In the eastern churches there is more a sense of all the people being gathered up into the praise of eternity.

We bless and praise the One who comes in the name of the Lord as we ready for our recognition of Christ's special presence among us.

We offer praise for creation and for God's continued presence with God's people. And now we especially recall the life, death and new life of

Jesus—Jesus offering himself, reconciling us. We remember the night he was handed over to suffering and death and how he gave thanks for the bread, broke it and gave it to his disciples. "This is my body, which is given for you." And then also the wine, "my blood of the new covenant...shed for you and for many for the forgiveness of sins." We do this in remembrance of him.

In response we proclaim "the mystery of faith"—that Christ had died, is risen and will come again. He also comes again in this Eucharist which anticipates the time of fulfillment of God's purposes for God's world and people.

Remembering Christ's death, resurrection and ascension we offer these gifts, and we offer ourselves, asking the sanctifying power of the Holy Spirit of our Creator and Redeemer God upon them and upon us. We ask that we may faithfully receive them and that we may serve God in unity, constancy and peace now and in the age to come.

Together we say the prayer that Jesus taught us and in awe and thanksgiving receive with the wine this bread for which we pray (part of "our daily bread," or, as the words also imply, "the bread of the coming day") which is our greatest need and joy. Mystically and mysteriously Jesus shares in our life and we in his in communion with God and with one another.

The elements are the self-giving life of Jesus. The bread and wine are the outward and visible signs of his body and blood given for us. The words "covenant" and "poured out" remind us that this sacrifice happened once at passover time, but help us also to realize that God is always giving of the divine life—never apart from the suffering of created life.

We call this celebration Eucharist (from the Greek word for thanksgiving) because in it Jesus gave thanks and because in it we offer our thanksgiving and praise. Like a gem with many facets it is memorial remembering; it is the Lord's Supper, sacrifice, communion and eucharist. It is our liturgy (from the Greek word for "public service"), a service we make together because our response is called for, but it is, first of all, what God in Jesus has done for us, reconciling us and making us ambassadors for Christ's love in the world.

And so with "thanks to God" on our lips and in our hearts we are sent forth in peace to our ministries in the world - forgiven, reconciled, refreshed and empowered, "to love and serve the Lord."

A Fundamentalist Liberal Catholic

Some years ago I was engaged in a difficult discussion with another seminary professor. After I had offered what I thought was one of my best arguments, he responded, "Well, that just goes to show what a Barthian you are!"

While I was and am grateful for many aspects of Karl Barth's massive theological work, I have my troubles with others. Nor am I an expert. I had never met Barth nor studied directly under teachers who would have called themselves Barthians.

I didn't want, however, just to respond, "No I'm not." Instead, rather nonplussed, I asked my colleague what he meant. But I also saw that the conversation had in his eyes reached an important turning point. He sat back in his chair and was clearly satisfied that my theological views, at least on this subject, had been helpfully categorized.

We all love labels. They can be a useful shorthand. They are, however, we also realize, often used to try to discredit the points of view of others and to avoid more strenuous and reflective discussion of significant matters. They can also have the effect of polarizing and absoluting any discussion. One is, for example, either Pro-life or Pro-choice as though the issues had no complexities, much less difficult particular circumstances.

Probably many of us find that we are from time to time on the receiving end of labels. Occasionally someone will even ask me which label I want to go under. Are you a this? they want to know. If I can respond "yes" or "no," they seem at least generally satisfied. Something in their mind has evidently been defined.

My favorite response is to say I am a practicing Christian. If they want more, I'll tell them I'm a catholic. That was the tradition in which I was raised in the Episcopal Church, and I believe, in any case, that it belongs to us all. We regularly profess our belief in the one, holy, catholic and apostolic church.

I love the heritage of the word and its ecumenical connotations, linking us with many other Christians throughout the world and with disciples before and after us in the Body of Christ. I value, too, the ancient understanding of catholics as those who together hold to the essentials of the faith but are also glad for a freedom and diversity of thought and practice in other matters.

At times, though I mostly keep it to myself, I want also to tell people that I am an orthodox protestant radical. Admittedly such a response may be puckish, but it also has its serious sides. I want to see myself as tenacious in protesting for the basic tenets of the Christian faith. Yet at the same time I recognize how challenging these essentials are to many of the ways we live, not only as a society but as a church as well. Such an orthodoxy at its roots (the Latin for root [*radix*] being the 'root' of our word radical) can cause us to recognize that much of what we call Christianity is more cultural than Christian.

Such cultural aspects of our life may or may not be helpful to the practice of our faith. If the latter, they ought to be dealt with. If the former, we can at least recognize that we could, if necessary, follow Jesus without them.

Such discernment can be particularly helpful when bringing the gospel to different cultures or when presenting it in our own increasingly secular society. We may see, for instance, how Christianity in the United States has, subtly or overtly, been linked with certain economic and class perspectives.

When I am feeling still more puckish, I want to bring together and refurbish two words that are often used pejoratively nowadays. The term "fundamentalist" has, of course, a rather specific historical reference to a movement within protestant Christianity which began in 1910 with the publication of twelve books called *The Fundamentals*. The movement grew in the period between the two world wars and still continues. It is, however, identified by many with a reactionary and rigid anti-modernism that causes most conservative and evangelical Christians to reject the label.

For some years, however, I have maintained that we ought to have a *fundamentalist* approach to the Scriptures, much in the sense to which the Fourth Gospel directs us. The evangelist is often pointing out how easily hearers can miss Jesus' true significance unless they listen and probe more fully into the meaning of his words and sayings. How easily we all can get caught up in the side issues of history and theology and lose our grasp on the *fundamentals* of our faith. And a genuine fundamentalism will certainly make us evangelical as well and open to and grateful for the gifts of the Holy Spirit.

The venerable word *liberal* has also fallen into some disrepute. There always was a difficulty with calling oneself a liberal in politics or in religion, because it didn't tell us what one was being liberal about. It was more a matter of attitude than content.

Its lack of reference has now been taken advantage of by detractors who see in *liberalism* a kind of vague openness to the latest trends and an association with increasingly questionable assumptions and sociological influences from a now passé modernism. It has come, too, to suggest its own rigidity, which is anything but liberal, in its attitude toward the perspectives of others who are considered illiberal.

In better days, however, liberal connoted positive virtues. A serious Christian liberalism signified a generosity of spirit toward other views, a special understanding and a care for those living in difficult circumstances, and a readiness to engage in thought and discussion with the arts, the natural sciences, literature and many other aspects of the human experience. In this way it, too, was catholic.

Finally, however, my name is Fred, and I find life and faith sufficiently mysterious, challenging and awesome so as not to want to lay myself down under any label or be crammed into anyone's category. You may well feel much the same way, but, if you want something to call me by, and are willing to link some of these labels together, I'll accept that.

Too Busy?

Avoiding the Tensions of Frenetic Living

There's proof that the Lord is returning soon," a vicar was told by one of her colleagues. "What should we do?" he asked her nervously. Quickly she responded, "Look busy, man. Look busy!"

Your life may also seem busy. It can even be hectic. Would you sometimes say it is frantic? Are you frequently anxious?

This is what I hear from a lot of people when I talk to them about the need for times of prayer and reflection, or just when we are talking about life in general. If I suggest the possibility of taking on some responsibility in the mission of the church, I can often see them eyeing me and saying to themselves, "One more thing for which I don't have time."

In her recent book, *The Overworked American: The Unexpected Decline of Leisure*, Juliet B. Schor points out that the amount of time most Americans spend on their jobs has been rising steadily over the past 20 years. The widespread predictions of the 1960s and 70s that there would be a surfeit of leisure time has not materialized for those who have work.

I am caught up in this cycle, too. But I also wonder why we live with such tension.

Many will point to the financial pressures people live under today. That is no doubt true. Yet it seems arguable to me that many of our parents and grandparents lived in more straitened circumstances. They had to worry about money, too, but they didn't seem to feel so harried in their daily lives.

The greater opportunities for women to have careers and often the necessity of their working has meant a critical change in their lives and in families. Longer commuting time affects many people today.

It is true, too, that the so-called "protestant work ethic" has a grip on many of us. A sound work ethic can, of course, be helpful, but not if we see our whole self-worth tied up in how hard we are working. "Look busy, man."

One can point to these and other factors as causes of frenetic living, but

I think there is another which is even more influential. To give it a name we can call it consumerism. Especially during the past 25 years a vast array of choices has opened out for us. There is more opportunity to take advantage of them, and a huge industry is dedicated to keeping our eyes fixed on the goods. There are 40 or 70 TV channels and hundreds of magazines. We are alway missing some good article or program, not to speak of the latest movies being advertised on TV. Constantly being spread out attractively before us are chances for travel and vacations. These appliances. This furniture. Places to go. Places to eat. Amusements. Things to do. If not for us, then for our children: things they need to experience if they are not somehow to be underprivileged.

Wear these clothes! Eat this food! Use these beauty aids! Drive this fancy car! Even send your kids to this special school or college!

Implied if not explicit in the message is, "Something is wrong with you if you don't have these things." It is even more insidious: "Something is wrong with you if don't want these things."

The message is hardest on the truly poor who can never have more than a few things from this constant display, but I feel it drives all our lives far more than we realize. We feel we need more of these things. There are so many places we haven't been and things we haven't done—things which all the beautiful people on TV and in the magazines seem to have.

We tell ourselves that we don't need all these things. The kids and the family don't need all these things either. Just being can be at least as important as doing. We don't have to live so competitively. What we need is more time for quiet, more time for friendships and conversations, more time for loved ones, more time to see beauty, more time for reflection and prayer, more time to help others. But just telling ourselves this doesn't always seem to work. If we still can't find the time, it may even make us more anxious.

What, in fact, we may need to do is to engage in a little spiritual warfare. Now there's an old-fashioned idea! The Bible speaks of "principalities and powers" that can dominate our lives. These are spiritual and psychological forces that may take us over and make us live selfishly, frenetically, consumed by our ownership of things and desire for more opportunities, even while we yet worry that we may not be getting our share, even while we know we are mortal. "In the shadow of the hawk we feather our nests," wrote Edna St. Vincent Millay.

This warfare is not all that easy, but as Christians we have some powerful weapons available to us. One is a kind of detachment. The things of this world may be nice, but far more important is the kind of person we are becoming and the quality of the communities we live in. The greatest adventures and achievements of life are finally moral and spiritual, not the mere accumulations of wealth or things or experiences.

It may at first seem odd, but one of the best ways to break the grip of anxiety's greed on our lives is to give more of what we have away—to give of our time, our talents and our money. It has been said that what finally counts in life is not what we have but what we have given away. This insight is about as far as one can get from the cynical idea that the one who dies with the most expensive toys wins.

Another spiritual and psychological weapon we have is the knowledge that we are loved. Apart from what we own, apart even from what we accomplish or how we behave, we still are loved by God and, one prays, within our families and communities of faith.

It is this security which enables us to involve ourselves in life at a deeper level and at least to begin to give priority to those most human fruits of the Spirit: love, joy, peace, patience, kindness, goodness, faithfulness, gentleness, self-control. So may much of the anxiety and hectic busyness drain out of our lives and we begin to know ourselves as more in harmony with ourselves and one another and in God's peace.

Sharing the Good News

Our English word evangelism comes from two Greek words meaning "good" and "to tell"; that is, "to tell a message," to announce. Angel comes from the same word as does "...-angelism." An angel is a messenger from God. So an evangelist is a messenger of good and exciting news. Evangelism means to tell good news.

Given this powerful meaning, it may seem surprising that some Christians seem to be suspicious of the word evangelism. Perhaps it makes them think of some of the gimmickry of some televangelists or of people who intrude upon the privacy of others.

Yet evangelism is a vital New Testament word that we should not let others take from us. It is what Jesus did. He went around all the towns and villages telling "good news" about the reign of God.

Jesus' basic message was that God's reign, that is, God's ways of rightness and mercy, of fairness, justice and harmony, were much more a part of the present time than most people realized. The demanding call and this great opportunity were already begun.

Some, of course, doubted. How could justice and mercy be known as the ways of God when so much evil and injustice seemed to prevail?

Jesus taught that those with eyes and ears of faith, those ready to trust in God's ways, could know justice by being people who hungered and thirsted for righteousness. They could know peace by being makers of peace. This could happen now and would be fully realized in the age to come as the will and purpose of the God of all creation.

Even to the disciples, however, Jesus' death seemed to prove that evil and cruelty won out in the end. Love and fairness and peacemaking were too weak.

But then the disciples' experience of Jesus as risen to new life convinced them that God's love could not finally be overcome. Although seemingly weak by many worldly standards, love formed unbreakable bonds. It lasted and endured. It was related to the power by which the amazing world of stars and suns and life was created. It was stronger even than death.

This was very good news which the disciples wanted to share with others. They couldn't help themselves. How could they do otherwise?

They didn't always know the right words. They knew their own lives were imperfect, and that in important ways they were only beginners in trying to follow the ways of Jesus. But soon new communities of thanksgiving and praise, and of caring and sharing were growing up all around the Mediterranean Sea.

These communities continue and go forward today. Although we are still imperfect and in important ways only beginners in being a people of justice and peace, each of our churches is meant to be a community experiencing the love of God and the call to right living and compassion. Our churches are places of thanksgiving and reconciling, where people discover a sense of belonging and of greater purpose for their lives.

That is good news—very good news! One certainly shouldn't be shy about it.

Yet quite a few Episcopalians do appear to be shy. Surprisingly, some do not ever seem to realize that it is part of their calling as Christians to be sharers of the good news, to be evangelists. Perhaps they think it is only a call for the clergy.

That is wrong on two accounts. First, it would make the churches very inefficient in evangelism since there are so many more lay people than clergy. Second, the lay people are far better evangelists. They are the ones out in the world with contacts with many different people on a daily basis. Unlike the clergy they are not viewed as professional Christians, but as volunteers acting out their faith. A primary task of the clergy is to help give the laity the understanding and insights that will enable them to share their faith so that others may know of God's work in Jesus and the power of the Spirit of God.

Ways of Evangelism

How do we actually do evangelism? What are some of the practical ways evangelism happens? In the last analysis, of course, we don't *do* evangelism. God—the Holy Spirit present in and among all our lives—is the one who changes people. By the working of God's Spirit people become converted within themselves; discovering what is now most important to them is the love of God and the capacity to reach out beyond themselves in care and service. Lives are changed and transformed.

Often that happens within a community of faith. It happens among people worshipping and serving together—where the Spirit is shared. The first and most important way of evangelism is to strengthen those communities of strong worship and prayer, where we are praying for evangelism. New and renewed faith happens with the help of education, in communities in which people are deepening their understanding and faith. It happens in communitites of service from which care and ministry reach out to others. It happens in communities of spiritual energy—where the real issues of life are being faced courageously with trust and hope in God's future.

How do we invite others to join us? First of all it is wise to have within the congregation a group that is regularly helping us think about evangelism. It could be the vestry or bishop's committee or a special taskforce. I do not mean that we should turn the whole responsibility over to them—evangelism and sharing our faith are every disciple's responsibility—but this group of thoughtful people helps us all to plan.

We should be sure we have effective signs around our church, and good advertising in the community. We should take care to see that our church building is attractively presented. We can go knock on doors in the areas around the church, taking surveys, respectfully asking people whether they have a faith or a church of their own, whether they might like to join us.

It is probably best to have lay people do this rather than the clergy—partly because there are so many more lay people than clergy, partly because clergy are regarded as professional Christians and may even be a little imposing or scary to people at first.

In fact, however, most new disciples and rededicated Christian lives come not from among strangers, but from people we already know; that is how churches grow—with friends, neighbors, family members, colleagues at work.

One thing I find Episcopalians are very good at is telling about their church: "You know, Sam or Mary—All Saints Church has just made all the difference in my life. I have friends there and a ministry and the opportunity to reach beyond myself in worship—service." Oftentimes that's all we need to say to begin with—to invite people to join us in the Christian community where they can find a new sense of our Lord's presence and promise for their lives.

Many times, however, it is listening that can be the beginning of evangelism, allowing others to tell us what matters most to them—their hopes and sorrows, what is missing in their life, the way they may have experienced God's presence and absences. Then we can share something of our story of faith with them.

I think every one of our churches ought to have a brochure—with color pictures if possible. It should not have a lot of words; there should be mostly pictures of the things we know bring people to church and hold them: Christian education for young people and adults, youth groups, worship, service and outreach opportunities, young adults, men's and women's groups—whatever things your church does best.

Sometimes when I am visiting a congregation parishioners tell me, "Oh, Bishop, we have such a brochure."

"Good," I reply. "Where do you keep it?"

"Oh, on a table in the back of the church."

"Great. So if someone stumbles in late at night they can get one!"

No, every parishioner ought to have a stack of the brochures. All should have them at home and even on their desk or table at work. Why not? We keep other important things on our desks. Friends may come up and ask about them.

When someone new moves into your apartment building or down the block, you can say a little prayer and go knock on their door. "Excuse me," you say. "I want to welcome you and be of any help if I can. You may have a faith or a church of your own, but Grace Church is such a great and important place in my life that I wanted to share that with you. I brought you this little brochure."

Or, if you're too shy for that, write a note on the brochure and stick it under their door.

I'll bet you can think of a lot more ideas than I can. You know your church and your community.

How about a special theme dinner event a couple times a year held in the church hall? It's all great fun, and at some point—just for two or three minutes—one of the lay leaders stands up and tells about your church and how glad you would be to welcome new participants. You can do something similar at other special events, like church concerts or plays. There are people waiting to be asked. They tell me that twenty-five percent of the unchurched people would go to church with a friend if they were asked. That's a lot of people.

If you have a school, at least once a year at parents' gatherings they should be told how much they and their childen are welcome at church and in church programs. I am frankly astounded that some of our churches don't do that—as though the church and school didn't belong together. It's a wonderful opportunity, and people often won't come unless they're invited.

People sometimes join churches because they first became involved in a service program—visiting the elderly, feeding the hungry, tutoring children, helping the homeless, trying to change wrongful conditions. The opportunities are almost endless for thoughtful disciples.

Cathedral for the
Twenty-First Century

*The new Cathedral Center of the Diocese of Los Angeles, built in
Echo Park just north of the city center, was dedicated in the fall of 1994.*

We face many challenges in this city and region. But it is worth
reminding ourselves that others have had it a lot tougher. As one
example, five hundred and eighty-seven years before the Christian era, the
city of Jerusalem was once more under siege from the Babylonians, and
Jeremiah, who had prophesied the city's fall, was under house arrest.
Zedekiah, the King of Judah, had repeatedly come to Jeremiah, trying to get
him to prophesy differently, but to no avail.

It was in these circumstances that Hanamel, Jeremiah's cousin, offered
him what must have seemed one of the worst deals of that or any other
century. Hanamel needed to sell a field which belonged to the family. It was
in the town of Anathoth. There, just a few miles north of Jerusalem,
Jeremiah himself had been born. Hanamel evidently had no brothers or no
brothers able or willing to buy the land. Tradition gave Jeremiah the right
and some sense of responsibility to purchase the field.

Clearly, however, it was a time to keep one's investments in silver or
jewels and not in land. The Babylonians had conquered Judah once before
and were advancing again. Jeremiah knew what was going to happen to
Jerusalem and certainly to little Anathoth as well.

Instead, however, we are told in detail—in more such detail than we
find anywhere else in the Bible—about Jeremiah's purchase of the land. We,
who have been through a lot of detail with the city and county agencies,
inspectors, lawyers, and the raising and paying of funds, can have some
sympathy.

There being no regular currency in those days, the silver bars or rings
had to be weighed to complete the purchase. Kristi Wallace, Pam Burrill,
Joon Matsamura and Peter Mann had to go through purchases only a little
less exacting.

The deed of purchase was made public in the presence of numerous
witnesses. There was a sealed copy which would have been rolled, tied and

encased in clay with a stamp on it and another open copy which could be more easily consulted. Both were placed in an earthenware jar for safe keeping.

What Jeremiah did is known as an enacted prophecy. Its message of hope and trust in God and God's future is summed up in the promise that "houses and fields and vineyards shall again be bought in this land." The building of a new Cathedral in this time and place may be seen as another enacted prophecy—a sign of hope and trust in God and in the future of God's people. Some would say that, with fire, drought, flood, a great civil disturbance, earthquake, too many broken families, poverty, murders— bizarre and all too familiar—refugees, gangs, joblessness and recession, this is not a time to build, or at least not to build here. But Jeremiah might well stand in our midst and tell us that it is the most important time to build — that, for us, this is not only part of rebuilding LA but a strong commitment to the faith and mission of our Church and, along with other men and women of faith and good will, a commitment to the center of our region and all of its life and work and ministries as well as a commitment of service to this neighborhood. It is a part of our "Hope in Youth" and inspiration for them. Nor has this been done by us just for ourselves, but for generations to come.

This twenty-first century understanding of a cathedral is resonant with the life of cathedrals of old. It is a place of worship, prayer, service and hospitality where many people will come and go on a daily basis—to learn a ministry, to buy a book, be on retreat, attend a meeting, plan a missionary work, celebrate Eucharist, take a class, eat lunch, pick up food, shoot a basketball, tutor a young person, help a family, say a prayer, hear a prophetic word, meet a friend, make a friend, find new hope and courage, —in some cases to be baptized or married or ordained or committed to God's unending love. In an ancient oracle the psalmist speaks of that time and place wherein God speaks and brings the divine presence close to the people. There "mercy and truth have met together; righteousness and peace have kissed each other." In our lives it is hard to find righteousness and peace, truth and mercy, fairness, justice and caring—the harmony of God's peace together. Today we pray that the Cathedral may be a place of God's righteousness and peace, of truth and mercy, coming together in God's love and reaching out to others. We pray that many people will come here, young people and older—many people out of the great diversity of this Diocese and region — and that here they will find God's mercy and truth, justice and peace and be strengthened to share them with others.

It is the people who are and will be the living stones of this cathedral of which St. Peter speaks in our lesson, for buildings of stone, metal and wood can only enable ministry. This Cathedral Center will make an enormous difference to our ability to be on mission together for our Lord and in service to others in God's name. But that mission must now be done by ourselves, living stones making a spiritual house of fairness and caring, of gracious adelante hospitality and invitation and peace, open and receptive and reaching out to all people—in this neighborhood and well beyond—as from the heart of our Church.

This Cathedral and its living stones are founded upon that rock of our hope and trust in God. It is built upon that living stone which many builders, and still a part of us, would reject. We would still reject because so many other things initially seem more important and chosen and enduring. It is only the experience of trust and service which enables us to see that the self-giving love known best to us in the life, passion, death and new life of Jesus, is that living stone which will endure. Other things—even noble things—will pass away, but it is this love, St. Paul reminds us, which "endures all things and never ends."

Like the ever-burning, unquenchable flame of the burning bush, it can be only such an ever-giving, unending power which is at the creative heart of universal being and life—of all its vastness and intricate smallness, simplicity and complexity, changing and rebirth—a power of love which moves the sun and all other stars and now moves in our hearts as we offer our thanksgiving and praise and renewed dedication to God. It is upon this faith that "all our hope is founded"—our hope for the years to come for the ministries of the Cathedral Center of St. Paul, and for ourselves as its living stones in service to all God's people —for whom we now are called upon to pray.

Our Offices

While still a priest of tender years, I went to see my confessor in the Diocese of Chicago, an older priest, known to be kindly but somewhat strict in the old Anglo-Catholic model. Although I'd learned to love him, he still made me a little edgy. Penance, I knew, was a sacrament of thanksgiving, but I always found myself most thankful after it was over. This time, however, I didn't worry too much because I didn't really have that much to confess, mostly those somewhat embarrassing flaws of omission and commission, with which one each time promises to deal, but which seem regularly to return like athlete's foot. Certainly, there was nothing that would startle the dear man.

I finished my little recital, which included the fact that I had missed saying some of my daily offices. To tell the truth I was secretly rather proud of my record. I hadn't missed all that many and had, I thought, some pretty reasonable excuses for the times I did. I'd even been tempted to include the excuses in my confession but decided that would be overdoing it.

There was rather lengthy pause—too long, I thought. He was obviously mulling something over. When he did speak, he fastened particularly on those offices I had missed. Maybe he was tired, but somehow he didn't sound all that forgiving. I hoped God was. He ended by telling me that he had never seen a priest go off the rails as long as that priest kept saying the offices.

The words of absolution flowed over me, and I hurried away into the main church to say my penance and thanksgiving. I felt a bit flushed and perhaps even hurt. It wasn't until I was driving home that I began to focus on his last words of advice. Then suddenly they held my attention. Here, after all was what I had been looking for. It was almost a magic formula—a guaranteed way to keep my priesthood on track.

For the next seven or so years I was incredibly "religious" about saying my offices—morning and night, rain and shine, well or sick, busy or not, on vacation, in busses, by candlelight. It didn't make any difference if I was tired. It also didn't make any difference if my wife was tired or the kids needed a little extra attention. Somehow the offices had to be fitted in.

239

Then one evening I just forgot. I can't imagine how it happened. When I realized it the next morning, I was thunderstruck. I think I even considered saying the office then, as though that might make up for it. But then something else happened. It was either the Holy Spirit or common sense or both that made me realize that I had been using the offices as a kind of talisman, sometimes perhaps more for the glory of my own discipline than as prayer.

With the help of other spiritual guides I learned to use the offices as a part of a healthier rule of life and not to be ruled by them. In later years, and with the new Prayer Book, I have found it sometimes helpful to modify their form by reading all the lessons in the morning and using a more meditative "Order for Evening" later in the day. Yet, while I trust I am a lot more relaxed about the offices, and confess to missing them from time to time, I find myself also still grateful for that confessor of almost 30 years ago. I do miss my offices when I miss them. I remember, too, words of Stephen Bayne about how the regular reading of Scripture shapes the architecture of our faith. There are, of course, other important aspects to a rule of life, but some form of regular morning and evening prayer—with Scripture, prayer and praise, intercession and thanksgiving—makes very solid foundation stones.

Wellness

I t's often tough. It's a challenge. We hear and read about it a lot—as if we didn't know. The work of the ordained ministry seems to take more effort. It is said there is less prestige than there used to be. Many of us could make more money in other professions. There are lots of financial pressures, personal and institutional, and now this stubborn recession (no matter who says it's over). The repetitiveness of some aspects of ministry can become dulling.

There are a lot of other pressures on everyone—congestion, commuting, both parents working in the family, crime, smog, the pace of life. The pressures filter through to the pastoral leaders and sometimes seem to hunt them like heat-seeking missiles. People bring their anger to church and may act it out. Anger is discharged in ways that would be more laughable if they didn't hurt others so much. At the same time, congregations may place even heavier expectations on their leaders for evangelism, stewardship and enthusiastic inspiration, while, at the same time, the ministry of the laity is on guard against misuse of authority, "clericalism" and defensive responses.

Some say faith is harder—that the cumulative forces of secularism and the lack of faith reinforcement in society slowly take their toll. The institutional church gets sidelined and faces its own problems and accusations of this and that in a flawed and fragmentary world.

A decade or two ago renewal might come through a move to a new ministry. But for some, that's now tougher too. Two career families, a kind of buyer's market out there, the competitiveness and cumbersomeness of the process from the clergy perspective and differing expectations about leadership have at least made it more difficult to make such transitions.

We've all heard this analysis enough times before that it has become boring and itself a burden. (And, if you think we've got it tough, you might want to check again on Paul's version of it in 1 Corinthians 4:9-13 and 2 Corinthians 11:23-29).

So what's the good news? Without minimizing the awareness that we have burnout, addiction, depression and casualties in our ranks, I give thanks that so many of you find wellness, and that for you wholeness and spiritual health are the paradigms for your ministry. The foundation, as always, is gratitude—gratitude for sunshine and running water, for friendships and laughter and opportunities for service. It rests in the knowledge that a lot of other people have it a lot tougher—poorer, more repetitive, more wearing—with less opportunity for creativity, and that they need hope and vision. It comes from learning new forms of ministry, continuing education, renewal, understanding of our own shortcomings, and the boundaries we must set, of insights into how communities, families and people function, of how to motivate and develop leadership in the 1990s. It is found in physical exercise, knowing the causes and dangers of overwork, self-discipline, colleagues, being an active part of the larger church, refusing to be complicit in the negativity that others may use to try to ameliorate their own disappointments and sadness.

It arises in adoration, in worship and prayer, ultimate trust in God and in living the ways of Jesus with their demands and gladness.

Our Secret Sharer

In his short story "The Secret Sharer" Joseph Conrad tells of a young sea captain who one night discovers a naked man hanging to the side ladder of his ship. Similar in age and build to the captain, the man, Leggatt, turns out to be an officer from another ship who, after having killed an insubordinate seaman during a storm, had escaped through a remarkable feat of swimming.

The captain makes the decision to hide Leggatt, and the story narrates their adventures and conversations while keeping the secret from the rest of the ship and also from the murderer's captain, who comes searching for him the next morning. Leggatt seeks understanding and the young captain's awareness that, in similar circumstances, he might have done the same thing.

After several harrowing days, the two decide that Leggatt should swim secretly from the ship and try to make out as best he can on the strange shore on which he will land. The next night the captain sails his vessel perilously close to the shore. With the towering coast looming over them, the stranger leaps from a sail compartment and swims away.

It is, of course, no accident that Conrad was writing his fiction while Freud and Jung were also exploring the unconscious and hidden depths of personality. Although Conrad was working independently, clearly a new consciousness was arising, and the novelist was fascinated by the awareness of a shadow side hidden in each individual—a kind of double, capable of doing things of which civilization could not and would not approve. Not surprisingly Conrad alludes several times in "The Secret Sharer" to the story of Cain and Abel.

Other psychologists and novelists bring us further insight into the energy that often comes from the shadow side. (And see Romans 7!) A will to dominate and have one's own way, anger, and more subtle ego demands can be the harmful aspects of deep drives and urges. When, however, brought into some measure of larger self-awareness and harnessed to more helpful goals, one's double life, as it were, can produce considerable power for health and sharing with others.

All people who have public roles of leadership and who are in helping professions have special responsibilities and opportunities to grow in such self-awareness. We who are clergy can learn that our double never really swims away. (Conrad, of course, recognized that the captain must now live with the knowledge of his sharer within him.) Suppressed and unrecognized, our sharer can undercut much of the good we want to do, harming family and collegial relationships and leaving us lonely. Prayer and spiritual reflection as well as psychology are, however, strong aids in helping us to recognize and accept our shadow and to open ourselves to grace, healing and new energy for faithful living.

Beating the Lone Ranger

Many of us have a strong tendency to see ourselves as the helpers and all others as the ones to be helped. Some say that on this basis we self-select for the ordained ministry and other helping professions. In any event, the Lone Ranger mentality among us is often noted.

Fortunately most of us now know enough about ourselves and the stresses of our vocations to make efforts to overcome this tendency. We look for good friends in whom we can confide; we look for therapeutic relationships. But from time to time we may still drift into more isolated ways of living. Recent studies suggest that many of us may depend too much on our life companions as persons to tell our problems and concerns to, perhaps placing unfair burdens on them and our relationships.

And how many times, after colleagues have gotten into serious problems with alcohol or sexual misconduct or whatever, have we not said to ourselves, "Gee, I hadn't seen old 'so and so' for quite a while"?

One can argue whether such keeping to oneself is cause or symptom or both, but it is rarely a good sign.

One of the best ways of overcoming tendencies to try to go it alone, and a way of also building up our shared faith, is through colleague groups. I am delighted that so many of you belong to such groups, and I have heard how much they mean to you. If you are part of such a group, you might think of extending it just a little, perhaps especially to include a sister or brother who seems to be trying to go it alone.

Also useful for sharing and deepening friendships and vocations are one-on-one clergy relationships in which reflection and evaluation is done on an annual or semi-annual basis. Many will, of course, do this with a spiritual guide. It can also be done with a colleague. You may choose to ask each other: "What are you reading?" "What are you praying about?" "How's your prayer life going?" "How's your family, and/or how's your circle of friends?" "What are you doing that is fun?" "What part of ministry are you finding most difficult?" "How are you taking care of yourself physically?" "Where are you growing vocationally and spiritually?" "Where would you like to grow?" "What might you do about it?"

245

How much grief and difficulty might be saved if we shared more often with one another in these ways! How much strengthening there can be when we do so! How much we need one another!

Gossip

My spiritual mentors have several times reminded me that what one gives up or takes on for Lent is very often something that should be part of a life-long discipline. Perhaps one intensifies an awareness of it during a particular Lenten season. Among this year's *awarenesses* for FHB I decided that the penchant to listen to and to join in gossip and the spreading of rumors could use some attention.

I suppose, like many other people, I am inclined to think of gossiping as a very minor sin, if, indeed, there is anything wrong with it at all. "It's just a way to pass some time—just talking things over." Perhaps I can even claim that I'm really only doing it out of pastoral concern for the persons or groups under discussion.

At the time, I may want to think of it as one of life's more innocent pleasures, but often when I reflect back upon it I realize it may not have been quite that innocent. Clearer insight comes when I ask about the motivation for sharing in gossip and the passing along of rumors. It is so often an insecurity—a fear that others may seem brighter, more competent or more generous than I. My response to that feeling is to listen to or to make remarks about others that show their feet of clay. Somehow, if I pull them down a little, then I think I'll feel a little taller by comparison, though—at the end of a day of gossip— I may actually end up feeling rather small.

I don't imagine that Church folk gossip any more than others, but I fear we certainly do our share—perhaps encouraged by our excuse that we are pastorally concerned and acting as responsible critics of our own institution. One way I find I can tell gossip and rumoring from responsible criticism and pastoral care is that the former is usually characterized by laziness and a certain lack of courage. When engaged in gossiping and the passing along of rumors, I am not really concerned to do the hard work of getting the facts. Nor am I ready to act courageously by challenging what I am hearing, by speaking out or by going directly to the parties involved.

Those of you who have been on the other end of gossip and rumors, as clergy often are, know how it can hurt. It may do the mission of the Church more damage than we think. "The tongue," James reminds us, "is a little member...How great a forest is set ablaze by a small fire!" (James 3:5).

The only real antidote I know is the healing medicine of remembering that my basic self-worth comes from the love of God and the love I know from others. It is not something I have to earn or deserve or compare with what others have. When I am thankful for this, my mind and heart can get on to other matters that do not leave much time or room for gossip.

By the time you read this, Easter will be upon us and Lent concluded. I will again have experienced my inability fully to live up to my rule of life. I will know the joy and the power of the resurrection again, but also, I trust, I will be more aware of an aspect of my life on which I must continue to work.

The Former Rector

"The problem in the Episcopal Church is the lack of any sense of authority. There is no authority in the Church today."

"Oh, yes there is," comes the response. "The former rector."

This joke in our Church is in some places not so funny. It can describe a difficult and sometimes sad pastoral situation. The better a priest and pastor the former rector was, the worse the problems can be if the rector is still around and about.

Congregations, like all other communities, are buffeted by change. Many people do not like change. The former rector often comes to represent stability as well as the days gone by. On important life occasions, for baptisms and weddings—and particularly in times of crisis—for illnesses and bereavements, many parishioners would like to have the former rector there to help out pastorally. It's also nice to be able to run into the former rector at the grocery store and, perhaps, just to boost his or her ego a little, to tell a few stories about the not-so-successful changes the next rector is making.

Former rectors have very human needs, too. As one grows older, the need to feel needed can grow. Even with the best intentions in the world, it would be hard not to listen and perhaps nod one's head understandingly. One can always say that one is only being pastoral.

And it is nice to be asked, if not to do the wedding, at least to come to the reception and to say a few words there. And how could one not visit the widow of a former warden in the parish and perhaps commiserate with her that the new rector seems to be too busy to come by more than once?

Maybe only a former rector who had a former rector in the parish could see the real dimensions of the problem: how much more difficult it was to establish oneself as the major pastoral figure for the congregation. Indeed, sometimes the next ministry has been all but ruined by a well-meaning former rector. And, again, the better the priest or former rector was, the worse the problem.

One of the most important acts of ministry is, when leaving, to leave. That's not easy advice to give. That's tough advice. It may be hardest of all on the spouse of the former rector, especially with so many close friends in the parish and maybe the need to leave a beloved home.

Yet it very often works out best for everyone to say good-bye—and not just for a year or two, but for good except for the occasional visit. It's best for the next rector(s) and family, for the congregation and its future, and for the former rector and spouse as well, who now have time to make new friends and associations independent of former roles. Yes, leaving can well be one of the most valuable contributions of one's ministry.

The Clergy and Sexual Immorality

The figures, to say the least, are alarming; and behind them lie many personal tragedies. Actually, we will never know the real figures since so many incidents, out of deep shame and embarrassment, remain buried in wounded hearts. It is claimed that as many as one in four clergy have at some time in their lives misused their office through forms of flirtation and other ways of toying with affections of parishioners or children. Some clergy do so with regularity. More than ten percent go further to sexual contact.

The figures are not much different for professors and other teachers, psychologists and doctors with respect to their students, clients and patients. The misuse of trust and authority of office is in no way limited to the clergy, but that is of no consolation. Somehow it seems that, when clergy misuse their office, they have breached a double trust—not only by abusing the esteem many people have for their office and the resultant projection of feelings on to them, but also by violating the sense that people can feel safe with clergy and know something of God's care and protection in their presence. Indeed, some clergy have used that safety as a screen for making their sexual exploitations more confidential, and even to convince their victims that what is happening is somehow sanctified by God because of who is doing it.

Afterwards, one hears the rationalizations: it is said that the priest was trying to help someone in need who was lonely; the priest acting as therapist is assisting someone to develop the ability of sexual expression; or we are asked to understand the pressures of the priestly office and how vulnerable clergy as humans can be in their own sexuality, especially given the temptations and opportunities of their vocation. We all live in an addictive society and in a culture deeply confused about sexuality.

One may understand but not excuse. Sometimes the clergy abusers are in other ways kindly and gentle people, but they nevertheless do great harm. Lives are severely, and sometimes irreparably, damaged.

What can be done? What must be done? In the first place, every one of us is forewarned and should be forearmed. Lonely, vulnerable, even adoring people will come our way. Sometimes they themselves will play seductive games. We are to know what is happening and the dangers involved. Spiritually and emotionally, we must strengthen ourselves.

We can talk more openly about the problem among ourselves. We can be alert to the danger signs of secretiveness and withdrawal among our brother and sister clergy.

And, we must be prepared to get help. When we see temptations developing, which seem to threaten us or overmaster us; or, if we have fallen into sin, now is the time to reach for help, to confess ourselves; to turn to God and to seek out tough love and professional help. There is plenty of help around.

Youth Leadership

During the 18 years I was teaching in Anglican or Episcopal Church seminaries, I was visited on a number of occasions by rectors who had come searching for curates or assistants. When I asked for a job description, I was fairly regularly told first off, "I'm looking for a young man or woman to do our youth work."

I tried to stifle the temptation to make a face. Most of the seminarians I knew were looking forward to teaching and working with adults. Indeed, the younger they were, the more likely they were not to want to be around the teenage group from which they had fairly recently emerged.

Then, of course, youth groups need stability both for individual members and if the group is to grow. Many curates or assistants stay for two, three or four years and are gone.

I've always thought that the best person to provide overall leadership for the youth group is the rector or vicar. They are usually at the right age. I believe youth relate better to older figures as leaders and mentors than they do to individuals close to their years.

Many rectors or vicars will say that they are too busy with other important matters to give much time to the youth. And, does that message get across to the youth loud and clear!

It isn't necessary that the rector or vicar be with the youth all the time. Best is to have a cadre of six to ten people from the congregation who will do much of the actual ministry and provide support and backup for each other. The rector or vicar can help provide leadership for that group and, with some regularity, a strong spiritual and teaching presence for youth.

And, it's fun! Compared to some of the other things we are charged with, it's one of the best ministries around.

The Diocese has a program for the education of full-time youth ministers, but I believe there never can be a substitute for the significant participation of the rector or vicar. We often talk about making ministries with and by youth more important in our churches. I am, of course, aware that there are many assistant and associate clergy and lay ministers who do splendid work in this area, but direct involvement by the rector or vicar can be a very important help.

While on the subject, when I visit congregations I ask to meet with the leadership. It is surprising how often no youth are present. Another clear message, we may fear.

When youth are asked to participate in leadership and to offer their ideas about the ministries of a congregation, it is surprising how new directions and energy can result. That is true for the adults, as well as for the sense of belonging and participation on the part of the young people.

Spiritual Reading

Merton, Nouwen, Julian of Norwich. The phrase "spiritual reading" often makes us think of writers who specifically address biblical themes, God's presence in the world, vocation, and the soul's relationship to God.

There is another way of spiritual reading, however, which we might also call reading spiritually. It involves the reading of novels, biographies and even scientific journals or a book on mathematics with spiritual perceptiveness and discernment. Such reading is a form of putting incarnational faith into practice by probing the fabric of life for the surprising presence of God. It is a way of expressing faith in the Spirit of God moving in many contexts—*The Go-Between God* (the title of John Taylor's 1972 book) bringing about the possibility of all manner of relationship, significance and community.

In his book, *Breaking the Fall: Religious Readings in Contemporary Fiction*, Robert Detweiler offers both method and insight for those who wish to engage in a form of such spiritual reading. Guided by contemporary critical understandings, he describes "religious reading" as a kind of deep play reminding us of how the text can never really be completed—that it and we are always open to that triumph of faith over nihilism. Sometimes more obviously, sometimes in hidden and complex ways, fundamental questions and a variety of religious themes are interwoven into much of contemporary literature.

On occasion a clergy woman or man will ask my advice on how a sabbatical time can be spent. I assume I am asked the question because of my years as a seminary and university teacher and the expectation that I will recommend this or that course in theology, spirituality or professional study. Sometimes I do, because such deepening and refreshment can always be valuable. Every once in a while, however, I like to surprise my questioner by asking about his or her major in college or another interest he or she would like to explore.

"Music," they might answer, or "painting" or "biology," they may respond. "Go do that for a time," I suggest. "Make that your spiritual reading. Refresh yourself with God's presence there and bring such spiritual gifts back to share with others."

Scars

I think I understand
How by combustion long, or swift and bright
The eyes and ears, my legs, hands, arms, each gland,
Then even teeth, bone at last, from all sight
Are gone to dust and sand.

Hard although to think
Of being not, and of these my fingers,
Which now move and write, and every link,
Perhaps saving this, whereby one lingers
With you, to gravely sink.

In faith one thinks, one hopes
Of that other tent, of some reclothing,
That not in nakedness, but with new tropes
Of sight and voice, and ourselves emerging,
All dressed in shining coats.

Yet still I think, would know
What happens to the scars I feel, I've earned:
The door, then shovel crossed on a child's brow;
More by sport and in a paned glass door turned
By a little girl, oh!

So I think of mother,
Phone again ringing, nearly once a year,
Some cut, or fracture when for her brother
Sister shouting, he fell so far, so near
To breaking heart of her.

Scars

As I think, too, of scars
Engravened on the bone of leg and arm,
How a cheekbone cracking in a fight mars
Now not at all (I laugh), nor the nose harmed.
All past now, all honors.

I think how it went on:
Of one of these fingers jaggedly gashed,
And finer lines of healing incision,
Gall bladder gone, back, lung repaired, but slashed.
Yes! quite a collection!

They must, I think, stand, too,
For colder wounds, acts that seemed unfeeling,
Undone and done, sharp words, as most I rue,
My cuts to others, for whose scars healing,
Too, I will pray anew.

Not least I think of times
Trying, trying to hunger and vying
For some modicum of fairness, those signs
For others, of just hands, a heart sharing,
Caring against our crimes.

Which has me think of night
Long wrestling with the one not letting go,
Who for some yet veiling love and its rite
Of wounds that may heal sends me limping so
Into the breaking light.

Then I can but think well
Of holes hammerd in palms and feet, his side,
And, why not, too? as saw slipped or chisel
While like us learning, so that when he died,
They after knew love still.

I think some way they're laid
In days to come, if not on our new selves,
Then in that life with whom as we are made
Hurts, known and knelled, are so reformed it tells
That they with we are saved.

257

Praying for Others

E very ministry has its surprises. I never understood how much I would need to pray in this ministry. There is, of course, prayer for my family, myself and my vocation—for wisdom and understanding, courage and faithfulness. There are prayers for the mission of this diocese, its congregations, institutions, programs. But it is not the need for these prayers that had surprised me so.

It is my particular intercessions which ask for so much time. Sometimes I am specifically requested to pray for people. Then the clergy and their families form a "parish" of their own, and there are lay leaders and their families as well. In such a large community there are bound to be illnesses and other concerns and problems. Still more often, however, it is some prompting by the Holy Spirit that asks me to pray for one of us. I see someone whose head is down, or hear second- or third-hand that the person is trying to discern something about vocation or battling with some demon.

What good are such prayers? Everyone must ask that question at one time or another. Would it not be more useful to use this time and energy in action and the pastoral care of others?

Two important things, I believe, happen in intercessory prayer. When we pause long enough to hold another up in prayer, we begin to see that person differently. I particularly need to pray for others whose views and attitudes may be different from mine. I need to understand their hopes, their sorrow or hurt, or sometimes their reasons for being upset and angry. It is often a form of compassion and sympathy—of sharing a little of their suffering.

Sometimes what I envision may seem silly, for, when I hold others up, I may get a picture of them up off the ground, legs dangling, jacket flapping, with all their vulnerabilities and strengths—in their full humanity. I ask that I might see them as God sees them—as the parent God sees the child, loving no matter what, always looking for the potential, the true needs. "Not who we are or have been, sees God with all-merciful eyes, but who we shall be."

I may only get a glimpse, but I cannot help but then be changed. Still more importantly, the relationship changes. Often I will be given something to do—a note to write, a mutual friend to contact, a word to share when we met.

There is something yet more mysterious, for you and I believe in the communion of saints and in the body of Christ. In ways we cannot fathom, we "live and move and have our being" in God. Even when we may be miles apart, we live and work in that interrelation. When we pray for one another, we become more aware that we are part of that body. What one member thinks or does or prays affects another.

Let us pray for our own needs and those of others.

One Another

The Greek word, which we usually translate as "one another" is used more than 80 times in the New Testament. I sometimes hear it in its various forms like a bell, ringing over and again. *Allēlōn. Allēlois. Allēlous. Allēlōn* and *one another* are lovely sounds, often a peaceful ringing of love and care. *Allēlōn. One another.* At other times the words seem a summons, a call to service. *Allēlōn. One another.* Then they can be a bell of hope, offering courage and new strength. *Allēlōn. One another.*

There are many places we could begin, but perhaps no place better than the picture of Jesus washing his disciples' feet.

> Do you know what I have done to you? You call me Teacher and Lord...If I then, your Lord and Teacher, have washed your feet, you also ought to wash the feet of one another (*allēlōn*). John 13:12-14

The call to serve and to love one another sounds often in John's Gospel.

> A new commandment I give to you, that you love one another (*allēlōn*); even as I have loved you that you also love one another (*allēlōn*). John 13:34

The Divine Life of the Universe present in Jesus makes known God's love for us. It is the purpose of the ever-giving power which creates the sun and all the other stars to make us lovely by love. We can only begin to love our neighbors as ourselves when we know ourselves as loved. That love becomes best known in human life—in the love of Jesus for his disciples.

> As the Father has loved me, so have I loved you....This is my commandment, that you love another (*allēlōn*) as I have loved you. No one has greater love than this—that one lay down one's life for one's friends. You are my friends if you do what I command you. John 15:9, 12-14

The love that originates with God and which can make us lovely is shared in our lives among friends, within the family, by faithful neighbors, seeking to make us lovable and so loveable, able to love one another. This love creates a community of caring relationships.

> For as in one body we have many members,...so we, who are

many, are one body in Christ, and individually members one of another (*allēlōn*). Romans 12:4-5

Love one another (*allēlōn*) with the affection of brothers and sisters; outdo one another (*allēlōn*) in showing honor.
Romans 12:10

Live in harmony with one another (*allēlōn*). Romans 12:16

Welcome one another (*allēlōn*) just as Christ has welcomed you.
Romans 15:7

I myself feel confident about you, my brothers and sisters, that you yourselves are full of goodness, filled with all knowledge, and able to instruct one another (*allēlōn*). Romans 15:14

Greet one another (*allēlōn*) with a holy kiss. Romans 16:16

When you come together to eat, wait for one another (*allēlōn*).
1 Corinthians 11:33

...that there may be no discord within the body, but the members may have the same care for one another (*allēlōn*). If one member suffers, all suffer together with it; if one member is honored, all rejoice together with it. 1 Corinthians 12:25-26

Again and then again we hear:

Greet one another (*allēlōn*) with a holy kiss.
1 Corinthians 16:20 and 2 Corinthians 13:12

Allēlōn. Allēlōn. Allēlōn.

...through love be servants of one another (*allēlōn*).
Galatians 5:13

Be kind to one another (*allēlōn*), tenderhearted, forgiving one another, as God in Christ forgave you. Ephesians 4:32

Bear with one another (*allēlōn*) and if anyone has a complaint against another, forgive each other. Colossians 3:13

Encourage one another (*allēlōn*) with these words.
1 Thessalonians 4:18

By this everyone will know that you are my disciples, if you love one another (*allēlōn*). John 13:35

Allēlōn. Allēlōn. Allēlōn. The loveliness of love rings in our lives, bringing peace, making us lovely, lovable, caring for one another and able to love others. And the bell is calling us to that love as well, summoning us, reminding us, *Allēlōn. Allēlōn. Allēlōn.*

For this is the message you have heard from the beginning, that we should love one another (*allēlōn*). 1 John 3:11

I am giving you these commands so that you may love one
another (*allēlōn*). John 15:17

This love is a special responsibility within the community of faith, but it also
extends out to others in the form of love's justice—in wanting the same
opportunities for others that one wants for oneself and one's near ones. The
love within the community is to generate a love which will reach out to
many others.

May the Lord make you increase and abound in love toward
one another (*allēlōn*), and to everyone, just as we abound in love
for you. 1 Thessalonians 3:12

Owe no one anything, except to love one another (*allēlōn*); for
the one who loves another has fulfilled the law. Romans 13:8

Allēlōn. Allēlōn. Allēlōn.

Let us no more pass judgment on one another (*allēlōn*), but
resolve instead never to put a stumbling block or hindrance in
the way of a brother or sister. Romans 14:13

Let us have...no competing against one another (*allēlōn*), no
envy of one another (*allēlōn*). Galatians 5:26

Bear one another's (*allēlōn*) burdens. Galatians 6:2

Allēlōn. Allēlōn. Allēlōn. Christians are called to build up the community in
love, kindness, peace and tolerance.

...leading a life worthy of the calling to which you have been
called, with all humility and gentleness, with patience, bearing
with one another (*allēlōn*) in love, making every effort to
maintain the unity of the Spirit in the bond of peace.
Ephesians 4:1-3

...let all of us speak the truth to our neighbors, for we are
members of one another (*allēlōn*). Ephesians 4:25

Be subject to one another (*allēlōn*) out of reverence for Christ.
Ephesians 5:21

Do not lie to one another...(*allēlōn*). Colossians 3:9

Confess your sins to one another (*allēlōn*), and pray for one
another...(*allēlōn*). James 5:16

Allēlōn. Allēlōn. Allēlōn.

Let us consider how to stir up one another (*allēlōn*) to love
and good deeds. Hebrews 10:24

Do not speak evil against one another (*allēlōn*). James 4:11

Do not grumble against one another (*allēlōn*). James 5:9

Now that you have purified your souls by your obedience to the truth, so that you have genuine mutual love, love one another (*allēlōn*) deeply from the heart. 1 Peter 4:22

Practice hospitality ungrudgingly to one another (*allēlōn*). 1 Peter 4:9

Clothe yourselves, all of you, with humility in your dealings with one another (*allēlōn*). 1 Peter 5:5

Greet one another (*allēlōn*) with a kiss of love. 1 Peter 5:14

One another. One another. One another. Allēlōn. Allēlōn. Allēlōn. The word chimes on—telling of God's love and the love in the community. It peals in summoning to the love of one another and love towards all. It also resounds with new hope and encouragement. Life, as we know too well, is not all loveliness. Sometimes we may feel very alone and unloved, and we may feel alone in our efforts to love and to do love's justice. Against the clangor of the world's confusion and the noise of all its cries of suffering, *allēlōn* may come to sound like but a forlorn and distant church bell. And our inner voice may warn us not to listen. There is no love, it tells us, which goes very far if at all beyond the self. What love there is for others may only be a form of self-interest, and one had better be careful even with that.

And then the bell sounds again. We hear it at first from that distance. *Allēlōn. Allēlōn.* Then it is again resonating among us. *One another. One another.* At the heart of human longing its song and hope will not be still.

Love one another (*allēlōn*) as I have loved you. John 15:12

In the face of all the powers of evil and death, it is only compassion's love that will never cease. "Love never ends." 1 Corinthians 13:8

...that we may be mutually encouraged by one another's (*allēlōn*) faith. Romans 1:12

May the God of steadfastness and encouragement enable you to live in such harmony with one another (*allēlōn*). Romans 15:5

Therefore, encourage and build up one another (*allēlōn*), just as you are doing. 1 Thessalonians 5:11

We must always give thanks to God for you, sisters and brothers, as is right, because your faith is growing abundantly, and the love of everyone of you for one another (*allēlōn*) is increasing. 2 Thessalonians 1:3

...we have community with one another (*allēlōn*)... 1 John 1:7
This love of one another comes from the Spirit of all life and leads to God.

Beloved, let us love one another (*allēlōn*); for love is of God,
and everyone who loves is born of God and knows God.
1 John 4:7

Allēlōn. The power and truth of love comes to life in receiving and giving love. The ones who love enter into life's greatest mystery—learning how love, which seems so weak and vulnerable, becomes the strongest power of life through which we share in life's most enduring meaning.

Beloved, since God loved us so much, we ought also to love
one another (*allēlōn*). No one has ever seen God; if we love
one another (*allēlōn*), God abides in us and God's love is
perfected in us. 1 John 4:11-12

Allēlōn. In the beginning and the end love is the only commandment.

...not as though I am writing you a new commandment, but
one we have from the beginning, let us love one another
(*allēlōn*). 2 John 5

Being made lovely by love. Love one another as I have loved you. *Allēlōn.*
"By this will everyone know that you are my disciples, if you have love for one another." Allēlōn.